W9-DAN-053

LITERARY INTERPRETATIONS OF BIBLICAL NARRATIVES

VOLUME II

LIST OF CONTRIBUTORS

James S. Ackerman is professor of religious studies at Indiana University.

Jonathan Bishop is professor of English at Cornell University.

Ira Clark is associate professor of English at the University of Florida.

Bruce Dahlberg is professor of religion at Smith College.

Michael Fishbane is professor of Near Eastern and Judaic studies at Brandeis University.

James Freeman is professor of English at the University of Massachusetts.

Edward L. Greenstein is professor of the Old Testament at the Jewish Theological Seminary.

Dolores Gros Louis is associate professor in the honors division at Indiana University.

Kenneth R. R. Gros Louis is professor of English and comparative literature, and vice president of Indiana University.

Jon D. Levenson is professor of religion at Wellesley College.

James Resseguie is associate professor at Winebrenner Seminary in Findlay, Ohio.

Phyllis Trible is professor of the Old Testament at Union Theological Seminary in New York City.

Thayer S. Warshaw taught high school English in Newtonville, Mass., and worked with the Indiana University Institute on the Bible as Literature from its inception in 1970.

LITERARY INTERPRETATIONS OF BIBLICAL NARRATIVES
VOLUME II

EDITED BY KENNETH R. R. GROS LOUIS

WITH JAMES S. ACKERMAN

Abingdon • Nashville

809.935
G913l
v. 2

LIBRARY
ATLANTIC CHRISTIAN COLLEGE
WILSON, N. C.

LITERARY INTERPRETATIONS OF BIBLICAL NARRATIVES

Copyright © 1982 by Abingdon

All rights reserved.
No part of this book may be reproduced in any manner
whatsoever without written permission of the publisher
except brief quotations embodied in critical articles
or reviews. For information address Abingdon,
Nashville, Tennessee.

Library of Congress Cataloging in Publication Data

Main entry under title: (Revised)
Literary interpretations of Biblical narratives.
(The Bible in literature courses)
Vol. 2 lacks series statement.
Includes bibliographical references.
1. Bible as literature. I. Gros Louis, Kenneth R. R., 1936–
II. Ackerman, James Stokes. III. Warshaw, Thayer S., 1915–
IV. Title. V. Series.
BS535.G76   220.6'6   74-12400   AACR2

ISBN 0-687-22131-5 (v. 1)
ISBN 0-687-22132-3 (v. 2)

Unless otherwise indicated, scripture quotations are from the Revised Standard
Version Common Bible, copyrighted © 1973 by the Division of Christian
Education of the National Council of the Churches of Christ in the U.S.A., and are
used by permission.

Chapter 11, "A Human Comedy," by Phyllis Trible, is from *God and the Rhetoric
of Sexuality,* copyright © 1978 by Fortress Press, and is reprinted by permission of
Fortress Press.

Chapter 13, "King David of Israel," first appeared in *Semeia,* No. 8, 1977.

Chapter 18, "Encounters in the New Testament," by Jonathan Bishop, is reprinted
from *Something Else,* published by George Braziller, Inc., in 1972, and is used here
by permission of the publisher.

The lines at the end of chapter 17, page 284, are from T. S. Eliot, *Collected Poems
1909–1962,* "Journey of the Magi," page 99. By permission of Harcourt Brace
Jovanovich and Faber & Faber Ltd.

MANUFACTURED BY THE PARTHENON PRESS AT
NASHVILLE, TENNESSEE, UNITED STATES OF AMERICA

CONTENTS

JAN 2 7 1983 9.20 Rel.

82- 1788

PREFACE

The first volume of *Literary Interpretations of Biblical Narratives* was published by Abingdon Press in 1974. In the preface to that volume, Jim Ackerman and Thayer Warshaw, two of my colleagues in a series of institutes on teaching the Bible as literature, which were held at Indiana University between 1970 and 1978, wrote the following:

> This book is a pioneering venture into relatively uncharted territory: we are not presenting biblical scholarship nor are we merely exploring the superficial esthetic surface of biblical literature. We feel strongly that we are opening up a new and very fruitful way of examining Scripture which will benefit both disciplines—on the one hand, enrich the insights gained from other existing interpretive methodologies and, on the other, offer to literature teachers ways of approaching the Bible within the usual categories of their discipline. We realize that this volume represents only a first step and hope that others will be encouraged to make further contributions in this area.

It is a pleasure to look back over the past seven years and to know that what we believed in 1974 to be a pioneering venture has indeed led to fruitful collaboration between biblical scholars and literary critics and opened up a new way of approaching and studying the Bible as literature. In 1979, for example, Jim Ackerman and I received a grant from the National Endowment for the Humanities for a Summer Humanities Institute for college teachers on the topic "The Bible as Literature: An Interdisciplinary Approach." The eight-week Institute involved ten teachers who had been trained in literature and ten teachers who had been trained in biblical studies. The literature scholars attended a series of seminars in which they learned how biblical scholars approach the Bible and what issues they have identified in key texts. The biblical scholars attended a series of seminars in which they discussed various literary approaches to poetry, drama, and fiction and their applicability to the Bible. Both groups met regularly to exchange their views and to explore how the disciplines represented in the Institute could contribute to each other, not only in developing one or more methodologies for studying the Bible as literature, but also for redirecting long held habits of mind about the Bible. The Institute concluded with each participant—some of them working jointly with scholars from the "other" discipline—presenting formal papers on biblical passages to the group as a whole. At the November, 1980, joint meeting of the American Academy of Religion and the Society of Biblical Literature, more than half of the participants from the 1979 Institute gave papers; indeed, several sessions at that convention were devoted to the subject "The Bible as Literature."

The 1974 volume was indeed a first step. Since its publication, a number of scholars trained in biblical studies—perhaps most especially David Gunn, Michael Fishbane, and Phyllis Trible—as well as scholars trained in both biblical studies and literary criticism—most notably Robert Alter, Frank Kermode, and David Robertson—have written provocative and insightful studies of biblical narratives. In naming these six, I am by no means overlooking the significant contributions of others to this new area of biblical scholarship. That it is new was suggested in part, I believe, by some of the reviews of the 1974 volume which implied that the literary technique employed in most of the essays marked the last attempt of Renaissance humanism to secularize the Bible and therefore to undermine its authority as a sacred text. Criticisms that Robert Alter received to his superb essays published in *Commentary* indicate the same attitude concerning a literary approach to the study of the Bible. I comment on this attitude in my essay describing my own methodological approach to the Bible as literature.

Preface

I believe that the contents of the present volume demonstrate a marked increase in sophistication (not to mention confidence) over the essays in the 1974 volume. Equally important, from my point of view at least, is the fact that the volume contains almost as many essays by biblical scholars as it does essays by literature scholars. The coming together of scholars from these two areas suggests to me that we have moved considerably beyond the 1974 venture and some of the initial responses to it.

Most of the authors in this volume use the Revised Standard Version of the Bible. Those who do otherwise mention so in the notes to their essays.

Many people need to be thanked for their help with the present volume. Much of the editorial work on the essays was done by two of my research assistants—Robert Glenny, now an assistant professor of German at Wabash College, and Michael Wilkerson, who also assisted me skillfully during my first year in my new position at Indiana University. Even before they reviewed the essays, however, each had been carefully edited by another long-time Institute colleague, Thayer Warshaw. The manuscripts were typed by various people, only some of whom I know because they are in Bloomington. These include Linda Fowler, Christy Beck, and Donna Harbstreit. Most of all, the essays by Jim Ackerman and myself owe a great deal to the teachers and students we have collaborated with over the years in our Institute and in our courses, as I suspect that the essays by our colleagues from other institutions are indebted to those with whom they have taught as well as those from whom they have learned.

I. METHODOLOGY

1. SOME METHODOLOGICAL CONSIDERATIONS

Kenneth R. R. Gros Louis

Much has happened in the new field of literary analysis of the Bible since *Literary Interpretations of Biblical Narratives* was published in 1974. The present essay is very much a personal assessment of how one literary critic proceeds in analyzing a biblical text. I am aware of, but do not discuss, the excellent work of Robert Alter, Michael Fishbane, Menakhem Perry and Meir Sternberg, David Robertson, and Leland Ryken (among others) who, I believe, share many of my basic assumptions about literary criticism of the Bible. The gap between literary critics and biblical scholars, however, even scholars who say they are endorsing this new approach to the study of the Bible, remains very great. Part of the reason for this gap results from the traditional definition of "literary criticism" in biblical scholarship, which is why I will discuss several of these definitions in this essay. But the main reason for the gap, in my opinion, is that some biblical scholars simply reject the notion that the Bible can be analyzed in the same manner as Shakespeare, Goethe, or Zola. These scholars have explained their position and will, I am sure, explain it again. Their emphases on the sacredness of the Bible and on the necessity of studying it in its historical contexts, however, are rejected by me, as they must, I believe, be rejected by any student of literature.

A literary interpretation of the Bible in no way replaces or invalidates other approaches—source analysis, anthropology, sociology, theology, archaeology, comparative religion—nor does it seek to rival in authority the centuries of interpretations in commentaries, or the more recent scholarly contributions of form criticism. Literary critics, in considering the Bible primarily and fundamentally as a literary document, believe in the creative power of language to affect our lives, and we deeply appreciate the Bible's portrayal of human situations and characters. The questions literary critics ask differ from those asked by biblical scholars. While we are certainly aware of the findings of biblical scholarship, we do not seek to explain any aspects of the text with the help of extraliterary information. The text to us is not sacred, and whether the events it describes are historical is not relevant to our purposes. The traditional disciplines of biblical criticism, important as correctives to flights of critical fancy, are not called upon to document any conclusions we might make. Our approach is essentially ahistorical; the text is taken as received, and the truth of an action or an idea or a motive, for literary criticism, depends on its rightness or appropriateness in context. Is it true, we ask, not in the real world but within the fictive world that has been created by the narrative?

I would like to outline my own critical assumptions in approaching the Bible as literature, describe the kinds of questions I ask myself in preparing to teach or write about biblical passages, and summarize how I deal with a specific text. Let me begin in the most general terms, with my most basic assumptions:

1. Not everything in the Bible is literary in nature.
2. Literary analyses of the literary aspects of the Bible are virtually nonexistent.
3. What has been called "literary criticism" of the Bible is not the kind of literary criticism teachers of literature do.
4. In fact, the biblical scholar's definition of "literary criticism" is virtually the opposite of the literary critic's definition.
5. Teachers of literature are *primarily* interested in the literary reality of a text and not its historical reality.
6. The literary reality of the Bible can be studied with the methods of literary criticism employed with any other text.
7. Approaching the Bible as literature, then, means placing emphasis on the text itself—not on its historical and

textual backgrounds, not on the circumstances that brought the text into its present form, not on its religious and cultural foundations.

8. The literary critic assumes unity in the text. To quote Northrop Frye: "A purely literary criticism . . . would see the Bible, not as a scrapbook of corruptions, glosses, reductions, insertions, conflations, misplacings, and misunderstandings."

9. The literary critic assumes conscious artistry in the text.

10. The literary critic, then, explores such topics as narrative structure, scene placement, selection and ordering of episodes, plot conflicts, image patterns, thematic emphasis, character development, and so on.

11. Literary criticism of the Bible is not biblical scholarship, it is literary criticism; the two are complementary.

(These assumptions underlie the essays in the 1974 volume; see especially Leland Ryken's "Literary Criticism of the Bible: Some Fallacies.")

Several of the most recent and widely used introductions to the Old Testament document my third and fourth assumptions. I am not trying to attack these views, but simply to illustrate the gulf that exists between biblical scholars and literary critics. Bernhard Anderson, for example, in the third edition (1975) of his *Understanding the Old Testament,* writes: "We cannot begin to understand the Old Testament as long as we regard it as merely great literature, interesting history, or the development of lofty ideas. The Old Testament is the narration of God's action: what he has done, is doing, and will do." Now whether or not I believe this statement, I feel obliged as a student of literature to alter Anderson's last sentence to read something like this: "*The basic assumption of the Old Testament is that it describes* the narration of God's action, what he has done, is doing, and will do." There is a world of difference between my sentence and Anderson's; for him, the Old Testament *is* the narration of God's actions; for me, that is the *fiction* which the Old Testament lays down as its basic premise. In using the word *fiction,* of course, I do not mean that it is necessarily *untrue.*

J. Kenneth Kuntz, in his very fine 1974 book, *The People of Ancient Israel,* describes the literary approach to the Bible as being concerned with genres, oral traditions, authors, editorial changes, dates, the intended audience, relation to historical events, chief rhetorical features, and the author's purposes. Kuntz here outlines a very respectable list of what literary scholars have long been interested in, but the list is appropriate to historical critics of literature, not to literary critics of literature.

Another good study, by James King West, *Introduction to the Old Testament,* published in 1971, reiterates Kuntz's understanding of what literary criticism is: "Higher criticism . . . is the interpretation of the text. Also called 'historical criticism' and roughly synonomous with 'literary criticism,' this discipline is concerned with the historical circumstances out of which the Biblical books developed—their authorship or the processes through which they were composed, the sources employed, their provenance (time and place of origin), and the purposes of their composition." West, like Kuntz, does not make any distinction between literary *scholarship* and literary *criticism.*

The gap between teachers of literature and biblical scholars can be seen even more strikingly in earlier, though highly respected studies. Gerald A. Larue, for example, in his 1969 book, *Old Testament Life and Literature,* writes that the literary approach to the Bible "may ignore the intention of the authors of the Bible and the relevance of what they said to their own time, or, in stressing literary characteristics, may slight the religious convictions of the writers." We know, as students of literature, that the author's intention, his goals in writing for his contemporary audience, and his religious convictions, play a small role indeed in literary criticism and, more important, in the analysis of literary texts. *We* may be familiar with all this information, but we do not depend on it for interpretation, even with an avowedly religious poet such as Milton. For us, in fact, Milton's Satan, Adam, Jesus, God, and Samson, are much more interesting than Milton himself. It is *their* views of themselves and their worlds, and not Milton's of his, on which we focus.

A final example also illustrates another of the chief difficulties in studying the Bible as literature. L. Berkhof's 1952 *Principles of Biblical Interpretation* might have been retitled "Principle of Biblical Interpretation," for the overriding thesis is that the Bible is divinely inspired. One result of this view is that there is no room for the literary notion of the persona in biblical criticism. Berkhof points out, for example, that the prophets often shift from the third to the first person and speak *as if they were God*. "This," says Berkhof, "would be unexampled boldness on the part of the prophets, if they were not absolutely sure that God was putting the words, which they were speaking, into their mouths as their own." Such a statement ignores not only the notion of persona, but also the possibility that an author could create a character whom he then identified as a prophet. Berkhof's extreme view also prevents him from acknowledging the existence of another crucial critical concept, that of the unreliable narrator: "The interpreter," writes Berkhof, "should gladly accept the explanations which the authors themselves give of their own words or of the words of the speakers whom they introduce. It goes without saying that they are better qualified to speak with authority in this respect than anyone else." What Berkhof seems unaware of is that writers develop specific strategies for presenting their material, and that these strategies often intentionally lead us astray.

I have not selected these examples perversely or hostilely. They accurately represent, it seems to me, biblical scholars' notion of what literary criticism is, as well as many biblical scholars' concern that literary critics are undermining the authority of the Bible as a sacred text. The issue, in a sense, may be whether we see literary criticism of the Bible as a further extension of its secularization and therefore as damaging; or whether we see literary criticism as a new means for introducing readers of the Bible to its richness. It may also be, of course, that by making the Bible more accessible, by teaching it like any other literary text, we may indeed be demystifying it in a way that will permanently damage its authority as Scripture. My own opinion is that this risk—if it exists at all—is worth taking.

It might be useful to go through the kinds of questions a literary critic considers in approaching a work of literature. Many of these questions will be known to readers; there is nothing unusual about the approach I am about to describe. Nevertheless, it seems to me that it is an approach that is rarely applied to biblical narratives. A literary critic begins by being primarily interested in how a work is structured or organized. Why, for example, does it begin the way it does? (It is sometimes helpful to consider alternate beginnings.)

What are the identifiable breaks in the text, either marked as such (chapters, verses, stanzas) or occasioned by changes in action, thought, language, setting? How does the ending differ from the beginning? In considering various breaks or units, we should be alert to parallels and contrasts, through reiterated speeches, reiterated actions, echoes of language, image, scene. The ending of a work of literature usually involves changes in characters, imagery, setting, tone, point of view. If, in fact, some of these do not change, the narrative may thus emphasize those which *do* change.

A literary critic is also concerned about tone—that is, the narrative's relation to its subject or its attitude to its subject, as well as the narrative's relation to us as audience. Is the narrative condescending or apologetic? Does it seek to arouse our interest in a topic, to excite our emotions, to compel us to action, to make us sad or happy? What information does the narrative give us and with what nuances? How much does the narrative intrude on the language of the characters and their conversations or actions? What information is not known to us or not given to those in the narrative? Do the omissions make a difference? Is there some information, for example, that we would like very much to know? There are major differences between first-person and third-person narration. First-person narration obviously involves limited knowledge in that the "I" teller is able to tell us about and comment on only what is within his or her vision. Third-person narration, however, can have complete knowledge, not only of the actions of the major characters, but of actions and incidents taking place far away from the primary events. In some instances, particularly in biblical narrative, we may not have a narrative voice distinct from the voice or voices of the speakers or characters. This situation presents a particular problem with regard to biblical narrative and the queston of narrative voice.

A literary critic is alert to changes in characters which occur during the progress of a work. We ask if characters feel different at the end toward certain people or topics or issues than they did in the beginning. We ask how their situation has changed, if it has—their physical situation, material, geographical, psychological, spiritual. In what specific ways have the changes occurred? What events or characters occasioned or forced or contributed to the changes? With whom and with what, in other words, did the characters come into contact, and to what end? In biblical narrative, for example, answers to some of these questions are often provided by parallel episodes or parallel incidents that help direct us to the issues of character development. At what point in the narrative do the characters change, if they do? In considering this question, we need to look carefully not only at what the characters say, but at how they say it. What images or metaphors do they use? What is their tone of voice? What words become more pronounced in their vocabulary or shift in meaning or are rejected or are emphasized? The assumption here is that characters in a work of literature—like us—reveal themselves and their backgrounds, their concerns, biases, attitudes, by what they say and how they say it. It is also important to note how characters react to one another, what they say and do.

The action of a narrative is in many ways less meaningful than how that action comes into being. We ask whether the action or pronouncement or decision is plausible in the context of a particular narrative. Is David's affair with Bathsheba, for instance, prepared for in the narrative? Is it plausible for David to call Bathsheba from the rooftop on which she is bathing? Is it plausible, given the terms of the story, that Cinderella should get to the ball? Is it plausible, given what we know of Hamlet, that he should not immediately or indeed perhaps ever obey the instructions of the ghost? Part of our job, in other words, is to explain why we believe in the plausibility of a narrative, no matter how fantastic its action or its "plot" might be. If the narrative is not plausible, then we should be prepared to consider the reasons for its very implausibility.

Literary critics also consider how readers respond to a work, how it affects them, what it makes them think about. Critics are concerned with exploring why it is that a work leads us to specific responses and specific thoughts, how it directs our reactions, guides and limits them. In this instance, literary critics frequently turn their attention to rhetorical devices and consider their effect on the work and on us as readers. The list of rhetorical devices, of course, is very long, and many of them are prominently used in biblical narrative.

All these questions, it seems to me, are directed toward

answering the question: How does this work of literature gain whatever meaning it has for us? If we do not answer this question, then we are dealing not with literature as literature, but rather with literature as philosophy, or as history or as theology or psychology, and so on—all of which disciplines are related to literature, influence it, and are influenced by it.

For all the questions I have suggested above, it may be more important to be able to demonstrate how we arrive at the answers than to know the answers themselves. The demonstration usually involves an awareness of a narrative's alternatives, choices, options: in terms of scene placement, choice of speaker, length of a character's speech, imagery, metaphors used by a character, individual words a character may emphasize and thus become associated with, and so on. We must constantly be asking: why does the narrative include this scene at this moment? Why does the narrative have this particular character saying these particular words at this moment? Why does the narrative remind us of an earlier scene or character or speech at a particular moment in the course of the narrative itself?

The crucial question of options and choices and alternatives is very well illustrated by the four Gospels. Here, after all, are four narratives essentially about the same subject; but clearly the narratives have made different choices, selected different options, worked with different narrative strategies. The Gospel of Mark, for example, whatever the sources, has selected and arranged narrative units in a particular order and to a particular end. As we know from reading the four Gospels, the narrative of Mark has designs and strategies that differ from those of Luke, Matthew, and John. In a concern with Mark's Gospel as literature, then, we are less immediately interested in sources, theology, philosophy, world view, or whatever. Instead, we ask questions having to do with narrative technique, organization and selection of material, character development, character motivation, character ambiguities. We ask why Mark decided to order his material in the way he did; why particular scenes or incidents are described and placed where they are in the text; in what directions the narrative is moving, toward what end; why certain incidents are repeated; what connections or transitions exist between one narrative unit and another; what relationships exist among the characters. And on such a list could go.

Of particular interest in the Gospel of Mark is the use of parables. A literary critic would ask why they are used at all. What do we learn from them that we would not learn from straightforward narration? We also wonder why the narrative selected these particular parables for inclusion in this particular narrative. We ask how they function, what their relation is to the narrative as a whole; why they appear in the specific narrative contexts in which they occur. We ask what the effect would be of moving them elsewhere in the narrative. All these questions are directed to the Gospel's narrative strategy—selections have been made, we must assume, from many parables; options and alternatives hve been rejected, both in terms of the material and in terms of its placement in the narrative as a whole.

As I consider these questions about the parables or indeed about any aspect of a biblical narrative, I also feel the need to be aware of what other disciplines have contributed to the issues. I must find out at some point, for example, the definition and use of parables in Jesus' historical setting as well as the historical circumstances, if any, that they reflect. For parables, I would discover in scholarship and criticism two divergent trends. Some scholars seek to discover the original form of the parable and the original meaning of its internal historical references (to persons, customs, cultural factors). Other scholars treat the parables as aesthetic objects and analyze them with the methods of structuralism or with the aid of the perspective of existentialism. Clearly a tension exists between these approaches: historical critics run the risk of leaving the parables in the past, with nothing to say to the present; and those who treat them as metaphors or as autonomous aesthetic objects perhaps do less than justice to them as parables, and particularly as parables of Jesus. My own approach, as is certainly evident by this time, attempts to view the parables as literary devices in a literary narrative. And yet I am aware that the assumption of this narrative is unique. I can never forget that the narrative believes it is describing the life of the Messiah, the Son of God. The Gospel, from a literary point of view, is creating a fictional world—but the word *fictional* is not meant to connote that the world may not be a true one. The fictional world of Mark, in other words, is based on specific narrative assumptions and intentions a critic cannot ignore.

The scholarship and criticism on parables illustrates the continuing gap that exists between biblical scholars and literary critics. Various essays tell us that we need to decide what class of parable a particular parable belongs to. Is it a figurative saying? A similitude? A parable of advent? Of reversal? Of action? All this may be useful information, but I am not sure that it is useful to me as a literary critic, any more than it is useful in understanding a particular sonnet to identify whether an image is a Petrarchan image or a Neoplatonic one. Another set of essays on parables might explain that parables tease us into thought. As a literary critic, I feel compelled to ask precisely how this occurs and why. Yet other essays say that Jesus used parables because truth in a tale is more readily remembered. Even if I accept this statement, I still need to demonstrate how it functions and whether it functions successfully in the narratives that make use of parables. More generally, biblical scholarship points out that Jesus obviously used parables to illustrate his teachings. As a literary critic, I must ask why Jesus used parables at all. He surely had at his disposal, as do we, many other ways and means of illustrating what it is he wanted to convey. Finally, it is generally agreed that parables appeal to readers because there is something in them that touches on broad areas of human experience. This again may be an accurate statement, but it seems to me that the job of the literary critic is to uncover precisely what experience is being touched on and what the relation then is between that experience, the parable, the narrative context in which the parable appears, and the narrative of Mark as a whole.

I have dwelled for a long time, perhaps too long, on parables and a literary critic's concerns and questions about them. I would like to close this essay on methodology by describing my own approach to a biblical narrative.

I begin by reading the narrative six or eight times, at various intervals. I then write an elaborate summary of it, a summary that frequently is longer than the narrative itself. I will then construct several summaries of the summary. What I am trying to do (using what may sound like a very mechanical process) is to familiarize myself so thoroughly with the text that I can detach myself from it and approach it as an object totally familiar to me but at some remove from me. Once I have this full knowledge of the text and the ability to separate myself from it, I can look at the narrative from a distance to see when one action or speech is an echo of another, when one scene is related to another or repeats a previous scene, and so on. It is at this point that I can begin to take notes, either mentally or on paper, of such things as repetitions in the narrative—repetitions of situations, of scene, of a motif or word, of individual phrases, particularly when they are attributed to a single character. This enables me to begin to understand the small changes that might occur in the repetitions and thus to begin to answer the question: Why is there repetition at all? Is it used for emphasis? to accelerate the action? to emphasize attitudes? to reveal a new aspect of a character or of the action? to foreshadow later action? In pondering the summary of my summaries, I am also looking for the kinds of concerns I described earlier—development of character, changes in a character's situation or attitude, tone or language, motives for a character's action or a narrative intrusion or digression, reasons for placing a scene where it is (by looking at what comes before it and at what comes after it). I am always thinking about alternatives, choices, options, always asking why a scene, a word, a phrase, a speech, occurs in a particular context and at a particular moment in the narrative.

At this point I read everything I can in biblical scholarship about the biblical narrative. I believe it is crucial to do this only after I have totally assimilated the narrative and identified most of its strategies. In reading through biblical scholarship, I am of course seeking background information; perhaps more important, I am also attempting to discover what has been of particular interest to biblical scholars and critics. I want to know what issues they have identified as crucial in the text, what emphases they have placed in their analyses of the narrative. This will lead me to make a list of the major issues as perceived from the perspective of biblical scholarship. The list will often coincide with the list of issues I have found important from a literary point of view. (In preparing for my essay on David, for example, I became aware during the first part of my analysis and before I had read biblical scholarship that there was a seeming inconsistency in the narrative in that Saul on two occasions has to ask who David is. I later discovered, as most readers will be aware, that biblical scholarship has been concerned with the very same issue. I also was aware during the course of my analysis from a literary point of view that David's relationships with Saul and Absalom dominated the narrative. I later discovered, again as most readers know, that biblical scholars devote much attention to David's relationships with these two characters.) After I have finished my review of biblical scholarship and compared it with my own initial analysis from a literary perspective, I am prepared to make a list of questions that, it seems to me, are central to an understanding of the narrative as a work of literature. These questions may range in number from 15 to 20 to as many as 40 or 50. Usually, it will be possible to cluster the questions into certain groupings. From this list of questions, the organization or structure of the lecture or essay that I hope to prepare emerges.

There is really no way to end an essay on methodology other than to say that the methodology I have described has led to the essays I have written for this particular volume. Since we are dealing with biblical narratives, however, there may be questions any consideration of methodology must take into account. These include the issue of divine inspiration; the problem of making value judgments about the Bible and its narratives; the question of what the text is—that is, is our text the entire Old and New Testaments? one of the narratives within one of the Testaments? a unit within one of these narratives? and so on. Behind all the present work on the Bible as literature there remains the question of the authority of the Bible as scripture. I have stated my own opinion about this issue earlier, and it may be helpful to close by repeating it here. The Bible is one of the great works of western culture. As a student and teacher of literature, I believe it is important to make the text of the Bible as accessible as possible to as many people as possible. In interpreting the biblical narratives as literature—and I believe many of them are great literature indeed—my hope is that the texts will be made more accessible, that the Bible will exert its proper influence in our culture, that the values it endorses and promulgates will, as they should, affect us all.

2. SOME PEDAGOGICAL CONSIDERATIONS

Thayer S. Warshaw

A. The World of the Text

"In the beginning God created the heavens and the earth." Thus we are introduced to the world of the Bible: The main character is God. The setting is outside of space and time. The action does not fit into the laws of nature.

Later, our cast contains angels, demons, and monsters. As for settings, a discussion between God and Satan takes place in heaven; and hell is specified as the place of the damned. Events include God's intervention in history: He speaks to human beings, turns the tide of battle, causes famine; he turns rivers into blood and divides the Red Sea; his Son turns water into wine and revives the dead.

Such supernatural elements of character, setting, and plot present no problem to students of literature, even to those who are strict empiricists or products of a nonbiblical religious tradition. Early training in literary criticism focuses their interest more on how the story is told than on whether it is literally true, more on how the book's teachings are presented than on whether they are binding upon readers. In approaching the Bible as an object of literary analysis, that is, nonbelievers avoid the question of whether the stories and teachings are about a God, and from a God, who actually exists. For students of literature, any text is a

25

LIBRARY
82- 1788 ATLANTIC CHRISTIAN COLLEGE
WILSON, N. C.

given, to be taken on its own terms. They enter its world with Coleridge's "willing suspension of disbelief."

If the nonbeliever must willingly suspend disbelief, must not the believer equally suspend his or her belief?

Before addressing that question, let us clarify the distinction between approaching the Bible as a religious document and approaching it as literature. In both cases, the Bible is understood to *be* a religious document; it arises out of deep theological, moral, and cultic beliefs and practices. It is preoccupied with God and with God-given moral imperatives. It has been, and still is, regarded as authoritative for the religious beliefs and conduct of millions of people.

The difference lies in one's approach to the book: what questions one initially asks of the text and where one looks for answers. When students examine the Bible primarily for its religious content, they ask, What did the people who set it down and the people it portrays believe about God; and how did their belief, or disbelief, affect their lives? To answer such questions, students not only examine the text itself, but also go beyond it, to its contexts. They draw on various fields of scholarly research that illuminate ancient civilizations—in particular, putative sources and analogues of the text. They also consult theologians and commentators for help with its meaning.

When students examine the Bible primarily as literature, they ask the kinds of questions discussed by Kenneth Gros Louis in the preceding chapter of this book. To answer these questions, students must restrict themselves fairly closely to the text and the special tools of literary analysis, limiting their requests for scholarly help almost exclusively to matters of precise translation.

Having made that distinction, let us restate our earlier question: Must the believer willingly suspend belief in order to approach the Bible as literature? Put another way, does religious commitment interfere with literary analysis of the Bible? If it were only a matter of whether one believes in God and in the Bible, the answer to this second question might be no. We might even accept the often-advanced argument that the believer has an advantage over the nonbeliever—that he or she has already entered, at least part way, into the world of the Bible. It is not so simple as that, however. What does it mean to "believe in God" and to "believe in the Bible"?

· Consider some questions as to just what the world of the Bible is: Does the Bible include both an "Old" Testament (OT) and a "New" Testament (NT)? Not according to Jews. Does the OT consist of thirty-nine books? Not according to Roman Catholics. Are the ancient stories told correctly? Not according to Muslims and Mormons. In what order do the books appear: Is Malachi the link between the two testaments? What translation is best to use? Does Isaiah speak of a virgin or a young woman? Believers (and nonbelievers) disagree.

If the Bible includes both testaments, how are they related? Should we read the OT through the lens of the NT, as the NT itself insists? If so, are the theology and morality of the OT to be taken as relatively undeveloped, needing the NT as a corrective? Again, believers disagree.

When is the Bible speaking literally and when figuratively? Some believers will deviate from a literal reading only where the text itself says it is speaking figuratively. Other believers are at pains to "explain" the Bible's prehistory and miracles as adaptations of natural events, as mythological truths, as parables, or as some combination of the three. Still others insist that the Bible can be read only allegorically.

How free are the characters in the Bible; and to what extent may they be acting out God's plans, almost like puppets? Joseph tells his brothers that God sent him on ahead to Egypt to preserve the family. God hardens the heart of Pharaoh. The devil puts it into the heart of Judas to betray Jesus. Believers argue about the degree of human free will, the specificity and inviolability of predestination, and the extent of God's immanence in history.

If students take sides on these issues of belief when reading the Bible, they are bound to come out with varied and probably conflicting *literary* answers to many of Gros Louis' literary questions. For example, if both testaments constitute one book, written under the influence of the same holy spirit, then many of the events of the OT must be read as instances of the writer's use of foreshadowing, a perfectly normal literary device. If Joseph is telling the truth to his brothers and not just soothing them about God's hand in his career, then he and his brothers have been controlled by God since childhood. We cannot use their words and actions as evidence of the writer's technique in the characterization of Jacob and his sons—to say nothing of the possibly providential promiscuity of Potiphar's wife.

I suggest that when students who are believers enter the literary world of the Bible, they should lay aside their beliefs just as deliberately, if not as willingly, as nonbelievers suspend their disbelief. Both kinds of students must agree to limit themselves, as far as possible, to the world of the text. Their challenge is to look for answers to their literary questions neither from the history of the text nor from their own religious or irreligious commitments.

If there are questions about translation—what the words meant in their original context—students should settle disputes or confusion according to some rules agreed upon in advance. They then can engage in discussion, for then they are talking about substantially the same textual world.

B. Beyond the World of the Text

All well and good as an ideal, perhaps even approachable by fairly sophisticated literary critics. Pedagogy, however, has to face two other problems. First, students who are approaching the Bible as literature for the first time may be hampered by other than their religious beliefs. Some habits of thought are less readily acknowledged, let alone set aside. Second, most people, including students, read literature for more than its craftsmanship. Great writing broadens and deepens the mind and spirit of its reader because of the issues it raises and the answers it proposes or exposes, and certainly the Bible is no exception.

Let us look at each problem in turn. Some beginning students have absorbed from their families, social groups, religious communities, and educational experiences certain interdenominational prejudices. Many of these forces support their biases with appeals to the "proper" interpretation of the Bible: The Bible doesn't sanction certain beliefs and cultic practices of those other people; they are blasphemers, heretics, immoral, evil, damned. The Bible is also looked to for proof to reinforce discrimination against atheistic communists, heathen Asians, black descendants of Cain and Ham, and miscreant Jews.

Other students reflect the strong political, social, economic, or educational views of their families and communities, based on their conviction that our society and our government should follow biblical teachings: Biblical morality implies that we must/must not permit abortions, prayer in public schools, censorship of textbooks and the media, social welfare programs, free enterprise, and specific positions on foreign policy. Such commitments can lead to harsh prejudice against people who disagree.

The extent, intensity, and self-consciousness of such semi-secular, Bible-related beliefs vary. At the more concentrated and socially discriminatory end of the scale, they affect a student's reading of biblical literature just as strongly as do the acknowledged religious beliefs that we have asked him or her to suspend. However successful a believer may become at reading biblical literature nonconfessionally, we cannot expect freedom from all cultural influences. Nevertheless, it seems that sound pedagogy—literary and extra-literary—requires some attention to these intrusive prejudices before or during students' examination of the Bible as literature. Beginning students should be exposed to alternative ways of thinking and to a broadening of their horizons.

Consider the example of anti-Semitism, which is deeply imbedded in our culture, even in our language. Webster defines the verb "jew" as "to cheat by sharp business practice." Jewish tradition reveres the Pharisees as the embodiment of normative post-biblical Judaism; but Webster's synonyms for "pharisaical" include "sanctimonious, self-righteous, hypocritical," and "making an outward show of piety and morality but lacking inward spirit." The dictionary is not making a judgment; it merely reports how the terms are used in our society.

The two most famous Jewish characters in English literature have entered our language as common nouns: a shylock is "an extortionate creditor or moneylender," and a fagin is "one who teaches children to steal"—again, according to Webster. A survey in this country not long ago found that most Christians identified only Judas, of all the apostles, as a Jew, the others being known only as Christians.

As for the biblical basis for such unconscious cultural

anti-Semitism, one of the most pervasive and sophisticated sources lies in the contrast between the God of the OT and the God of the NT. The stereotypical OT God is to be feared; he embodies and encourages retributive justice; and he favors his chosen people against the world. The stereotypical God of the NT is to be loved; he exhibits and rewards mercy; and he is open to all people.

Many, if not most, students bring these stereotypes with them. Nevertheless, such initial impressions about the OT and NT portraits of God might not, in themselves, be harmful to the students or to their literary analysis of the Bible. The process of education and maturation is largely a matter of learning that things are not as simple as they seem, that gray is a more common color than black or white. Closer reading will show that the stereotypes do not hold up. Loving, merciful, and universalistic aspects of God appear in the OT; and the NT has its passages in which God (or Jesus) is vengeful and harsh toward people who oppose, persecute, or reject him.

The harm comes from the tendency to transfer these stereotypes of the OT and NT portraits of God to our modern context. The values of Judaism and of Jews are contrasted with those of Christianity and of Christians. The essential Jew is seen as harsh and merciless, clannish and xenophobic, valuing the flesh and Mammon. The ideal Christian is seen as loving, merciful, universalist, and committed to faith and the Holy Spirit.

With such stereotypes, unconscious though they may be in most cases, students who approach the Bible, especially the Gospels, are bound to have their prejudices reinforced: The Jewish priests and elders deliver Jesus to Pilate; and the people/crowd/Jews join in to accuse him, call for his crucifixion, accept responsibility "on us and on our children" (in Matthew's account), and imply that they would do the deed themselves if the law allowed it (John).

If teachers feel an obligation to their students and to society beyond the teaching of literary criticism, they must face this problem of prejudice. In order to meet it, they must go beyond the literary world of the text. Students should be exposed to a possible explanation of the anti-Semitism in the NT. It is not necessary to violate the integrity of the text nor to attack the literalist position of religious conservatives. The intent should be to help students uncover and examine their own prejudices, without devaluing the text or destroying the students' faith.

It seems proper, therefore, to direct students to the consensus of critical scholars regarding the circumstances under which the Gospels were written. These theories suggest reasons for the anti-Semitic polemics: that the evangelists reflect fierce first-century antagonisms within the Jewish community, that traditional Jews and the followers of Jesus were mutually hostile, and that each side in the increasingly bitter family feud was in effect reading the other side out of the family. (For a more detailed exposition, addressed to beginning students, see Juel, *et al., An Introduction to New Testament Literature,* Abingdon, 1978.)

True, this explanation is not acceptable to literalists who believe that the writing and the content of the Bible were free of temporal influences. True, also, that the explanation takes students outside the literary world of the text and into its history. For an examination that is supposed to be limited to literary craftsmanship, such a departure is suspect, because it opens the door to a host of possible nonliterary distortions of the text. However, in the case of students' antisocial prejudices (of whatever kind, anti-Semitic or other) that might, without guidance, be reinforced by the literature, the extra-literary obligations of teachers justify, if they do not require, an occasional exception. Teachers are not merely literary critics, even when on the platform. They have a moral obligation to open the minds and spirits of their students and to foster our society's nobler commitment to a harmonious pluralism.

C. Issues in the Text

One enters the world of the text in several ways. One avenue leads the reader to become empathetically involved with the characters. It is not unusual for a teacher to say, rhetorically or as an assigned paper: Imagine how Abraham felt when God asked him to sacrifice "your son, your only son Isaac, whom you love"—through whom the meaning, purpose, and promise of Abraham's life was to be justified and fulfilled. Or imagine how the apostles felt when they finally realized that Jesus, for whom they had left everything behind and who had given them new faith and hope, was not going to reestablish the longed-for Jewish monarchy—that he would not deliver them from oppression but would succumb to it and probably drag them down with him.

The teacher invokes the students' humanity: Why do you suppose the characters acted as they did? How would you feel if you were in their place? What other course of action might they have pursued? What might they have done if circumstances had been a bit different? Have you ever had, witnessed, or heard of a similar moral situation?

The purpose of such questions is to engage the students with the text. The questions make demands upon their experience, imagination, intellect, and values. If the exercise is successful, the students' speculations will deepen their appreciation of the literature. The teacher will have taught them that reading good literature is a creative experience, to which the reader must contribute his or her mind and spirit and through which both mind and spirit grow.

As a matter of fact, critical analysis of literary craftsmanship is not a matter of merely uncovering the writer's technique and use of literary devices. These are aspects of form, and great literature does not live by form alone; the form must be appropriate to the content. How the writer expresses himself or herself should support, and be justified by, what the writer has to say. Manipulation of point of view in telling the story, placement of emphasis in presenting the teaching, use of parallelism in the poem—all these must suit the theme to make for well-crafted literature.

Therefore, students of the Bible as literature must attempt to understand its themes: its view(s) of the nature, meaning, and purpose of the universe, of society, and of the individual; its view(s) of human values and morality. What *is* the answer in Job? Why do the righteous suffer? Why are thanks for blessings so often related to destruction of enemies in the Psalms? What is the NT position on the relative importance of faith and works: On which should one concentrate one's energies? Such questions of matter must be raised before weighing the suitability of the manner.

In sum, to understand the literature, students must enter fully into its world with empathy. Second, to appreciate its craftsmanship, they must examine its ideas so that they can judge the appropriateness of form to content. Third, students cannot avoid confronting the Bible's themes if they are at all open to personal growth: The theological and moral questions posed by Job, the Psalms, and Paul in the preceding paragraph are equally vital today.

These three circumstances add up to our second problem. Students read literature for more than its formal craftsmanship; they become involved in the issues it raises. In the educative process of facing moral dilemmas, considering alternatives, examining their own experiences and assumptions, and broadening their perspectives, students often enhance and reinforce their values and received opinions. Sometimes, the process seriously disturbs them. In either case, studying the issues of literature in general and of the Bible in particular stimulates a reaction.

The pedagogical problem is how students are to be invited to notice, understand, comment on, and even offer judgments about the theology and moral values in a book that is sacred to a large part of our society. These are not unusual pursuits in the study of secular literature, whether they are assigned or not. In the case of the Bible, especially in a school or university supported by the government, which is committed to separation of church and state, such activities ought to be pursued with care and sensitivity. Even in a private institution one has a moral, if not the legal, responsibility to respect the religious beliefs of others. The grove of academe is not so secluded from society, nor literature from life, that one may ignore such sensibilities.

Reading the Bible as literature is, in a sense, like reading Shakespeare. Teaching the Bible as literature, however, differs from teaching Shakespeare in one important respect. With Shakespeare the teacher does not have to take into account attitudes of students toward a holy book whose teachings and interpretation have come to affect their eternal salvation or damnation.

When teaching the Bible as literature, it may be well to keep in mind these suggestions: (a) that those who believe (in whatever sense) in the Bible should temporarily suspend their beliefs when they enter the literary world of the Bible; (b) that one should look into the historical background of the Bible for possible explanations of social prejudices that the Bible seems to sanction; and (c) that, in confronting theological and moral issues raised by biblical literature, one should remember the religious sensibilities of others.

I submit, even further, that these concerns are not only pedagogical, directed to student and teacher. The general reader who approaches the Bible as literature might also find these cautions useful.

II. GENESIS

3. GENESIS 3–11

Kenneth R. R. Gros Louis

Now the serpent was more subtle than any other wild creature that the Lord God had made. He said to the woman, "Did God say, 'You shall not eat of any tree of the garden'?" And the woman said to the serpent, "We may eat of the fruit of the trees of the garden; but God said, 'You shall not eat of the fruit of the tree which is in the midst of the garden, neither shall you touch it, lest you die.'" But the serpent said to the woman, "You will not die. For God knows that when you eat of it your eyes will be opened, and you will be like God, knowing good and evil." So when the woman saw that the tree was good for food, and that it was a delight to the eyes, and that the tree was to be desired to make one wise, she took of its fruit and ate; and she also gave some to her husband, and he ate. Then the eyes of both were opened, and they knew that they were naked; and they sewed fig leaves together and made themselves aprons. And they heard the sound of the Lord God walking in the garden in the cool of the day, and the man and his wife hid themselves from the presence of the Lord God among the trees of the garden.

When we look at this passage as literature, we are left with a number of questions. From where does the serpent come? Why is he more subtle than any other wild creature? What motivates him to tempt Eve? By what thought process does Eve arrive at her decision to eat the fruit? How does she reveal her disobedience to Adam? What is Adam's initial response? What then leads him to eat the fruit? What happens when the eyes of both are opened? What goes through their minds as they hide among the trees concealing themselves from the Lord God walking in the garden?

And if we fleshed out the story into a narrative of our own, what would we write in answering these questions?

In Genesis 3, it is not necessary, as it was with chapters 1 and 2, to consider whether we believe in this account of the Fall of Man or not. From a literary point of view, all we need to accept is that we are given a story of temptation and fall. The pattern described is clearly a universal one which raises questions having nothing to do with the historical validity of the content of chapter 3. How, for example, is a person tempted? What arguments does a tempter use to persuade us to break laws and codes of behavior? What processes do we go through before making the choice to do the wrong thing? How do we persuade ourselves that we had no other choice under the circumstances? How do we justify to ourselves the actions we have taken? How does the wrongdoing affect our way of thinking and our attitudes toward those around us?

The answers to these questions in relation to the opening of Genesis 3 will be literary answers; they call attention to material omitted, hinted at, and consciously ignored; they draw attention to what is emphasized in the text, to what has been selected for inclusion in the text, in part by noting what *is* there and in part by noting what is *not* there. Similar questions could be asked about the remainder of chapter 3. Why, for example, does the Lord God need to ask, as he looks for Adam and Eve, "Where are you?" Why do Adam and Eve respond to God's pointed questions the way they do? Why does God assign particular punishments to the serpent, to Adam, and to Eve? The curse on the serpent must be particularly puzzling to Adam and Eve. What does the enmity between her seed and the serpent's seed mean to them? Why the emphasis on the pain of childbearing for Eve? What does it mean that the ground is cursed because of Adam? Why does God make them coats of skin and clothe them? Why does he feel the need to guard the garden with a cherubim and his flaming sword?

What we are seeking, as literary critics, is not the anwers to these specific questions, but rather conjectures about and explanations of why these details are included at all, why our attention is drawn to them. Do they initiate a narrative pattern? Will they be echoed later in the story? Is the narrative consistent in its selection of details? If we were to write narratives based on these chapters, we would need to answer the questions specifically, but as critics we are more concerned with the selection of the material and the emphasis given in this particular narrative. In the story that follows, for example, one might ask these questions: Why does Eve say, seemingly with delight, "I have gotten a man with the help of the Lord," when she presumably knew that she would have children? What is the significance of the distinction made between Abel as shepherd and Cain as farmer? Why is Cain's offering less pleasing to God than Abel's? Is this not arbitrary favoritism on God's part? Why does God not seem to understand Cain's anger and tell him instead to suppress it, to do well, and to be aware of sin couching at the door? Why does Cain then kill Abel? What does he hope to gain? Why does God ask Cain where Abel is, a question to which he already knows the answer? Why does Cain lie to God? Why does God curse Cain in the way he does, then alleviate it somewhat by the mark? Why does Cain protest the punishment? Why do his descendants live in tents, play musical instruments, and forge bronze and iron tools? What is the point of Lamech's statement to his wives: "Adah and Zillah, hear my voice; you wives of Lamech, hearken to what I say: I have slain a man for wounding me, a young man for striking me. If Cain is avenged sevenfold, truly Lamech seventy-sevenfold"? Why is it only after this episode that the narrative takes us back to Adam and to his son Seth? What evidence do we have that explains why "at that time men began to call upon the name of the Lord"? Why is there an allusion to the creation of Adam at the opening of chapter 5? And why is that allusion then echoed in the account of the birth of Seth? Why are we given the long genealogies of Adam's descendants, all of them, until Noah, only names? Finally, why does Lamech say that Noah will bring man relief from the cursed ground? What does he mean? What does he believe is going to happen? Underlying all these questions is our basic concern as literary critics: What has led to the selection of these details and to the arrangement of the material in these ways? Is there an identifiable pattern in the narrative?

If we return to the opening of chapter 3 and proceed through chapters 3–11 of Genesis, we begin to perceive the literary artistry of the biblical narrative. The serpent's first question to Eve plants in her mind the suggestion that God has been unjust, that somehow God has been holding back some of his favors. "Did

God say, 'You shall not eat of any tree of the garden'?" asks the serpent. And Eve, responding in a straightforward way to what she believes is a straightforward request for information, replies, "God said, 'You shall not eat of the fruit of the tree which is in the midst of the garden, neither shall you touch it, lest you die.'" Eve's response is striking for two reasons. She does not mention that the tree is the tree of the knowledge of good and evil, but simply says that it is the tree in the midst of the garden. More important is the fact that she makes a slight alteration in God's command, at least as we have been given it in chapter 2. There God said to Adam, "You may freely eat of every tree of the garden; but of the tree of the knowledge of good and evil you shall not eat, for in the day that you eat of it you shall die." If there is nothing in God's command about touching the tree, then from where does Eve get that information? Is it an elaboration for the sake of the serpent? Does it indicate how serious, how dangerous the tree is? Is it possible that Adam, not trusting Eve and delighting in the opportunity to exercise intellectual powers, elaborated on the command as he passed it on to her, saying in effect: don't eat the fruit; don't even go near it; don't, in fact, even touch it?

Eve may believe that she is less than Adam, that she is his inferior. She is pleased to be able to teach the serpent something he had previously not known; but, of course, what Eve does not know is that the serpent is waiting for just this opening, is waiting for her to say exactly those things: touch the fruit, eat the fruit, we will die. And the serpent responds to her, expanding on the hint he has already planted in her mind, on the suggestion that in some way God is unjust: "You will not die." He is saying to her that God is a liar, that God has a selfish reason for not wanting them to touch or eat the fruit: "God knows that when you eat of it your eyes will be opened, and you will be like God, knowing good and evil." Eve must be struck by the fact that the serpent uses that phrase "knowing good and evil," for she knows that the tree is in fact the tree of the knowledge of good and evil. She has not told the serpent that; she simply had called it the tree "in the midst of the garden." The fact that he uses that phrase indicates to her and surely helps to persuade her that the serpent is right, that indeed it may be the tree of the knowledge of good and evil. She looks at it; it looks good; it seems pleasant to the sight; she is hungry. The narrative suggests that the tree may make her wise, perhaps, as Milton suggests in *Paradise Lost,* even a little wiser than Adam, a thought that Milton's Eve does not find unappealing. So Eve eats the fruit, then gives it to Adam, who also eats, although we are not told why.

After eating the fruit, both Adam and Eve feel shame and guilt; they hide in the garden. God comes walking through the garden and asks, "Where are you?" Since God presumably knows where Adam and Eve are and what they have done, there is no reason for that question. As there may have been nothing special about the tree—it perhaps simply represents a test of Adam and Eve by God to see if they could follow one command from him—so God's question may now be another test of Adam: Will Adam respond at all, will he remain hidden, will he lie? Adam answers, but not entirely honestly: "I heard the sound of thee in the garden, and I was afraid, because I was naked; and I hid myself." There is no mention of what he had done, simply that he had heard the sound and had been afraid. God then asks the question directly: "Have you eaten of the tree of which I commanded you not to eat?" And now, confronted with the direct and true accusation that he has been disobedient to the Lord God, Adam evades responsibility, brushes off the blame, and somehow suggests that the fault is shared between God and Eve: "The woman whom thou gavest to be with me, she gave me fruit of the tree. . . ." The fault is in part God's for creating the woman in the first place, and in part Eve's for giving him the fruit. When God asks Eve, "What is this that you have done?" she also evades responsibility: "The serpent beguiled me, and I ate."

God then curses all three, giving particular punishments to the serpent, to Adam, and to Eve. The curse on the serpent, which tells of enmity between the serpent's seed and Eve's seed and of the time when Eve's seed will bruise the head of the serpent, must be particularly puzzling to Adam and Eve at this time. God tells Eve that she will have pain in childbearing, and he tells Adam that the ground is cursed because of him, that he will be able to eat, but that he will need to sweat, that there will be thorns and thistles, that there will be much toil. God tells Adam and Eve, "You shall eat bread till you return to the ground, for out of it you were taken; you are dust, and to dust you shall return." He thus announces to them the death that he had promised them in his command, although it is not certain that Adam and Eve are aware that this is that death. God shows them mercy by making them garments of skin, and then, as the final result of their disobedience, he banishes them from the garden and sends them forth from Eden "to till the ground from which [man] was taken." (The charge to till the ground is an ironic reminder of God's charge to Adam when God first placed him into the garden of Eden, "to till it and keep it.") Finally, God places a cherubim with a flaming sword as a guard at the entrance to the garden, perhaps because Adam and Eve still have enough intellectual power and enough authority to return if they choose, perhaps simply to remind them, and us, of the permanence of the banishment.

At the beginning of chapter 4, Adam and Eve are outside the garden. Adam is toiling, sweating, getting some bread among the thorns and thistles. Eve bears Cain, saying, "I have gotten a man with the help of the Lord." She says this only when Cain is born, not at the births of either Abel or Seth. It may be that she says this with delight and wonder, believing of Cain (as Lamech may believe of Noah later) that *this* is the man who will bruise the head of the serpent. We are told that Abel is a keeper of sheep and that Cain is a tiller of the ground. The ground, however, has been cursed because of Adam, and so we can imagine the toiling of Cain as he tries to bring good things from it. From that cursed ground he brings to the Lord an offering of fruit, selecting the best. We have heard about fruit before in this narrative, the fruit that led to Adam's and Eve's fall, and perhaps it is for this reason that God has no regard for the offering. It also may be that God rejects the offering simply because he wants to see how Cain will respond. As the tree may have had no significance other than to test Adam and Eve, so may this be a test of Cain. The Lord says to him, "Why are you angry, and why has your countenance fallen? If you do well, will you not be accepted?" God may be saying, you do not need to be praised every time you do something; if you continue to do well, I will accept you. "And if you do not do well, sin is couching at the door," God continues. In some translations this reads, "sin is *crouching* at the door," implying that there is something bestial (perhaps serpent-like?) waiting at the door. "Its desire is for you, but you must master it"—as Adam, and especially Eve, presumably should have mastered their desire to eat from the one tree forbidden them.

Cain, however, kills his brother in the field, although we are not told why. The Lord asks him, "Where is Abel your brother?" The question is similar to that asked of Adam and Eve: "Where are you?" As in the earlier question, God already knows the answer; but what will Cain say? Cain not only answers deceptively, as did Adam; he actually lies: "I do not know; am I my brother's keeper?" The parallels between this story and the story of Adam and Eve are striking. God's curse on Cain even echoes the curse on Adam. "What have you done?" asks the Lord God. "The voice of your brother's blood is crying to me from the ground. And now you are cursed from the ground." God had cursed the ground for Adam, but now he tells Cain that he is cursed *from* the ground, and extends the curse yet one step further: "When you till the ground, it shall no longer yield to you its strength; you shall be a fugitive and a wanderer on the earth." Adam at least could get bread from the ground, though with much toil; Cain will receive nothing from it. Being a fugitive and a wanderer on the earth also marks an extension of the prior banishment from Eden.

Unlike Adam and Eve, who said nothing when they heard God's punishment, Cain challenges it, and voices his great distress: "My punishment is greater than I can bear." He is distressed for four reasons: he is driven away from the ground, the source of his livelihood; he will be hidden from the face of God; he will be a fugitive and a wanderer on the earth; and climactically, he will be killed: "whoever finds me will slay me." Cain seems most concerned about the possibility of death. Adam and Eve had said nothing of that, perhaps because they, unlike Cain, did not know what death was. But God rejects the notion of blood for blood: "'If any one slays Cain, vengeance shall be taken on him sevenfold.' And the Lord put a mark on Cain, lest any who came upon him should kill him." This is a kind of mercy, similar to that shown to Adam and Eve when God made them garments of skin.

Adam and Eve had been banished from Eden; they left the garden, living possibly where they could even see the flaming sword that guarded its entrance. Cain, however, moves further away from God; he dwells "east of Eden," where he builds a city, naming it, perhaps pridefully, for his own son. God had planted a garden; Cain now constructs a city. The little civilization develops: Cain's descendants practice trades and skills, live in tents, raise cattle, play musical instruments, forge instruments of bronze and iron. Only one of Cain's descendants, Lamech, comments on this civilization. He says to his wives, "You wives of Lamech, hearken to what I say: I have slain a man for wounding me, a young man for striking me." These two lines are sufficient, however, to suggest to us the state of the civilization in which Lamech lived, and they help to explain why, at the end of chapter 4, the narrative tells us, "At that time men began to call upon the name of the Lord." Lamech says further, "If Cain is avenged sevenfold, truly Lamech seventy-sevenfold." Lamech, like Cain, is anxious to avoid death, and he reasons that if Cain, who killed for no reason, would be avenged sevenfold should anyone slay him, then surely he, Lamech, who killed a man who had actually struck him, should be avenged seventy-sevenfold. His statement represents a corrupt misunderstanding of the mark on Cain and of God's implied concern that blood should not be shed for blood. The murder, the fear of death, the fear of revenge, and the gross misinterpretation of God's words all suggest the sad nature of this civilization. The narrative reports that a third son, Seth, is born to Adam and Eve. Eve does not now say, "I have gotten a man with the help of the Lord," but only, "God has appointed for me another child instead of Abel, for Cain slew him." Unlike the wonder and joy expressed at that other birth, this statement is one of resignation and perhaps acceptance of the fact that the serpent's head may not be bruised soon.

Chapter 5 then returns us ironically to the beginning with an allusion to the first chapter of Genesis, an allusion that reminds us of the enormous potential that existed when Adam was placed in the garden of Eden: "When God created man, he made him in the likeness of God. Male and female he created them, and he blessed them and named them Man when they were created." The potential has now been destroyed; the pattern planned by God has been broken. Thus, we recognize the irony when we are told that Adam "became the father of a son in his own likeness, after his own image." Seth is born in the image of Adam, not in the image of God.

After a long account of Adam's genealogies and the passage of generations, Noah is born. At Noah's birth, Lamech recalls the cursing of the ground and anticipates a new beginning with Noah: "Out of the ground which the Lord has cursed this one shall bring us relief from our work and from the toil of our hands." In a sense, of course, Lamech is right, but he surely does not expect the relief to be the destruction of the earth. It is now, at the beginning of chapter 6, "when men began to multiply on the face of the ground," that several details, a series of incidents, a series of statements are given which prepare us for God's decision to destroy the world in the flood. In 6:3 we hear the Lord say, "My spirit shall not abide in man for ever, for he is flesh, but his days shall be a hundred and twenty years." God may have decided that a hundred and twenty years is quite enough for men such as Cain and Lamech. God also sees that there is wickedness: "The Lord saw that the wickedness of man was great in the earth, and that every imagination of the thoughts of his heart was only evil continually." And then, in a voice that echoes the opening of chapter 5—"When God created man, he made him in the likness of God"—and also echoes the account of the sixth day of creation, the narrative now tells us that "the Lord was sorry that he had made man on the earth, and it grieved him to his heart. So the Lord said, 'I will blot out man whom I have created from the face of the ground, man and beast and creeping things and birds of the air, for I am sorry that I have made them.'" He announces that he is going to reverse the process that was described in chapters 1 and 2 of Genesis by destroying everything that was created, except that "Noah found favor in the eyes of the Lord."

The earth is corrupt, but, for reasons unknown to us, God decides to salvage Noah. He says to Noah, "I have determined to make an end of all flesh; for the earth is filled with violence through them; behold, I will destroy them with the earth. Make yourself an ark of gopher wood . . ."; and God then gives very specific instructions on how to construct that ark. God also tells Noah that he will establish his covenant as a special personal relationship between Noah and himself, just as there was a special personal relationship between Adam and God earlier. The narrative is suggesting that the creation process described in chapters 1 and 2 is going to be reversed and then started again.

If we consider the settings in chapters 2 through 6, we see that the narrative has carefully prepared us for this reversal of the process of creation and that it is preparing us for what follows the flood. We begin with a garden planted by God, into which he puts man, "to till it and keep it." He then brings to the garden beasts, birds, cattle, and so on. After Adam's and Eve's disobedience, that setting shifts to outside the garden, where man must "till the ground from which he was taken." That setting shifts again after Cain's murder of Abel still further away from the presence of the Lord, east of Eden, and into a city built by Cain and named for his own son. The next distinct setting we hear about is the ark that was built by Noah but with detailed and specific instructions from God, an ark in which Noah and his family are to be secure and into which God commands Noah to bring beasts, birds, cattle, and so on. We have moved, then, from the secure garden of Eden, planted by God for Adam, to the secure ark, built following God's instructions for Noah. In between are the ground outside of Eden, which Cain tills, and the city east of Eden, which Cain builds. We are going back to the beginning, then, and we return fully when we come to the phrase, "all the fountains of the great deep burst forth, and the windows of the heavens were opened," for at that moment we recall chapter 1, verse 7 of Genesis, "And God made the firmament and separated the waters which were under the firmament from the waters which were above the firmament." That separation of the waters is now canceled out, and the waters return again over the earth from below and from above. The chaos caused by the flood as it sweeps over the earth, blotting out "everything on the dry land in whose nostrils was the breath of life," is like the chaos that preceded the creation. But this time, shut up in the ark, is a remnant of that creation maintaining itself at God's command to begin anew.

That the flood and its aftermath mark a new beginning, an echo of the creation, is obvious on the narrative level. The language describing the flood, however, confirms the conscious artistry of that echo. The repeated phrases in the account of the flood—"birds according to their kind," "animals according to their kind," "every creeping thing according to its kind"—recall for us the creation of creatures in the first chapter of Genesis. The emphasis on the death of all things in the account of the flood, the account of the blotting out of all flesh, recalls with irony the life given to creatures at the creation, the filling of the earth and sky with creeping and flying things. God's command to Noah after the waters have subsided, "be fruitful and multiply upon the earth," clearly echoes God's blessing to man in chapter 1, "Be fruitful and multiply, and fill the earth and subdue it." Finally, God's deliverance of all the beasts, birds, and fish into Noah's hands echoes his charge in chapter 1 that man will "have dominion over the fish of the sea and over the birds of the air and over every living thing that moves upon the earth."

It is as if Noah retrieves man from the point prior to Adam's disobedience. God created Adam, the narrative tells us, because "there was no man to till the ground." He put Adam into the garden with the command "to till it and keep it." After Adam's disobedience God had said, "Cursed is the ground because of you." Cain, a tiller of that cursed ground, kills his brother and is cursed *from* the ground. Lamech, not fully understanding the import of his words, had said of Noah, "out of the ground which the Lord has cursed this one shall bring us relief from our work and from the toil of our hands." After the flood, God, pleased by the odor of Noah's sacrifice, thinks in his heart, "I will never again curse the ground because of man," and in chapter 9, verse 20, the narrative tells us, "Noah was the first tiller of the soil." We have moved in a circle controlled by the word "ground" and all its connotations and are back with a second first tiller of the soil, to whom God has said, as he once said to Adam, "Be fruitful and multiply, and fill the earth." This time, however, God does *not* say, as he said to Adam, "and subdue it." With this phrase omitted, we know that God has learned something about man.

There is indeed a greater distance between God and Noah than there was between God and Adam. Adam was put into a garden prepared for him; God then decides Adam needs a helpmate and experiments until he finds the right one. Adam, in other words, takes no initiative. But Noah, instead of hearing from God that the flood is over and that his family and the animals can leave the ark, discovers that fact for himself by sending out the raven and then, three times, the dove. Only after Noah has removed the covering of the ark and determined by the dove that the waters have subsided does God give him new instructions. It is as if God were waiting to see what Noah did, to see what decisions he made on his own. Only after Noah builds the altar and prepares the sacrifice does God agree not to curse the ground again because of man; and even as he says that, God acknowledges to himself that "the imagination of man's heart is evil from his youth."

God's expectations for man seem to have changed. Perhaps because of the trades and skills developed in Cain's city, God seems to know that man will create and conquer; hence, he knows that the animals, birds, and fish will go in fear and dread of man. Perhaps because of Cain's murder of Abel, God seems to know man's capactiy for wickedness; hence, he explicitly states, in clear echo of his conversation with Cain, "of every man's brother I will require the life of man. Whoever sheds the blood of man, by man shall his blood be shed." Perhaps because of Adam's and Eve's disobedience, God seems to know that a verbal agreement between man and God is insufficient; hence, he offers man a visible sign, the rainbow, of his covenant with Noah and all future generations. God, too, is developing as a character in this narrative.

If this represents a conscious literary pattern in the opening chapters of Genesis, then we would expect that pattern to continue. In chapter 9, verse 20, when Noah is called the first tiller of the soil, reminding us, of course, of Adam, he chooses to plant a vineyard (earlier, it was God who "planted"). Noah takes the fruit of his vineyard, and from the fruit (we recall the "fruit" of Genesis 3 and Genesis 4), he makes wine. He drinks of the wine and becomes drunk, losing control of his self just as Adam and Eve (and Cain?) had lost control of their selves; and he lies uncovered in his tent, naked as Adam and Eve were naked. "And Ham," the son analogous to Cain, "saw the nakedness of his father, and told his two brothers outside." The two sons, like Seth and Abel, remain loyal; they tell their father what has happened, and Noah then curses the son of Ham. Up to this point there are parallels between the story of Noah and that of Adam and Eve as well as that of Cain. The curse is perhaps more similar to the curse on Cain, which indicated that his descendants would be outcasts from society. The fact that Noah delivers the curse instead of God, however, suggests a further change in the relationship between man and God: man, it seems, must now share in the administration of human justice.

After the flood we hear that Noah lived 350 years, and at the opening of chapter 10 and through chapter 10 we receive an account of the generations of his sons. As in the accounts of the generations of Seth and of the son of Cain, the descendants of Noah develop trades and skills. Some of them live on the coast, we are told; Nimrod is a mighty hunter; they build a great city (we may recall the city built by Cain). In verse 20 we read, "These are the sons of Ham, by their families, their languages, their lands, and their nations." In verses 31 and 32 we read, "These are the sons of Shem, by their families, their languages, their lands, and their nations. These are the families of the sons of Noah, according to their genealogies, in their nations." Unlike the account of the generations of Adam, where the important phrase "in his own likeness, after his image" occurs, the accounts here are more straightforward: "These are the sons of. . . ." No longer is there any echo of the creation; we sense that the distance from the garden of Eden is now much greater. That distance is underscored at the end of chapter 10: "from these the nations spread abroad on the earth after the flood." People are migrating from east of Eden, where Cain once was; and they say to one another as they come to the location of Shinar, "Let us make bricks, and burn them thoroughly." "Come," they say, "let us build ourselves a city, and a tower with its top in the heavens." Why would they want to build such a tower? One possibility is that they want to challenge or imitate the rainbow, which is God's and which stretches from heaven to earth. (We shall build a tower, they say, and it will stretch from earth to heaven.) "Let us make a name for ourselves," they assert, exhibiting the pride that led Cain to name his new city for his son. "And the Lord came down to see the city and the tower, which the sons of men had built." The Lord "came down," we are told, but the distance between man and God seems so much greater now than in the garden of Eden, where God had walked in the cool of the garden. He decides that he needs to scatter the people, to confuse their languages. The people had feared being "scattered abroad upon the face of the whole earth"; yet, ironically, their actions have led precisely to this end.

The account of the descendants of Shem, which immediately follows this episode, is clearly comparable to the earlier account, in chapter 5, of the descendants of Seth. That account had led to

Noah; this one leads finally to Abraham. At the opening of chapter 12, the Lord says to Abraham something similar to what he had said to Noah earlier: "Go from your country and your kindred and your father's house to the land that I will show you. And I will make of you a great nation, and I will bless you, and make your name great, so that you will be a blessing." Adam, in a sense, had left his father's house, too. Abraham is another of many who will leave their fathers' houses in the narratives that make up the Bible.

If we consider the settings once again, we see that the patterns of Genesis 3–11 continue. We begin with the garden of Eden, move to the ground outside that garden, move then to Cain's city, to the ark, to the ground outside the ark, then to the city and tower of Babel, and finally, to Abraham's great nation. The garden, the ark, and the promised land of Abraham are settings identified by God as special, secure, and protected. God puts Adam and Eve into the garden, he outlines the construction of the ark and shuts Noah into it, and now he directs Abraham to the promised land. But we notice a gradual distancing between man and God. As man is more on his own, he is forced to use his own ingenuity and to make his own decisions. We have already noted that Noah exercised more initiative than Adam, and it is clear that Abraham will take much more initiative than Noah. Why that distancing occurs is perhaps explained by the other settings, which stand in opposition to the garden, the ark and the promised land: that is, the ground tilled by Adam and Cain and Noah outside the secure, protected places, the ground of Egypt occupied by the Pharaoh, the cities built by Cain's and Noah's descendants. These are man-made places which seek to rival in pride and splendor the settings created or constructed or identified by God.

We can also see a pattern in the arrangement of characters and in the genealogies. Adam and Eve, created by God, have three sons. One of them is killed; one of them is wicked. We are given the genealogies of the two surviving sons, and among the descendants of Seth is Noah, destined to bring man relief from the cursed ground. Noah, like Adam and Eve, also has three sons. One of them is, like Cain, sinful, and he is cursed. One of them is, like Seth, favored, and among his descendants is Abraham, destined to bring man relief from the enemies of his people. The long genealogies of the generations of Adam and of Noah are therefore extremely important. They suggest not only the passage of time but also the possibility, in time, of someone who will provide relief, someone who, perhaps, in terms of this narrative and from the perspective of those in this narrative, may be the one to bruise the head of the serpent. The genealogies and their potential make the election of Abraham by God more striking; for at this point in Genesis we are told that Abraham's wife, Sarah, "was barren; she had no child." How, then, can Abraham's line be continued in the same way Adam's and Noah's were, to lead to another Abraham and to another Noah?

There is also a unity in the thematic pattern of sin and punishment. Eve, tempted by the sensuous appeal of the fruit and the desire to be wise, disobeys God's command. After Adam also eats the fruit, the two feel shame in their nakedness; they feel guilt as they hide from the Lord God and as they evade responsibility for their actions. God punishes them, but he also shows them mercy by making them garments. Cain is tempted by his desire to surpass Abel, jealous as he is for God's favor. After he disobeys God's warning and kills Abel, he feels shame, and he, too, evades responsibility for his actions. God punishes him, but he also shows him mercy by marking him so that he will not be slain. Adam's descendants are tempted by the wickedness in their hearts and in their imaginations to do violence. God punishes them in the flood, but he is again merciful, for he saves a representative remnant of man's world. Noah's descendants are tempted by their skills and craftsmanship to build a great city with a tower that reaches to heaven. God punishes them by confusing their language, but he is ultimately merciful in leading Abraham to a promised land.

The poetic interpretation of history is unified by the different kinds of disobedience described in these chapters. Adam and Eve sin directly against God; Cain sins against his brother and neighbor; Adam's descendants sin against their own nature; Ham sins against his father; those at the tower of Babel sin against art by abusing man's skills in order to secure a name for themselves. Gradually the human community is broken down. Gradually man is separated from God and from Eden; brother is separated from brother, man from his own heart and imagination, son from father, nation from nation. Eden becomes increasingly distant, and man becomes increasingly alone. The metaphorical Eden, a place of security and protection, of order and harmony, of timelessness, must be recreated by man, as in the ark and in the promised land. The narrative indicates that man, forever outside of Eden, is, like Adam, in exile; like Cain, a wanderer and a fugitive; like those drowned in the flood, in darkness; like those at the tower of Babel, in confusion; like those in the long genealogies of Adam and Noah, trapped within the slow movement of time and human history. The poetic interpretation of history also holds out hope for man: the serpent will be bruised; Cain will not be killed; the rainbow will signify the covenant; Abraham will bless all the families of the earth. Man, because of his potential for sin, will not return to Eden; but God, because of his potential for mercy, will return Eden to him.

4. ABRAHAM: I

Kenneth R. R. Gros Louis

It seems ironic that Lot, who had chosen that portion of land which looked most fruitful and most comfortable to dwell in, "well watered everywhere like the garden of the Lord, like the land of Egypt," is, because of his choice, taken prisoner by the victorious kings in the battle described in Genesis 14, a chapter most commentators find peculiarly out of place in the collection of incidents that make up the Abraham legend. When Abram followed the Lord's instructions and separated himself from his country, his kindred, and his father's house, we recall that Lot went with him, as well as Sarai his wife, along with all their possessions and servants. We do not know, of course, if Lot—or for that matter Sarai—is aware of the Lord's promises to Abram, promises that in themselves arouse our curiosity because Sarai, we have been told, is barren, and because the land Abram's descendants will possess is occupied by the Canaanites. Our curiosity and concern are further aroused, as perhaps are Abram's and certainly Lot's, when we discover that the land promised to Abram's descendants is experiencing a famine. Abram must leave the promised land, which is, at this point, as barren and unfertile as his wife Sarai, to journey to Egypt, where presumably the land is fruitful and productive enough to support Abram's large household.

With the immediate danger of starvation solved, Abram is confronted with another problem, this one caused by the beauty of

Sarai. Fearing for his own life (and how can he have descendants if he is killed? How can he lay claim to a promised land if he is away from it?), Abram must introduce Sarai as his sister and permit her to be taken into Pharaoh's house. If Lot does not know of the Lord's promises to Abram, all these events must strike him as odd—the leaving of their country and kindred; their settling in a mountainous area that is suffering from famine; their moving into Egypt; Abram's deceiving of the Pharaoh and apparent abandoning of Sarai. If Lot does know of the Lord's promises, he must be uneasy anyway—Sarai and Abram are advanced in age and childless; the land to which Abram is directed is barren and occupied; the family becomes separated in the distant land of Egypt. Therefore, after Lot has escaped from Egypt for reasons he may or may not know and has begun to prosper in the land where Abram "had made an altar at the first," it is not surprising that, given a choice, he selects the well-watered Jordan valley for his home, the cities of the valley for his dwelling place. Whether he is defecting from Abram's vision or not, he has had enough of wandering, famine, and the nomadic life. He chooses fertility, comfort, and civilization. But, as we have seen, as a consequence of his choice of land that is "like the garden of Lord, like the land of Egypt," he becomes a captive, he loses his freedom. To this seeming irony, we must return.

The narrative's reference to "the garden of the Lord" invites us to consider the patterns that have been established in the first eleven chapters of Genesis. Abram is descended from Shem, one of Noah's three sons, as Noah was descended from Seth, one of Adam's three sons. Abram, like Shem and Seth, has two brothers. The Lord speaks to Abram as he had spoken to Adam and to Noah, promising him special treatment, which, initially at least, compares favorably with the special treatment given to Adam, for whom the Lord had planted a garden, and to Noah, whom the Lord saved from the otherwise devastating flood.

But the differences, even from the beginning, are more striking than the similarities. Unlike the gifts given to Adam and Noah, Abram's gift is not immediately to be his. Adam had been put by the Lord into the garden of Eden, surrounded by "every tree that is pleasant to the sight and good for food"; Noah had been given specific instructions on how to build his ark and ordered to bring with him representative pairs "of every living thing of all flesh." Abram's gift, on first reading, seems analogous—he is told to go to the land the Lord would show him and is promised that he will head a great nation and be blessed. But when Abram—and we as readers—arrive at the land, it is barren and unfruitful; indeed, it is plagued by a severe famine. Whatever the Lord has in mind for Abram clearly will not be given to him soon; it may not, in fact, be given to him in his own lifetime, as the narrative suggests when the Lord, speaking to Abram a second time, adds a potential qualifier to his first statement: "To your *descendants,*" says the Lord, "I will give this land."

And what descendants might Abram have? Adam had three sons, the youngest of whom began a long line that culminated in Noah. Noah had three sons, one of whom began a long line that led eventually to Terah, who fathered Abram, Nahor, and Haran. Nahor disappears temporarily from the narrative when Terah moves away from his territory; Haran is dead; Abram's wife is barren. And yet, we read that the Lord appears to Abram and promises to make his name great, even while for us the memory of the fate of those who built the city and tower of Babel to make their own names great remains fresh. What do we make of this juxtaposition, in the context of Sarai's barrenness?

Clearly, our perspective and expectations have been given several jolts. The fruitfulness of Adam's descendants has been suspended as a result of Sarai's barrenness; the land's fecundity and productiveness, which supported Noah so well and which was Adam's gift even after it required the "sweat of his face," has failed; the possession of a secure place, like the garden of Eden or the ark of Noah, will come to Abram's descendants only at some distant time.

The opening verses of chapter 12 thrust us into the future, for the present, unlike the past, even for those for whom God has a special concern, is barren, unproductive, insecure. Abram is promised land and progeny, told that he will be fruitful and have a secure place in a promised land. But the Lord does not fulfill his promises instantly, as he had with Adam and Noah. Perhaps, the narrative is telling us, the Lord is going to be more cautious this time, having seen the results of his generosity to Adam and his concern for Noah. Unlike Adam and Noah, Abram, it seems, is going to be tested by the Lord to prove himself worthy of fruitfulness and security. From a literary point of view, God impinges on Abram's personal life and offers him what, under the circumstances, seems not only fantasies, but impossibilities. Even Abram and Sarai, when they later are told that Sarai will bear a son, laugh.

So it is not without some reason, in the context of his own life, that Lot chooses the well watered Jordan valley. His father is dead; he has followed his uncle in his wanderings to a barren land occupied by Canaanites and to an Egypt ruled by Pharaoh. He and Abram are doing quite well after their return—both are very rich in cattle, silver, and gold. Since Abram gives him his choice, why should Lot not select the most fertile land, the land closest to the cities? Lot, however, does not know as we know from the earlier chapters of Genesis, that there are, paradoxically, dangers in fruitfulness, possessions, luxuries, and civilization. Cain had built himself a city and pridefully named it after his son. Those in the land of Shinar had planned to build a great city, with a tower to rival the Lord's rainbow in touching both heaven and earth. It was the very fruitfulness of Adam's garden which in part led him to desire more; the Lord had rejected Cain's offering of the fruit of the ground; the wine made from the fruit of Noah's vineyard had made him drunk; Abram, the narrative tells us, "was very rich," but surely he knows that his wife is barren and that the land promised to him is occupied by others; Sarai is beautiful, but her very beauty poses a threat to Abram's life. "Pleasure," Keats wrote, "turning to poison while the bee-mouth sips." Lot is so rich that he has to separate himself from Abram. He is so desirous of more comforts that he is unaware of the echo and the foreshadowing of his own thoughts as he surveys the Jordan valley—"watered everywhere like the garden of the Lord, like the land of Egypt"—an echo, for us, of the garden where Adam and Eve fell, a foreshadowing, for us, of the land where Abram's descendants will be slaves for four hundred years. Such recollections are forced on us by the narrative, which concludes Lot's survey of the land with the ominous phrase, "this was before the Lord destroyed Sodom and Gomorrah."

A great deal happens between the time the Lord planted his garden for Adam and the time Abram's descendants will be led from their bondage in Egypt. The length and dangers of the journey are only gradually revealed to Abram—and to us. The difficulty is demonstrated by Lot, who will defect from hardship when he can and select what seems the easier and more comfortable route when a choice is offered. The daring imaginativeness of the narrative lies in its attempt both to depict what it presents as a Lord who creates and controls history, and at the same time to describe independent individuals who live out that history, who must survive on a day-to-day basis, who have the ability to choose between alternatives. To achieve congruity between the seemingly incongruous concepts of a controlling divinity and individuals capable of making choices is an enormous undertaking. But as we have already seen in Genesis and can see throughout the Old Testament, the narrowing of the gap between what seems to be and what is, between appearance and reality, creates that harmony of incongruities that leads us, and the characters who participate in these historical developments, to understand the true meanings of such concepts as beauty, fruitfulness, possession. The microcosmic response of Lot as he surveys the Jordan valley, which invokes so many images in our minds—and certainly invoked images in the minds of the audience who first heard it—turns out also to be myopic, for there exists in the same valley, in the same sentence, both the likeness of Eden and the destruction of Sodom and Gomorrah.

Lot, however, never understands the necessity of this coexistence, never sees beyond himself and his own needs. After he is rescued from the "victorious" kings by Abram, he presumably returns to Sodom, since that is where we find him sitting by the gate of the city when two angels of the Lord come to Sodom one evening. Although he is warned—and twice—that the city is to be destroyed, the narrative tells us that "he lingered," and the angels are actually forced to seize him and lead him by the hand away from his own death. "Flee for your life," they tell him; "do not look back or stop anywhere in the valley; flee to the hills." But Lot, even at this moment, thinks of his comfort: "I cannot flee to the hills," he says. "Behold, yonder city is near enough to flee to, and it is a little one." That the narrative is aware of how Lot is being characterized is made clear in the repetition that follows. Lot has already pointed out that the city he wishes to go to is a "little one," but he adds the rhetorical emphasis, "Let me escape there—is it not a little one?" He had earlier chosen the more comfortable life, and he will not easily abandon it, even under crisis circumstances. Once in the city, however, given his past experiences and his knowledge that Sodom and Gomorrah were indeed destroyed, he seems uncertain about his choice, and then moves into the hills. "He was afraid," the narrative tells us, "to dwell in Zoar; so he dwelt in a cave with his two daughters." In that cave his daughters, the daughters Lot had offered to the sinful men of Sodom, in imitation of their father's concern for self and in a final perversion of the concepts of fruitfulness and possession, make Lot drunk with wine, sleep with him, and bear his children. That is the last we hear of Lot in the Old Testament.

Now that Lot has fulfilled his function in the narrative, chapter 20 immediately returns us to the beginning, that is, to chapter 12. Abraham again changes the place of his dwelling, again claiming that Sarah is his sister, this time deceiving Abimelech. We are reminded, of course, of Abram's initial movements and of his permitting Sarai, his "sister," to be taken in by the Pharaoh of Egypt. Most commentaries on Genesis cite these parallel passages as evidence of the various sources that were combined to make up the book. Evidence of different sources and compilers is persuasive, but from a literary point of view, repetitions in a narrative are not necessarily the result of clumsy or inconsistent craftsmanship. Commentators never tire of pointing out the "repetitions, stylistic irregularities, and inconsistencies" in the Pentateuch. "In Genesis 15:5," writes one biblical scholar, "Abraham is promised many descendants, and in Genesis 17:2 the promise is needlessly repeated." Repetition in narrative is rarely needless, as the final shapers of the Genesis material seem to be aware. Many incidents usually occur between an initial account of an event and its repetition, and these incidents affect our second reading of the event. Subtle or obvious changes may be made in the retelling which help advance our understanding of the narrative. Or, as may be the case with chapter 20, the narrative consciously brings us back to its beginning, signaling to us that a pattern or theme has been completed and that a new, but parallel, one is about to begin. The narrative has given us Lot as a foil against which to compare Abraham. With Lot now in the background—indeed eliminated—we should accept the suggestions of chapter 20, return to the beginning, and consider a second major structural pattern of the first half of the Abraham legend—the changing relationship between Abraham and God.

Anyone who reads Genesis 12 is surely struck by Abram's immediate acceptance of the Lord's directions. Presumably he knows, as do we, that his wife is barren; yet, he does not ask the question that must have come into his mind. Presumably, too, he notes the slight shift in the Lord's promise when he arrives in Canaan—"To your *descendants* I will give this land." Abram himself is not necessarily excluded from possession of the promised land, but the statement implies that he *may* be. Still, Abram asks no questions. He remains silent again when the famine in the land forces him to journey to Egypt leaving the possession and the altar he had built to the Lord.

Commentaries on Genesis point out that Abraham represents a model of faithful obedience to the Lord, and so he surely does. But we need, I think, to explore the concept of faithfulness more fully to understand the complexity of the insights offered by the Abraham legend. The compilers of the narrative do not seem to be advocating blind obedience or passive faith; Abram's faith, for example, is not that of the Christian martyrs. A complex relationship is being suggested between a God who has a plan for human history and the individuals who participate in the unfolding of that plan. Incremental tension exists in the conversations between Abraham and the Lord as the Lord gradually reveals more of his plan and Abraham reveals more of his human questions and concerns. That faith by itself is not sufficient is indicated in Egypt, when Abram, remembering the Lord's promises and *believing* in them, must act to ensure that they are not thwarted by Pharaoh. In avoiding possible death because of Sarai's beauty, Abram demonstrates the need for initiative on man's part, for imaginativeness—a word, it may be worth noting, that is metaphorically interchangeable with the word *fruitfulness*. His initiative not only saves his life, but also enhances his authority—Pharaoh, the narrative tells us, "dealt well with Abram" for Sarai's sake and gave him sheep, oxen, he-asses, menservants, maidservants, she-asses, and camels. Abram demonstrates—and for similar motives—the same initiative, imagination, and belief when he suggests to Lot that they separate from each other. For purely pragmatic reasons, he does not want any conflict with Lot that might interfere with the Lord's promises. In giving Lot his choice of land (and since Abram is his elder it would seem appropriate for Lot to decline the offer), Abram illustrates his understanding of his relationship to the Lord's historical design. Abram's job is to keep himself and Sarai alive and well and the family together; the Lord has promised descendants and land, and will, Abram's actions suggest, provide them at the proper time. As we have seen, the narrative emphasizes the rightness of Abram's instincts by juxtaposing the attractive description of the Jordan valley—Lot's choice—with that allusion to the destruction of Sodom and Gomorrah, the cities that, because of Lot's choice, are distant from the place where Abram dwells.

Abram's dependence on the Lord, epitomized by his belief in the Lord's promises, in no way affects his own independence. On the contrary, it makes him more alert in his dealings with others, more cautious in responding to what seem to be reasonable propositions. Chapter 14 may seem out of place to some biblical scholars, but from a literary perspective, it is very important. For one thing, it suggests to us, more than any other episode in the narrative, the turbulent, uncertain world in which Abraham moves. Although he is living a semi-nomadic life, he is hardly isolated and alone in the wilderness. The chapter enlarges our understanding of Abram in other ways, too. Again he initiates action in rescuing Lot from his captors. As in the incident with Pharaoh, Abram uses his imagination, this time deploying his 318 men and attacking by night to overcome what is presumably a much larger force. His concern for Lot, the nephew who had chosen the most fertile land, illustrates his sense of responsibility to the concept of the family and provides the basis for our understanding of one of the reasons why he later bargains with the Lord over Sodom and Gomorrah—he wants to save Lot's life.

Most important, perhaps, chapter 14 makes explicit Abram's belief in what the sources of fruitfulness and possession really are. Upon his victorious return Abram is greeted by the kings of Sodom and Salem and complimented in the most flattering terms. The king of Sodom offers him all the goods he has recaptured. But

Abram declines: "I have sworn to the Lord God Most High," he says, "that I would not take a thread or a sandal-thong or anything that is yours, lest you should say, 'I have made Abram rich.'" Abram may know, as we know, that the men of Sodom are "wicked, great sinners against the Lord." Yet his response is also consistent with his previous decisions—to journey to Egypt, to deceive Pharaoh, to give Lot his choice of land, to rescue Lot. They all reveal his guiding principle, one not stated until the most dramatic moment of his life—"the Lord will provide."

The difficulty Abram has—that anyone might have—in maintaining this principle unquestioningly is what makes the Abraham legend significant as literature. Living as we do, and as Abraham did, in a world of uncertainties, it is not easy to stand and wait. The development of Abraham's relationship with the Lord is in a real sense the development of his coming to terms with the possibilities and limitations of human experience and human understanding. The two have many conversations in the narrative up to the point at which, in chapter 20, the narrative takes us back to its beginning. After that, however, the Lord speaks to Abraham only once: "Take your son, your only son Isaac, whom you love. . . ."

We have already noted the apparent gap between the Lord's magnificent promises to Abram and what we know of Sarai and soon learn about the unproductive land occupied by the Canaanites. The gap between promise and probability of fulfillment strikes us again when Lot chooses the well watered Jordan valley. But the narrative, as if in response to our puzzlement—and perhaps Abram's—has the Lord appear to Abram immediately after Lot has separated from him. The Lord not only repeats his promises, but enlarges on them: "I will make your descendants as the dust of the earth; so that if one can count the dust of the earth, your descendants also can be counted." The land that Abram is to receive is more particularly specified: "Lift up your eyes, and look from the place where you are, northward and southward and eastward and westward; for all the land which you see I will give to you and to your descendants for ever." In a dramatic suggestion, the Lord encourages Abram to "walk through the length and the breadth of the land." It takes little imagination for us to enlarge on this simple direction and wonder what Abram thinks as he strolls through the promised land, aware of Sarai's barrenness, of the Canaanites, of Lot's fertile valley. It is a walk that tests patience and challenges faith. Had Abram maintained such silent acceptance to the end of his life, he would not be as interesting a character as he is; indeed, he would not be as believable as he is. But the compilers of the Old Testament are always conscious of the beating heart. The repetitions of the Lord's promises to Abram are in no way needless. They are central to the gradual understanding that Abram must achieve. Each visit from the Lord provides Abram—and us—with new information.

"After these things," chapter 15 opens—that is, after Abram has rescued Lot and rejected the possessions offered by the king of Sodom—the Lord comes to him in a vision. "Fear not, Abram," says the Lord; "I am your shield; your reward shall be very great." The words are striking. The metaphor the Lord uses to describe his relationship to Abram recalls the battle of the kings and Abram's daring recovery of Lot, and indicates the Lord's acknowledgment of the turbulent human world in which Abram lives. The promised reward, coupled with the "fear not," echoes the Lord's earlier promises, but in a more personal way. The change may be occasioned by Abram's continued concern for the welfare and safety of Lot, and by his refusal to be made rich by the king of Sodom. If Abram is being tested, he seems to be doing well, providing for Lot but waiting for the Lord to provide for him. The simple words "fear not" begin to bridge the gap between Abram and his God, recalling as they do the more intimate relationships the Lord had with Adam and with Noah, indicating the Lord's concern for Abram's thoughts and emotions.

Abram does not miss the significance of the comforting phrase and is emboldened by it to ask the questions that must have been on his mind from the start. "O Lord God," he says, "what wilt thou give me, for I continue childless. . . . Behold, thou hast given me no offspring." Since the Lord has told Abram on three occasions what he will give him, the question itself is superfluous; but its motive, a desire for more information, for greater clarity, is psychologically credible. After all, Abram's wife is barren; and, as he points out, it seems as if a slave born in his house will be his heir. The Lord might not have answered Abram's question earlier, but Abram's confidence in the Lord—when in Egypt, with Lot, with the king of Sodom—is now, it seems, to be reciprocated. "This man shall not be your heir; your own son shall be your heir." For the first time, Abram receives a specific promise of a son, although we note that the Lord does not indicate to him—or to us—that the son will also be Sarai's. The grandeur of the earlier promise is described in another simile, as the Lord tells Abram that his descendants will be as numerous as the stars. Earlier, he had told Abram that his descendants would be as numerous as the dust of the earth. The very metaphors, so carefully chosen, bridge the gap between the divine and the human, merging heaven and earth in images rich with echoes from the earlier chapters of Genesis. Do we recall, even subconsciously, the image of the rainbow? Abram, the narrative informs us, believes the Lord, "and he reckoned it to him as righteousness." Abram seems to perceive the inevitable congruity of the Lord's gifts and his own faith.

Given the new quality of their relationship, Abram is prompted to ask the second question, which must have been on his mind from the start—"O Lord God, how am I to know that I shall possess it?" Notice that the question is not "When will I possess it?" or "How will I come to possess it?" but rather, How can I know this is going to happen, how can I be certain that my knowledge of this information is valid? In part, the Lord's answer to Abram's epistemological concern is unsatisfactory; his knowledge must be accepted on trust and faith, for it is not demonstrable. In retrospect, of course, the knowledge and the means of knowing its validity are certain and clear for the audience for which the Abraham legend was first written down. They know, for example, of the birth of Isaac and of the Exodus. But for Abram the answer comes in the form of a covenant, an oath. Abram is to know he will possess the land because the Lord has made a formal agreement with him. That, however, is only the superficial aspect of the Lord's reply. Abram's knowledge comes from two other factors. First, the Lord himself, as he had with Adam and Noah, participates in the ritual by appearing to Abram, and by passing between the pieces of flesh when the sun had gone down, narrowing the bridge between divinity and humanity in a visibly dramatic way. Second, and perhaps most important, Abram knows his descendants will possess the land because they will earn it. What a difference for Abram between the Lord's initial promise, "I will make of you a great nation," and the details now offered: "your descendants will be sojourners in a land that is not theirs, and will be slaves there, and they will be oppressed for four hundred years." Surely Abram, when he left his country, his kindred, and his father's house, did not expect such a history for his family and descendants; surely he did not know that he would not possess the promised land himself. What a difference, too, between Abram's descendants, who must earn the promised land by being slaves in Egypt, and Lot, who simply takes the fertile valley because it looks like Egypt. Having observed Abram's actions and seen demonstrations of his faith, we can imagine his response to this information. We can imagine as well how Lot, who chose the fertile valley and begged to be permitted to go to his "little" city rather than the hills, would have responded.

The destinies of Abraham and Lot are moving in different directions because of the values on which they base their lives. Lot, concerned primarily for himself, is shrinking as an individual, being reduced to the narrowness of his vision. His life fulfills his being, as he moves away from Abraham's grand vision to the Jordan valley, to the city of Sodom, to the little city of Zoar, to the cave in the hills, to the smallness of his own family and the inbreeding of his own descendants through his daughters. The space within which he lives literally gets smaller as the narrative progresses until he literally disappears; we never hear of his actual death. Abram, on the other hand, expands in space and then in time, his descendants to be as numerous as the dust of the earth, as the stars of the heavens. But always there is the coexistent pain, the coexistent puzzlement: his descendants will be slaves for four hundred years, yet the land they will inherit will stretch "from the river of Egypt to the great river, the river Euphrates"; "Sarai, Abram's wife, bore him no children," yet his son shall be his heir.

The expansion of Abraham's destiny continues in chapter 17. Although some biblical scholars claim that portions of the chapter contain needless repetition, the few alterations are extremely significant. Earlier the narrative had told us that the Lord made a covenant with Abram, but now the Lord says, "I will make my covenant between me and you." The Lord's loyalty, in other words, is to be reciprocated by Abram and his descendants: "Every male among you shall be circumcised," a charge which, we are told twice, Abraham fulfills "that very day." Earlier the Lord had spoken of Abraham's descendants in metaphors, but now he explicitly says that Abraham will "multiply . . . exceedingly," be "exceedingly fruitful," with obvious echoes for us of previous blessings in *this* narrative of Adam and Noah. Earlier he had promised to make Abram "a great nation," but now he changes his name to Abraham and reveals that he will be "the father of a multitude of nations." Earlier he had promised to give the land Abram could see to his descendants for ever, but now he speaks of an "everlasting covenant" in which he will be God to Abraham and to all his descendants. The incremental progression of the Lord's promises reaches its culmination in this chapter. For Adam and Noah, no trial period was required; but for Abraham twenty-four years have passed since he left his father's house and country. The relationship between him and the Lord has grown increasingly intimate, and it reaches a climax in this chapter through the personal covenant between them, confirmed by rituals in which each participates.

The Lord's appearance in chapter 17 comes in an important narrative context, too. Between his promise to Abram of a son in 15:4 and his promises in this chapter, Abram has fathered a son—"Hagar bore Abram a son; and Abram called the name of his son, whom Hagar bore, Ishmael." From Abraham's perspective, part of the Lord's promise seems to have been fulfilled. That he assumes Ishmael is to be his heir is indicated by his laughter when the Lord tells him, for the first time, that Sarah will bear him a son. He dismisses the notion—"Shall a child be born to a man who is a hundred years old? Shall Sarah, who is ninety years old, bear a child?"—and he says to the Lord, "O that Ishmael might live in thy sight!" Ishmael is, after all, now thirteen years old and Abraham has grown very fond of him. Surely he is the promised son. But in another of the ironies that underline these differences between human and divine perception which the narrative is exploring and seeking to bring into some kind of congruity, Abraham has been mistaken. The fruitfulness of which the Lord has recently spoken will, like the "everlasting possession" of the land of Canaan, be the Lord's gift. Others can rival fruitfulness, like those who attempted to build the tower of Babel; or they can imitate it, like Sarah, who gave Hagar to Abraham as a wife; or they can offer it, like the king of Sodom, who offered all the captured goods to Abram; or they can persuade themselves they have found it, like Lot, who chose the well watered valley; but they will not have fruitfulness in its fullest sense, in its luxuriance and generousness, without the Lord. Abraham, in his dealings with Pharaoh, Lot, and the king of Sodom, has demonstrated that he understands this; yet, even such understanding leads him to assume wrongly that Ishmael is his son and heir.

There are certainly possibilities for beauty and fruitfulness and possessions in human life, but there are also limitations over which we may have no control. Abraham seems to have learned this lesson by the time he bargains with the Lord over Sodom and Gomorrah. He does not say, "But my kinsman Lot is in the city and his life should be spared," nor does he say, "You cannot kill everyone because a majority of the city-dwellers are sinners." Instead, he probes cautiously, as if to see whether or not his expectations and hopes might converge with the Lord's, to see where they might intersect. "Suppose there are fifty righteous within the city; wilt thou then destroy the place and not spare it for the fifty righteous who are in it? Far be it from thee to do such a thing. . . . Far be that from thee! Shall not the Judge of all the earth do right?" Out of context, Abraham's speech is a bold one. But in the context we have just been considering, his question is in large part rhetorical. He may, as some commentators point out, be suggesting that the god of justice should also be a god of mercy. He may, as I have suggested, essentially be pleading on behalf of Lot. Neither interpretation has to be discarded, however, if we also acknowledge that Abraham is being more cautious in finding out the specifics of the Lord's plan, knowing as he now does that the Lord's promises may be fulfilled only in the distant future (the promised land) and that even what seems to be their fulfillment (Ishmael) may not be that at all.

In pressing his case with the Lord, with open flattery and no little wit, Abraham seeks to find the point of convergence between his desires and the Lord's plans. It is not like Abraham, given his previous, long relationship with the Lord, to become so much the courtier, the intimate associate: "Behold, I have taken upon myself to speak to the Lord, I who am but dust and ashes," he says, as he cuts the number of righteous from fifty to forty-five to forty to thirty to twenty, and finally, to ten—"Oh let not the Lord be angry, and I will speak again but this once." "The Lord went his way," the narrative concludes with wit of its own, "when *he* had finished speaking to Abraham."

The conversation is important in illustrating the new kind of relationship that exists between Abraham and the Lord as a result of their covenant. In one sense, it is not out of place for Abraham to bargain with the Lord. He now knows that he will not dwell in the promised land, that Sarah will bear him a son, and that he will die and be buried in peace and in a good old age. His destiny and fulfillment are set. His bargaining is also successful—Lot's life is saved, even though the latter is reluctant to go and must be dragged away from Sodom by the angels. But in another sense, Abraham's intimacy and knowledge of his future may not be a good thing, for if he can second-guess the Lord or persuade him to alter his plans, however slightly, then perhaps the gap between human initiative and divine design has grown too small. Abraham—indeed any person—cannot become too much an insider, too greatly detached from the history that he must with his own ingenuity and imagination help to create. The danger in Abraham's position is not to the Lord, but to Abraham himself, who, by being "in," so to speak, on the the Lord's plans, loses his independence and might forget the necessity of being alert and cautious, of being prepared for the unexpected, of being constantly ready for the fulfillment without knowing when it might occur. It is certainly important, for their credibility to us as readers, that Abraham and Sarah laugh when the Lord tells them that they will have a son. It is important, too, for Sarah to deny that she laughed and for Abraham to ask the Lord how he can know that he will possess the land. If Abraham had had the confidence earlier that leads him to bargain with the Lord for the lives of the righteous—perhaps particularly for Lot—in Sodom, he would not have asked his questions or been moved to laughter; he would not, in other words, have responded in the most human and natural way to the unexplained and the unexpected. As Abraham surveys the destroyed cities in 19:28, knowing that Lot has been saved as a result of his bargaining with the Lord, we know how close Abraham came to not even hearing about the destruction of Sodom and Gomorrah. The Lord had debated whether to tell

Abraham of his plans and decided to do so only at the last moment. We are made aware, because of this exceptional decision, of how little we usually know. Abraham had not known, for example, that there would be a famine in the land to which he was led or that Lot would be captured, or that Ishmael was not to be his heir, or that Sarah would bear him a son. Perhaps Abraham is thinking as well of the uniqueness of his opportunity to save Lot, of having known in advance what, for others, came unexpectedly and unexplained. It is perhaps worth noting that the Lord, who has spoken to Abraham throughout the narrative to this point, speaks to him only one more time: "Take your son, your only son Isaac, whom you love. . . ."

That chapter 20 opens with Abraham again pretending that Sarah is his sister is appropriate. The preceding chapters of the Abraham legend form a compete unit of their own. The unit begins with general promises of fruitfulness and possession, promises that are juxtaposed with barrenness and famine; the unit ends with the season of the birth of Isaac and the specifications of the boundaries of the promised land, specifications that are, however, juxtaposed with perversions of fruitfulness and possession, by the daughters of Lot, by the men of Sodom who attempt to break down Lot's door so that they might know his male guests.

If we were to chart the events that have occurred in the human world in these chapters, we would become aware of destinies moving in inverse proportion to what seemed their possibilities. For Abraham, the barrenness of Sarah is soon to be converted into fruitfulness, the land that was occupied and unfertile at the first will become an everlasting possession for his descendants, flowing with milk and honey. For those in the fertile Jordan valley and the civilized cities, however, come death and destruction—the Lord "overthrew those cities, and all the valley, and all the inhabitants of the cities, and what grew on the ground." The interlacing of fruitfulness with barrenness, possession with desolation, runs through the entire narrative. The word "interlacing" suggests the simultaneity of what seems to us, and to those in the narrative, to be opposites. Inherent in what those in Abraham's world seem to value most is its opposite. That is why the line from Keats' "Ode to Melancholy," indeed perhaps the entire poem, contains insights not unrelated to the Abraham legend—"Pleasure turning to poison while the bee-mouth sips." The promised land, for which Abram leaves his country, his kindred, and his father's house is barren and occupied; the beautiful woman whom Pharaoh brings into his house causes him to be afflicted with great plagues; the well watered valley chosen by Lot is filled with sinners and fought over by kings; his secure and fertile land is the site of his capture; Sarah's generous decision to give Hagar to Abram as wife causes her anger and pain; Hagar's obedience to her mistress leads to her being driven into the wilderness; the pleasure the men of Sodom seek in surrounding Lot's house and assaulting its entrance makes them blind; the little city Lot bargains for fills him with fear; the secure cave he moves to arouses the perverse scheme of his daughters. Each seemingly attractive opportunity also contains within it barrenness, pain, destruction, perversion.

As these human events and choices interlace, suggesting to us the difficulty of seeing clearly the precariousness of human existence, the Lord and Abraham, initially separated by the differences between divine and human perceptions and concerns, move into closer—almost too close—harmony and congruity. The movement of human history involving pleasure and pain impinges on Abraham less and less in the narrative. His detachment from the events around him—a psychological, not a real detachment— is suggested by the narrative's placement of the Lord's promises to him. He is promised descendants and land after the narrative informs us that Sarai is barren shortly before we learn of the famine; the promise is repeated and expanded after the destruction of Sodom and Gomorrah is foreshadowed and before the battle of the four against the five kings; he is promised a son and told of his descendants' oppression after he rejects the king of Sodom's offer and before Sarai drives Hagar into the wilderness; the covenant is made with him after Hagar is saved by the Lord and before the destruction of Sodom and Gomorrah. The distance between these future-oriented and incrementally specified promises and the depressing, at times catastrophic, events that surround them in the narrative and with which Abraham lives, gradually moves Abraham out of time, enabling us to interpret figuratively the significance of his look down toward Sodom and Gomorrah, watching the smoke of the land rise like the smoke of a furnace.

As Lot loses his possessions in nearly every sense of that word, Abraham gains self-possession, equanimity. As Lot and those from his city pervert the meaning of fruitfulness, Abraham receives fruitfulness as a gift. As Pharaoh and Lot and the king of Sodom place value on beauty in its physical and material manifestations, Abraham in chapter 18 demonstrates the beauty of service and simplicity, running from his tent door to greet his vistors, hastening to his tent to tell Sarah to "make ready quickly three measures of fine meal, knead it, and make cakes," selecting a calf, tender and good, standing silently by while his guests eat under a tree. Lot, we recall, serves his guests unleavened bread.

Abraham is not the same man in chapter 20 when he introduces Sarah as his sister to Abimelech as he was when he made the same introduction to Pharaoh in chapter 12. His knowledge of his destiny is obviously greater, but more important, he has discovered—and the narrative has identified for us—the denotations of a beauty, possession, and fruitfulness, which narrow the gap between a Lord who has a design for history and the individuals who must retain their independence as they fulfill it, between human possibilities and human limitations. Abraham's understanding prepares him well for the test in which he is asked to sacrifice his son, his only son, whom he loves.

5. ABRAHAM: II

Kenneth R. R. Gros Louis

It is difficult to discuss chapter 22 of Genesis without being influenced by Erich Auerbach's brilliant analysis in his 1946 study, *Mimesis: The Representation of Reality in Western Literature.* Auerbach compares the Abraham and Isaac narrative in chapter 22 with the scene in Homer's *Odyssey* in which the nurse Eurycleia, washing the feet of a guest in Penelope's house, recognizes a particular scar and knows that the guest is the long-wandering, long-lost husband of Penelope, Odysseus. The primary emphasis of Auerbach's analysis, to reduce his subtle and sophisticated argument more than is perhaps fair, is to point out the differences between the leisurely, present-dominated Homeric account, and the tense, abbreviated narrative of Isaac's near sacrifice, in which foreground information is reduced to an absolute minimum. Auerbach, of course, as his subtitle suggests, is concerned with more than Homer and the Bible; he uses these specific scenes, he says, "in order to reach a starting point for an investigation into the literary representation of reality in European culture." For him, the styles in these scenes represent basic, though opposite, types:

on the one hand [speaking of Homer] fully externalized description, uniform illumination, uninterrupted connections, free expression, all events in the foreground, displaying unmistakable meanings, few elements of historical development and of psychological perspective; on the other hand [speaking of the Abraham and Isaac episode], certain parts brought into high relief, others left obscure, abruptness, suggestive influence of the unexpressed, "background" quality, multiplicity of meanings and the need for interpretation, universal-historical claims, development of the concept of the historically becoming, and preoccupation with the problematic.

To summarize Auerbach's interpretation of Genesis 22, the episode is "a homogeneous narrative produced by the so-called Elohist." The narrative opening, he writes, startles us: "Where are the two speakers? We are not told. . . . Whence does [the Lord] come, Whence does he call to Abraham? We are not told. . . . Unexpected and mysterious, he enters the scene from some unknown height or depth and calls: Abraham!" Similarly, continues Auerbach, we do not know where Abraham is: "Whether in Beersheba or elsewhere, whether indoors or in the open air, is not stated; it does not interest the narrator, the reader is not informed; and what Abraham was doing when God called to him is left in the same obscurity." The story itself is stripped bare of Homeric-type details: "It is unthinkable," writes Auerbach, "that an implement, a landscape through which the travelers passed, the serving-men, or the ass, should be described, that their origin or descent or material or appearance or usefulness should be set forth in terms of praise; they do not even admit an adjective." A journey takes place, but we are told nothing about it. "The journey is like a silent progress through the indeterminate and the contingent, a holding of the breath, a process which has no present, which is inserted, like a blank duration, between what has passed and what lies ahead, and which yet is measured: three days!" In the narrative itself, Isaac is not characterized—he is Abraham's only son, whom he loves, but, says Auerbach, "this is not a characterization of Isaac as a person. . . . He may be handsome or ugly, intelligent or stupid, tall or short, pleasant or unpleasant—we are not told." It is worth noting that Auerbach says nothing about what happens *after* Abraham prepares the altar and wood and takes the knife to slay his son—a moment about which John Calvin wrote, "I could not have looked." "In the story" of Abraham's sacrifice, Auerbach concludes, "the overwhelming suspense is present; what Schiller makes the goal of the tragic poet—to rob us of our emotional freedom, to turn our intellectual and spiritual powers . . . in one direction, to concentrate them there—is effected in the Biblical narrative."

It is certainly difficult to quarrel with Auerbach's analysis of the eight verses of Genesis 22 on which he chooses to concentrate. He is obviously right in pointing out the lack of details in the episodes, the lack of characterization and of psychological processes (especially in regard to Isaac), and the highly concentrated or compressed way in which time and space are treated. But it is curious to me that Auerbach, who is so concerned with the context of the Eurycleia-Odysseus episode and who contrasts the Homeric style with the Old Testament style by drawing examples from other scenes in the *Odyssey* (and indeed, from a few scenes in *The Iliad*), says so little about the narrative context of the Abraham and Isaac story. Auerbach does not deal with the entire narrative; his discussion concerns what happens from the moment of God's command to the time of Abraham's arrival at the appointed place of sacrifice. It is curious, too, that such a fine critic, and one who elsewhere in *Mimesis* emphasizes the necessity for critical detachment and objectivity, advances certain interpretations of the narrative that have no textual justification. Abraham, Auerbach tells us, was "sorely tried. . . . Bitter to him is the early morning in which he saddles his ass, calls his serving-man and his son Isaac, and sets out." On a purely human level and considering the scene by itself, Auerbach's point is obviously not unreasonable; still, there is nothing in the text to support his assertion that the morning for Abraham was "bitter." Later in his essay, Auerbach, after noting that Abraham's actions are explained in part by his previous history (but not elaborating on this insight), contends that Abraham "is constantly conscious of what God has promised him and what God has already accomplished for him—his soul is torn between desperate rebellion and hopeful expectation." I find no textual evidence that Abraham, at any moment, considers "desperate rebellion"—the dialectic Auerbach imposes on Abraham's soul seems to me solely a twentieth-century interpretation. If Auerbach is looking for what the narrative keeps obscure, it is precisely not this point which he develops about Abraham—for despite circumstances that are indeed exceedingly trying, the narrative contains no mention, not even a hint, that Abraham thinks of rebelling; on the contrary, the text is emphatic in stressing how quickly and unquestioningly Abraham carries out the Lord's various commands.

As students of literature we must, it seems to me, be concerned with the narrative context of the Abraham and Isaac story. And by that I mean not only the episodes that precede and follow it, but also that entire "previous history" of Abraham to which Auerbach so briefly alludes. In discussing Genesis 12–19, I tried to describe the growth of Abraham as a personality and the slow development of his complex relationship with the Lord. Abraham's personal growth is depicted in the narrative through the contrasts between his actions and decisions and those of Lot. The lingering final image for me is of Abraham looking down toward Sodom and Gomorrah, watching the smoke of the land rising like the smoke of a furnace. At that moment in his life, he seems psychologically as well as physically removed from the events around him, spatially and temporally detached. What the Lord had told him would happen to Sodom and Gomorrah has happened, and we can only assume, as Abraham himself has assumed throughout, that all the Lord had promised for the future will also come to pass. Abraham's destiny, his "fulfillment," to use a word from Auerbach, has been set prior to the destruction of Sodom and Gomorrah. Sarah will bear him a son whose name shall be Isaac, and it is with *Isaac,* the Lord has told Abraham, that "I will establish my covenant . . . as an everlasting covenant for his descendants after him." Only two verses later in chapter 17, after the Lord has promised to make Ishmael fruitful as well, the promise is repeated: "But I will establish my covenant with Isaac, whom Sarah shall bear to you at this season next year." If there is a single climactic moment in the Abraham legend—and there may be several—I believe it is when Abraham views these smoking ruins, knowing, as we know, what has passed between himself and the Lord, knowing, as we know, what is to come for Isaac and his descendants, understanding, as Lot never understands, the true meanings of barrenness, beauty, fruitfulness, and possession.

Surely as readers of a literary narrative, we must keep the previous history detailed in Genesis 12–19 deeply in mind as we read chapter 22. We may not know where the Lord speaks from, but we do know that he has spoken to Abraham before; we may not know where Abraham is or what he is doing when he answers—"Here am I," but we do know that he has answered the Lord before; Isaac may not be characterized for us, but we do know that the Lord has made a covenant with Abraham concerning him and his descendants, as he had earlier made covenants with Noah and Abraham. What Abraham does in chapter 22 is not an existential act, but part of a coherent continuum that is not obscure to us as readers; indeed, given what has gone before in the narrative, what he does seems less a climactic moment and more like a coda, a final refrain that recalls for us the themes of Abraham's life and epitomizes them in a highly compressed scene, the tone of which is quiet, direct, simple.

We must also consider, of course, the immediate contexts of the Abraham and Isaac story. No matter how the version of Genesis that we have was finally formed, the job was not done haphazardly. As in any other narrative, the placement of scenes can be crucial to our understanding of the Abraham legend. The near-sacrifice of Isaac, for example, is preceded by a controversy between Abraham and Abimelech over a well of water, a conflict whose resolution is confirmed by a covenant made between the two men. The Abimelech-Abraham covenant invites us to consider the role "covenant" has had in structuring the entire Abraham cycle of stories. The concept of covenant is, in fact, woven carefully into the fabric of the Abraham narrative.

Despite the Lord's promises to Abram at the opening of chapter 12, it is only *after* the sojourn in Egypt, *after* the capture and rescue of Lot, *after* the prophetic account of the oppression of Abraham's descendants, that the Lord, in chapter 15, makes a *covenant* with Abram. Two chapters later, the narrative distinguishes carefully between the Lord's plans for Ishmael—"I will bless him and make him fruitful and multiply him exceedingly"—and his plans for Isaac. The Abimelech covenant immediately preceding the test of Abraham surely leads us to remember these previous covenants and thus affects our response to Genesis 22. Not only does the present incident with Abimelech demonstrate Abraham's bringing of the concept of covenant into the human community, thereby creating harmony and peace—Abimelech and the commander of his army, we note, *return* to the land of the Philistines—but it also connects by a narrative link the Lord's command to slay Isaac to the Lord's earlier statement: "I will establish my covenant *with* Isaac. . . ."

The near-sacrifice is followed in the narrative by an account of the children born to Abraham's brother, Nahor, and then, at the beginning of chapter 23, by Sarah's death. We have heard nothing of Nahor and his wife Milcah since the end of Genesis 11, a chapter that also contained the last of many genealogies of the descendants of Adam. The reintroduction of Nahor here provides a frame for the Abraham narrative, and indicates to us that the account of Abraham's complex interrelationships with the Lord is coming to an end. The allusion to Sarah's death confirms the gradual winding down of the Abraham legend, as does the fact that the Lord does not again speak to Abraham. (Careful readers should further be struck by the special attention given to Rebekah in the account of Nahor's family, and thus be alerted to the match between Isaac and Rebekah, which soon takes place.) The near-sacrifice of Isaac, then, is framed in the narrative by accounts that recall for us two of the critical moments of Abraham's life: the covenant with Abimelech recalls the covenant with the Lord; the reintroduction of Nahor recalls Abraham's separation from his brother, when the Lord had told Abraham to go from his country and his kindred and his father's house.

If, as I have suggested, Genesis 22 is a kind of coda that epitomizes the themes of the Abraham narrative, then it is appropriate that it be framed by episodes that reiterate some of those themes by recalling similar episodes from earlier in Abraham's life. The opening of Genesis 20, as we know, echoes the earlier episode in Egypt when Abraham had also said that Sarah was his sister. There is nothing remarkable in narrative repetition, particularly in the Old Testament, which depends so heavily on repetitions to advance and enhance its narratives. Here, however, is the *first* repetition or echo in the Abraham narrative; and, more important, nothing occurs in Genesis 20 and 21 that does *not* echo an event in the "previous history" of Abraham. These chapters provide us with a review in miniature, and by echo, of Abraham's life and thus prepare us to read chapter 22 in the larger context of his previous history. What does not appear in Genesis 20 and 21, appropriately, is any echo of Abraham's relationship with Lot, who, having served his narrative function as a foil to Abraham, and his thematic function as one who misunderstands and perverts the concepts of beauty, fruitfulness, and possession, disappears from the narrative at the very point at which the narrative returns us to its beginning. Everything else that happens to Abraham before the narrative begins to echo itself is reiterated in chapters 20 through 23 of Genesis. In fact, the only completely *new* information is in the eight verses on which Auerbach concentrates. There is no way, therefore, that Genesis 22 can be read as a complete or self-sufficient narrative, no way that the text can support Auerbach's assertion that the early morning in which Abraham saddled his ass was bitter for him.

At the opening of Genesis 20 Abraham is journeying toward the Negeb, as he was in Genesis 12. The further similarities between these two chapters are obvious. Abraham introduces Sarah as his sister; the rulers of the land, Pharaoh in 12 and Abimelech in 20, are apparently struck by Sarah's beauty and take her to their homes; plagues afflict Pharaoh, the threat of death frightens Abimelech; both rulers are puzzled by Abraham's action; both return Sarah and give Abraham sheep and oxen, manservants and maidservants. We are obviously invited by the incidents of chapter 20 to recall the events of chapter 12. In doing so, however, we also become aware of the differences between the two chapters. For one thing, the retelling of the episode is longer than its original, which is in itself unusual, for we normally expect a narrative repetition or echo to be a briefer version of what we have been told previously. Why is this repetition longer? How does it function in the larger narrative context? What is different? Pharaoh, we remember, had been afflicted with great plagues. But in Genesis 20, the Lord appears to Abimelech in a dream and tells him he is a dead man because the woman he has taken is another man's wife. Abimelech is warned, in other words, as Pharaoh was not, and has the opportunity to correct his error *before* he is punished for it. "Lord," says Abimelech, "wilt thou slay an innocent people?" We remember at this point Abraham's earlier conversation with the Lord about the righteous in Sodom and Gomorrah, and we might consider that the Lord, in giving Abimelech a chance to avoid punishment, has been affected by Abraham's argument. The Lord acknowledges Abimelech's innocence, but orders him in another dream to restore Sarah to Abraham. And Abimelech, like Abraham in Genesis 22, "rose early in the morning" to carry out the Lord's command. The expanded echo enables us to see a new aspect of the Lord, who admits that he prevented Abimelech from touching Sarah. His intervention and warning balance the vengefulness he displayed in destroying Sodom and Gomorrah and the anger he displayed in afflicting the equally duped Pharaoh with plagues.

The expansion of the episode also illustrates a different aspect of Abraham. Earlier he had explained to Sarah that he would introduce her as his sister because she was beautiful to behold; now he tells Abimelech, "I did it because I thought, There is no fear of God at all in this place. . . ." He also explains that in a sense Sarah really *is* his sister. The important point is that Abraham emphasizes not Sarah's beauty, but rather the fear of God, which has become for him a higher order of beauty. The leisurely repetition further enables the narrative to recall the time when "God caused [Abraham] to wander from [his] father's house"; and it recalls for us the circumstances of his wandering—the barrenness of Sarah and of the promised land—by commenting on the barrenness of Abimelech's people—"For the Lord had closed all the wombs of the house of Abimelech because of Sarah, Abraham's wife." This final piece of information, which might have been inserted more logically earlier in the episode rather than being introduced at its close, is immediately followed by the sentence, "The Lord visited Sarah as he had said, and the Lord did to Sarah as he had promised." The juxtaposition between barrenness and fruitfulness again reminds us of the pattern of Abraham's previous history, compressing into two sentences experiences that for him had spanned many years.

The first seven verses of chapter 21 describe the birth and naming of Isaac and Sarah's response to the birth, the fulfillment of the Lord's culminating promise to Abraham. But the verses also recall thematically, through echoes and subtle allusions, most of Abraham's conversations with the Lord: the promise itself, of course—"Sarah conceived, and bore Abraham a son in his old age at the time of which God had spoken to him"; Isaac's circumcision, the sign of the covenant, given by God in chapter 17; the initial responses of Abraham and Sarah in chapter 18 when they laughed at the thought that they would bear a son—"who would have said to Abraham," asks Sarah now, "that Sarah would suckle children?"—this is the fruitfulness that the Lord offered as his gift after Abraham had permitted Lot to choose the fertile valley, and again offered him after he had rejected the wealth offered him by the king of Sodom. Like chapter 20, chapter 21 reverberates with echoes of Abraham's past. The birth of Isaac epitomizes the rightness of Abraham's earlier decisions and the fulfillment of the Lord's covenant with him.

As *these* echoes impinge on us as readers, we are then reminded of Sarah's earlier conflict with Hagar the Egyptian. For a second time in the narrative, Sarah deals harshly with Hagar. Earlier Abraham had given her free rein—"do to her as you please," he had said—but this time, "on account of his son" Ishmael, he is displeased when Sarah wants to drive Hagar and her son away. But God intervenes, as he had intervened with Abimelech, and tells Abraham to follow Sarah's wishes; for "through Isaac," the Lord says, "shall your descendants be named." And Abraham, like Abimelech, rises early in the morning to send Hagar and Ishmael away. "Thou art a God of seeing," Hagar had said earlier when an angel of the Lord had stopped her flight in the wilderness and told her to return to Sarah. Her words are recalled and confirmed in the episode in chapter 21: The God of seeing hears the weeping of Ishmael, knows of Hagar's distressing cry, "Let me not look upon the death of the child," and intervenes to save them in the wilderness by opening Hagar's eyes and revealing to her a well of water. The episode precedes so closely the command to sacrifice Isaac that we must have it in our minds as we read chapter 22. Indeed, the only narrative incident between the saving of Ishmael, with its echoes of the Lord's previous intervention on his behalf, and the ordered sacrifice of Isaac, is the controversay and covenant between Abraham and Abimelech, which itself echoes Abraham's covenant with the Lord and the Lord's promise of a covenant with Isaac.

How else, then, can we read Genesis 22 except as Abraham's testing of the Lord, as well as the Lord's testing of Abraham? What more can the narrative do to remind us of Abraham's past and to indicate to us the nature of the Lord in this narrative? Everything that the Lord has promised or done for Abraham is

recalled for us before the Lord says, in Genesis 22: "Abraham!"
Everything that Abraham has learned from his relationship with
the Lord is recalled before Abraham answers, "Here am I." There
is nothing sudden or mysterious about this exchange—we have
been prepared for it all along. What initially may seem mysterious,
and will certainly seem so out of context, is the Lord's specific
command, "Take your son, your only son Isaac, whom you love,
and go to the land of Moriah, and offer him there as a burnt
offering upon one of the mountains of which I shall tell you." But
in the context of the entire Abraham narrative, the command is
demystified. This may be the same Lord who inflicted Pharaoh
with plagues and who destroyed Sodom and Gomorrah, but it is
also the same Lord who has intervened on behalf of Abimelech,
who has made Sarah fruitful, who has saved Hagar and Ishmael
and even Lot, who has formally announced a covenant with
Abraham and his son, his only son, whom he loves. If what the
Lord has promised for Isaac is to happen, Isaac cannot die. If, on
the other hand, Abraham has been mistaken, if his vision has been
false, if his successful bargaining with the Lord over the righteous
in Sodom and Gomorrah has misled him, then his lord is a false
god, a slayer of children, a breaker of covenants. We know from
the chapters immediately preceding Genesis 22 that the Lord *is*
concerned for the innocent and for his oath. Abraham must
assume this, too, based on his own previous history. At last, the
Lord's command gives him a definitive opportunity to find out. If
Isaac dies, then the Lord has failed Abraham, whose life will have
been wasted. If Isaac lives, then Abraham's confidence in his
Lord, demonstrated throughout his "previous history," is
confirmed, and he can, as he does in the succeeding chapters,
prepare for his son's marriage and his own death, convinced that
his descendants will indeed possess the promised land.

There can be nothing bitter about the early morning when
Abraham saddles his ass. On the contrary, he must be tense and
anxious, provided as he is with an unusual opportunity to confirm
the justness and righteousness of his Lord, to find out, on a starkly
realistic level, if the Lord's covenant with him concerning Isaac's
descendants is true or not. What he does in the episode is fully
consistent with the principles on which he has based his life's
actions and decisions. The narrative is not abrupt, but condensed.

The journey to Moriah is a microcosm of Abraham's longer journey, which began when he immediately obeyed the Lord's command that he leave his country, his kindred, and his father's house (indeed, the very language of 22:2 echoes that of Genesis 12:1-2). The principle that guided him then—and with Pharaoh, with Lot, with the king of Sodom, with Hagar the Egyptian—guides him still: "God will provide himself the lamb for a burnt offering, my son," he says. There is no suspense in this episode, but rather an enormous sense of relief, a slowing of the pulses. It would be irrelevant for the narrative to describe where the Lord comes from, or what Abraham is doing, or the serving-men and ass, or the geographical location of the place of sacrifice, or even the journey itself. This information is irrelevant in the context of the previous history of Abraham, a history that has been echoed for us in the verses immediately preceding the Lord's command. Abraham's entire life has been his journey, and his response to the command to sacrifice his only son whom he loves epitomizes the selflessness that has characterized it. When he tells Isaac that the Lord will provide the lamb for a burnt offering, he *means* it; he is not evading Isaac's question or attempting to conceal the truth from him. The voice of the angel of the Lord, which interrupts Abraham as he raises the knife to slay Isaac, not only vindicates Abraham's vision and values, but also vindicates the Lord, who has, after all, very shortly before this scene, reminded Abraham and us, "through Isaac shall your descendants be named." Abraham has been *right,* the narrative is telling us, in fearing and trusting God; he has been right during his entire journey, even in his answer to Isaac's question, "Where is the lamb for a burnt offering?" "Abraham called the name of that place The Lord will provide," says the text, but we know that this location reminds us of many places over which Abraham might have intoned the same words. The covenant between Abraham and the Lord has been confirmed on both sides; it is appropriate, therefore, that the angel of the Lord should, for the first time in the narrative, link the metaphors that were earlier separated (13:16 and 15:5) and that suggest a link between heaven and earth—"I will multiply your descendants as the stars of heaven *and* as the sand which is on the seashore."

Genesis 22 is not the climactic moment of the Abraham legend, but rather its summary. The narrative does not need to echo further the *events* of Abraham's life; it needs now to recall the values that have made that life meaningful and affecting, to remind us of Abraham's understanding of the significant connotations, in the context of this narrative world, of *possession, fruitfulness,* and *beauty.*

The episodes that follow the near sacrifice of Isaac are concerned with these concepts and, like the episodes that preceded Genesis 22, recall for us earlier events in Abraham's life, but this time with an emphasis on the values advanced through them. Genesis 23 describes Abraham's bargaining with the Hittites for property so that he may bury Sarah. The unusually long chapter 24 explains Abraham's desire that Isaac marry a woman from his own country and then details the journey undertaken by his faithful servant to fulfill that desire. The themes of these chapters preceding Abraham's death are those central ones of possession, fruitfulness, and beauty.

Abraham makes clear in his conversations with the Hittites that he wants to *purchase* a burying place. "For the full price let [Ephron] give it to me in your presence as a possession for a burying place." When he here rejects the Hittites' offer that he bury Sarah in the choicest of their sepulchres, we are reminded of Abraham's rejection of the king of Sodom's offer in chapter 14. Then he had said, "I have sworn to the Lord God Most High, maker of heaven and earth, that I would not take a thread or a sandal-thong or anything that is yours, lest you should say, "I have made Abram rich."" Presumably, the same principle operates in his discussion with Ephron, even though the price Ephron sets is ourageously high. Indeed, Ephron seems to realize that, and his statement seems almost intentionally hyperbolic, and if he may *want* Abraham simply to take the land—"a piece of land worth four hundred shekels of silver, what is that between you and me? Bury your dead." But Abraham weighs out the amount of silver, "according to the weights current among the merchants." The echo of the king of Sodom's offer, like the echo of Sarah being taken in by Pharaoh, is longer than the narrative event that is being echoed. Here, the length enables the narrative to underscore Abraham's insistent belief that he receive gifts only from the Lord. His insistence further illustrates his sense of the importance of the family, given its need at this time for a burying place that is, as the text tells us over and over, a *permanent possession*. Lot, it seems to me, would have accepted Ephron's offer.

After he has buried Sarah, Abraham calls the oldest servant of his house, "who had charge of all that he had," and makes him swear that Isaac shall not marry a woman from among the Canaanites, but will take one from his own country and his own kindred. The moving episode that follows interlaces the concepts of fruitfulness and beauty as they are understood and practiced by Abraham. The servant is at first doubtful that a woman will be willing to return with him, but Abraham knows better: "The Lord . . . who took me from my father's house and from the land of my birth . . . he will send his angel before you, and you shall take a wife for my son from there." (Notice that Abraham does not mention the Isaac episode at all in attempting to assuage the servant's doubts.) The beauty of the scene comes from its simplicity and from the loyalty the servant shows to his master, in imitation, it seems, of Abraham's loyalty to his. The journey of the servant, in fact, is almost a low-keyed imitation of the journey of Abraham, illustrating as it does how one not called to be a prophet can nevertheless follow a prophet's example. The oath the servant takes recalls other oaths in the Abraham narrative; the immediacy with which he leaves for the city of Nahor emphasizes his willing service; the simple plan he designs draws attention to aspects of beauty that are often ignored—generosity and selflessness. It is appropriate, too, that the test of Rebekah should go beyond giving the servant a jar of water; her concern must extend to his animals as well, and she must seek no reward. She does all that the servant had hoped for, and she does it, the text tells us twice, "quickly." It is interesting to note, finally, that the servant's perspective on his journey is that it successfully illustrates not Abraham's faithfulness to the Lord, but the Lord's faithfulness to Abraham.

The entire episode calls into question Auerbach's contention that Genesis 22 illustrates the narrative style of the Old Testament. Auerbach argues that in the Old Testament the overwhelming suspense is present, that some parts are left obscure, that events unfold abruptly, that psychological processes are ignored, that the text is preoccupied by the problematic, that it contains the suggestive influence of an unexpressed background quality; in short, that it is vague and mysterious. But the journey of Abraham's servant is described in a style directly opposite to these qualities, even if we admit that they exist in the near sacrifice of Isaac when that episode is read out of the context of the entire Abraham narrative. There is little, if any, suspense in the episode; events unfold leisurely and logically; we are invited into the psychological processes of the servant's mind; the foreground is properly full. If anything, the episode might be criticized for being too drawn out. The servant's plan to find Isaac's wife-to-be is announced in verse 14; it is then fully played out by Rebekah in verses 17 through 20, and both plan and action are then repeated at length to Rebekah's family in verses 42 through 46. The conversation between Abraham and the servant is also repeated for Rebekah's family, as is the conversation between the servant and Rebekah. We are given details of the procedures of the oath made by the servant, of the time and place where he stops for water, of Rebekah's beauty and virginity, of the gift given to Rebekah and her family, of the arrangement made by her family to welcome the servant, of the departure of Rebekah from her country, her kindred, and her father's house.

The utter simplicity and quietness of the description of the dramatic meeting between Isaac and Rebekah provide a fitting end to the Abraham narrative. Isaac, out in the fields to meditate, lifts his eyes and sees camels coming; Rebekah, lifting her eyes, asks the servant, "Who is the man yonder, walking in the field to meet us?" The end of the journey, for the servant, for Abraham, and for us, may recall the simplicity of Abraham's entertainment of the Lord by the oaks of Mamre. Forgotten for a moment is Isaac's destiny, forgotten for a moment is the Lord's warning to Abraham that his descendants "will be sojourners in a land that is not theirs, and will be slaves there, and they will be oppressed for four hundred years." At this moment, we are struck instead by the unquestioning loyalty of the servant, by the generosity of Rebekah, by the fruitfulness of which her family speaks as she leaves them; struck by what Abraham has known and demonstrated—the source of true beauty, the source of true fruitfulness, the source of equanimity, the most exquisite possession any of us can have.

6. JOSEPH, JUDAH, AND JACOB[1]

James S. Ackerman

Scholars have long noted the unusual amount of doubling in the Joseph story: three sets of dreams occur in pairs—by Joseph, by his fellow prisoners, and by Pharaoh. Joseph is twice confined—in the pit and in prison. The brothers make two trips to Egypt for grain, have two audiences with Joseph on each occasion, twice find money in their grain bags, make two attempts to gain Jacob's permission to send Benjamin to Egypt, and finally receive two invitations to settle in Egypt. Both Potiphar and the prison keeper leave everything in Joseph's hands. Potiphar's wife makes two attempts to seduce Joseph and then accuses him twice. Joseph serves two prominent prisoners (and two years elapse between their dreams and those of Pharaoh). Joseph twice accuses his brothers of spying, devises two plans to force the brothers to bring Benjamin to Egypt, and on two occasions places money in their sacks. Finally, the same goods (gum, balm, and myrrh) are twice brought from Canaan to Egypt—first with Joseph and later with Benjamin.[2]

Doubling appears in speeches as well as actions. In some instances characters repeat a phrase in one episode (eg., 41:25/28; 42:15/16; 43:3/5). Elsewhere, speeches recapitulate and supplement events reported earlier in the story (e.g., 40:15; 42:21-22; 42:31-34; 43:7; 43:20-23; 44:3-7; 44:18-34; 50:17).

The common assumption has been that much of the doubling is a result of the conflation of sources—an assumption I shall not question here. My concern is to point out the effect that doubling has as a literary device in the story. D. B. Redford, for example, has noted that doubling can often be used for emphasis: "The certainty of the dreams' fulfillment is thus stressed, as well as the stubbornness of Jacob, Joseph's determination to treat his brothers as spies, Egyptian initiative in making possible Israel's settlement in Egypt, and so on."[3] A second effect of doubling, Redford believes, is plot retardation in some crucial instances. For example, while the doublets are emphasizing Jacob's stubbornness and Joseph's determination, they are also delaying the recognition scene in which the brothers will discover the identity of the Egyptian lord.[4]

Acknowledging the many instances of these kinds of doubling, I would argue that there is a deeper, structural doubling in the Joseph story—occasioned by the unexpected turn of events in chapter 42 when the brothers first come to Egypt to bring grain. "And Joseph's brothers came, and they did obeisance to him—nostrils to the ground. . . ."* (All asterisked biblical quotations have been made directly from the Hebrew text.) This is the outcome envisioned in Joseph's first dream of ascendancy over the rest of his family (37:5-7). We hadn't known what to make of those dreams: had special favor been thrust on the youth, or did he grasp after it by tattling on his brothers? Did the dreams indicate divine choice, or were they the ambitious imaginings of a lad who would play the role of deity? Like Day Star, who had tried to replace the deity, Joseph is cast into the pit (Isa. 14:12ff); and then he is taken down into Egypt. But a recurring motif is God's presence with Joseph in Egypt, whether he is in Potiphar's house or in Pharaoh's prison. The reader notes with satisfaction that Joseph's rise to power in Egypt results from a combination of pious behavior, divine help, and his wise advice at court.

When the brothers come to Egypt for grain, the reader is prepared for the denouement. When they do obeisance before Joseph, we remember the dreams before he does. We assume that the story will soon end, showing how human beings cannot thwart the divine purpose. We have been prepared for this conclusion by chapter 41: after hearing and interpreting Pharaoh's dreams, Joseph tells him that the matter is fixed by God when a second dream repeats the first (41:32). Then, as Joseph predicted, the seven-year cycles of plenty and drought take place. Thus as the brothers fulfill Joseph's dreams by bowing down before him, the lesson of God's control of history is played out again, and the reader may consider the main story at an end.

The denouement does not fulfill our expectations, however, as Joseph turns with apparent vengeance on his brothers. Scholars who question Joseph's morality or who see him reverting to his earlier adolescent behavior are overlooking a literary device used by the storyteller: "And Joseph recognized his brothers; but as for them, they did not recognize him. And Joseph *remembered the dreams* that he had dreamed about them. And he said to them, 'Spies you are—to see the nakedness of the land'"* (42:8-9*a*).

At this crucial moment of confrontation, the prostrated brothers bring to his mind an image from the past. Like the reader, Joseph remembers not the betrayal or suffering wrought by his brothers, but his dreams.[5] We have been seduced by the baker-butler and the Pharaoh dream sequences into assuming that dreams indicate that what has been fixed by God will inevitably come to pass. Here is the climactic instance: Joseph's brothers are bowing down before him. We are not prepared for further plot complications.

In the unusual description of Joseph's thoughts in 42:9, the syntax connects his remembering the dreams with his accusing his brothers, launching a new series of events. That syntactical connection suggests that everything that follows is related to his dreams. We have just been told how Joseph, in naming his Egyptian-born sons, had put the past behind him: "God has made me forget all my hardship and all my father's house (and) made me fruitful in the land of my affliction" (41:51, 52). Now events remind him of his dreams. And somehow, from Joseph's point of view, the dreams have not yet been *completely* fulfilled.

As we read further it quickly becomes clear that Joseph's immediate purpose is to have the brothers bring Benjamin to Egypt. Then we recall: *all* the brothers' sheaves had bowed to Joseph's sheaf, and Benjamin is still in Canaan. The lad must join the brothers in Joseph's presence. And Joseph must continue to dissemble, since the first dream depicts his being treated as lord rather than brother.

We might wonder why Joseph focuses on bringing only Benjamin to Egypt. He does ask after Jacob's welfare, but makes no effort to include the patriarch in his machinations with his brothers. When we look more closely at Joseph's dreams, however, we see that they were not so closely doubled as were Pharaoh's. The motif of obeisance appears in both dreams; but the first points only to the brothers, while the second includes the whole family. Thus Joseph's dream sequence establishes the pattern for his course of action after his brothers come to Egypt: obeisance of all the brothers is of first importance.

Joseph may not yet be conscious of the full meaning of his dreams. With the dreams of the butler-baker and Pharaoh, the pattern had been dream-interpretation-fulfillment. In Joseph's own case, however, the interpretation will not be clear to him until after the dreams have been fulfilled—possibly because he himself must play a role in bringing the dreams to fulfillment.

Both the recognition of the brothers and the recollection of the dreams are one-sided. As a plot device, they force the reader to see what follows in the light of what has preceded. But what of the actors in this drama? Will Joseph come to understand the connection between his dreams and the new sequence of events? Will the brothers come to the same understanding? Will they not have to relive Joseph's suffering so they can fully realize what they did to him?

The brothers soon recall their past crime and interpret their present misfortunes as a long-delayed retribution, but there is room for further growth. Joseph recalls his dreams, but is not yet able to interpret their meaning. Thus after the climactic meeting the story is so arranged that Joseph, in acting out his dreams, will embark on a twice-told tale through which he will both fulfill and learn the divine purpose for his life.

One result of this plot device is a series of dramatic ironies, some apparent to Joseph, some appreciated only by the reader:

(a) "We are all sons of one man," say the brothers in 42:11, not realizing that their statement includes the strange lord standing before them.

(b) "You will be tested. . . . Send one of you and let him bring your brother . . . so that your words may be tested, whether *'emet* [a word that means both *truth* and *faithfulness*] is with you,"* says

Joseph in 42:15-16. The brothers pass half of the test in chapter 43. There was *'emet/truth* with them: they have proved they were the family unit they had claimed to be, rather than a group of spies, by producing the youngest son. But they will soon discover that the test has not ended. It is yet to be determined whether or not *'emet/faithfulness* was with them.

(c) When Jacob finally relents and agrees to send Benjamin, he prays in 43:14 that God will prosper the journey "so that he will send to you your brother, another, and Benjamin."* The father may be referring to Simeon, the brother kept hostage in Egypt. But Jacob did not say "your other brother." The syntax leaves the meaning just ambiguous enough for the reader to know that it can also refer to Joseph.[6]

(d) In 42:21 we are told that Joseph had earlier pleaded for "favor" *(ḥnn)* for himself, but his brothers would not listen. When Joseph first meets Benjamin, he gives the pious, traditional greeting "May God grant you faovr *[ḥnn],* my son"* (43:29). Those words will have a deeper significance as the plot develops. Will the other son of Rachel find "favor" from the brothers when they are asked to leave him enslaved in Egypt and return to their father?

(e) When the brothers return to the Egyptian lord after the divining cup has been discovered in Benjamin's sack, Judah's defense should be *nolo contendere:* they cannot defend themselves against the charge, even though they consider themselves not guilty. Instead, however, Judah exclaims, "God has found out the guilt of your servants" (44:16). Does he mean that the Egyptian should accept the statement as an admission of guilt regarding a deliberate theft, or something else? The guilt that Judah acknowledges God has "found out"—we and his brothers know—is for an incident that took place long ago.

A second result of the narrative device of delayed fulfillment is the doubled plot. Readers can see the brothers suffering, in part at least, measure for measure for what they did in the past:

(a) In Genesis 37, as Joseph approached his brothers in Dothan, "they *saw* him . . . and they conspired *[vayyitnakkᵉlû]* against him." Finally they returned with the bloody garment to their father, saying "This we have found; *recognize* now—cloak of your son—is it or not?"*[7] Twenty years later, when the brothers first appear before Joseph, "he *saw* his brothers, and he *recognized* them; but he acted unrecognizably *[vayyitnakkēr]* unto them"*—the significant pun, in a technique characteristic of the whole story, reinforcing the moral pattern of measure for measure. Joseph's dissembling echoes the brothers' conspiring. In 37:4 "they were not able to speak peaceably to him."* Now Joseph "speaks harshly to them"* (42:7). Those who had duped their father into "recognition" are now recognized. The deceivers are deceived. The ones who had seen Joseph and conspired against him are now on the receiving end, and the key to the deception is Joseph "acting unrecognizably."

(b) Joseph then falsely accuses the brothers of coming "to see the nakedness of the land"* (42:9). In the biblical tradition "nakedness" consistently occurs in texts referring to sexual misconduct.[8] Are we not being asked to recall Joseph's plight in Genesis 39, when Potiphar's wife falsely accused him of sexual misconduct, causing his angry master to throw him in prison? Now Joseph falsely accuses his brothers and has them bound over into prison for a period of three days.

(c) In 40:15 Joseph, interpreting the butler's dream, uses language that equates his Egyptian imprisonment with an earlier event in his life: "For I was indeed stolen from the land of the Hebrews, and also here I have not done anything that they should place me *in the pit.*"* Joseph is linking his brothers' betrayal with his imprisonment, so that the memory of his suffering is doubly tied to the pit. Thus when he imprisons his brothers, he is forcing them to relive two separate experiences from the past: his imprisonment by Potiphar, and his being cast into the pit by his brothers.

(d) While in prison, the brothers must decide which one will return to tell Jacob that nine more of his sons have been taken and that Benjamin must also come down to Egypt; they realize that Jacob will hold back. Desolately, the brothers in the prison/pit contemplate the prospect of death or slavery—just as Joseph had earlier sat in their pit awaiting death. He is meting out, measure for measure, what he had suffered in the past.

The outburst of "measure for measure" activity soon ends. After three days Joseph changes his mind and allows the brothers to return to Canaan, keeping only Simeon as a hostage. Why do we find the seemingly unnecessary change of plan after this short interval? Joseph's first response to his brothers had been punitive. He had wanted his brothers to relive in part the hardships that he had experienced. But his major purpose is to bring his dreams to fulfillment, and this necessitates a change in strategy. He also must realize that sending only one brother back home would be a certain overkill that would cause Jacob to dig in his heels, frustrating his intention. Thus he carefully modifies his course of action.

This change initiates a chain of events that will be part of a third plot doubling. The result of Joseph's changed course of action is to bring the brothers' long-repressed guilt to the surface. Only now will there be discussion and recriminations among them concerning what had happened twenty years before. Why does this happen? It is unclear whether Joseph intends it or not, but the changed course of action—ostensibly aimed at fulfilling the dreams—is subtly forcing the brothers to relive their earlier crime.[9] Thus with 42:18ff we move from a "measure for measure" punitive reaction to a more subtle "play within a play" in which, like Hamlet's uncle, the brothers will be forced to relive the past and face its horror.

The first expression of guilt comes as soon as they learn that they must return to their father to fetch Benjamin (42:21-22). Why is this? Surely part of the reason is a growing sense of *déjà vu* among the brothers. They must return to their father with the dreadful news of a second lost brother—this time, Simeon; and at the same time they must demand that Jacob surrender the other son of Rachel. Their imprisonment had forced them to relive Joseph's pit/imprisonment experiences. Now they must reenact their earlier crime.

On the homeward journey one of the brothers discovers silver in his sack. "What is this that God had done to us?" they exclaim. They are horrified by the discovery of what, in other circumstances, could have been construed as an act of kindness. Surely, their reaction is to some extent caused by fear that the money is part of a setup: it will be used as an occasion for a second false accusation that will result in imprisonment, slavery, or death when they return to Egypt. But the silver gained in the context of losing another brother also echoes their grim plan to sell Joseph into slavery for silver. That time, the Midianites had foiled their plan and received the silver instead. Now as the brothers return to their father minus another brother and with silver in their sacks, we (and possibly also the brothers) may well feel that the payoff for their earlier crime was twenty years delayed in coming.

The brothers have changed. As the story repeats itself, we must notice the great difference between their attitude toward Jacob's suffering over the report of Joseph's loss with the bloody garment and their description of why Simeon was taken and what they must do with Benjamin. They are now sincere, compassionate for their mourning father, desperate to set things straight. Reuben offers the lives of his two sons if Benjamin does not return. But Jacob pitifully turns them away. If Benjamin is lost, "you would bring my gray hairs in sorrow to Sheol."* This echoes Jacob's response to the loss of Joseph: "I will go down to my son mourning—to Sheol"* (37:35).

The parallels continue, as the reader picks up an irony that must elude the brothers. Jacob, after a long struggle, has finally been convinced that the family will not survive if Benjamin is not sent to Egypt. The wily father hopes for the best and does what he can by sending gifts to the Egyptian lord (43:11). Thus Benjamin departs for Egypt; and with him go balm, honey, gum, myrrh, pistachio nuts, and almonds—the very goods that accompanied Joseph twenty years before (37:25). The brothers had been indirectly responsible for Joseph's earlier descent into Egypt. This time they must take Benjamin in their own caravan. The allusion to the items of transport suggests that this time the brothers are reenacting the role of the Ishmaelite traders, bringing the other son of Rachel to an uncertain fate.[10]

When the brothers arrived in Egypt with Benjamin, "they did obeisance before him to the ground"* (43:26). With this statement, the narrator stresses that the first dream has been completely fulfilled. We can assume the same of the divine purpose contained in the dream. As for Joseph's own reported purpose, the brothers have demonstrated that 'emet is with them by producing Benjamin; they have told the truth. Joseph generously provides a banquet for his brothers; and they all feast, drink, even become drunk together. As chapter 43 draws to a close, the writer would have a perfect opportunity to describe Joseph's revelation of his true identity; but Joseph bypasses it.

Why not tell all right now? Joseph proceeds on a course of action that is puzzling (why pick on Benjamin, the one innocent brother?) and that goes beyond the dreams. We should remember, however, that Pharaoh's dreams told only what was fixed by God: seven years of plenty, followed by seven years of famine. They did not hint at the appropriate mode of human response to the fixed divine action, so that the human community would gain the maximum benefit. The appropriate response required a discreet and wise person in whom was the spirit of God. Similarly, Joseph's dreams had disclosed only the course of events that God would ultimately bring about within the family of Jacob: the young Joseph would rise to ascendancy over his brothers and parents. His dreams did not disclose the appropriate response to what they foretold. May we not assume that, as Joseph's response to Pharaoh's dreams had benefited all of Egypt in chapter 41, his mysterious course of action with the divining cup in chapter 44 will somehow benefit the family of Israel?

The first allusion to Joseph's dreams in 42:8-9 begins a plot doubling in which the brothers go through two distinct stages:

A. Measure for measure. First they suffer fit retribution for their crime against Joseph and for his tribulations in the land of Egypt—false accusation and imprisonment, with the fear of death or slavery.

B. Reenactment of the crime. As they return to their father minus a brother and with silver in their sack, hear their father's renewed anguish, and bring the second son of Rachel into Egypt, they are forced to relive painful scenes from the past that bring their guilt to the surface.

Both stages take place as part of Joseph's need to bring his dream to fulfillment. Note also that the brothers' experience is the chronological reverse of the earlier plot: first they suffer what had happened to Joseph during and after the crime; then they relive the crime. Chapter 43, verse 26 describes the literal fulfilling of Joseph's dream and initiates the final doubling that must precede the great climax and denouement of the story. In Aristotle's terms, we have had the major reversal and a one-sided recognition scene.

Yet to come are the full recognition scene ("I am Joseph") and the final working out of the plot.

The third stage of the doubling is carefully planned to push events back to the point before the crime took place. When the brothers return to the Egyptian lord after the divining cup has been discovered in Benjamin's sack, the chronology has suddenly shifted. They are no longer acting out an earlier crime. Instead, they are given a chance to commit a new one. The plot doubling has structured events so that history can repeat itself and they can again be rid of the favored son.[11] This time, however, they will be guiltless. All they have to do is go home and tell their father exactly what happened. Despite Judah's offer that all the brothers remain enslaved, Joseph tells them to return to their father "in peace." They surely recall Jacob's reaction to the loss of Joseph and their fruitless efforts to console him; the loss of the only other son of Rachel would destroy their father. Realization of this leads to Judah's moving speech in which he offers himself as a slave in Benjamin's stead so that the younger brother can return to his father.

When Joseph saw his eleven brothers bowed before him in 43:26, he knew that the divine plan foreshadowed in his first dream had been fulfilled. As a youth he could not have known why his ascendancy to power would be an important part of the divine plan to keep alive the family of Israel. As Joseph proceeds with the divining cup ruse, the narrative gives no indication that he has plumbed the relationship between his past suffering and his present power. Joseph's ploy with the divining cup is in no way related to the explanation he finally expresses to his brothers in 45:5-7. In chapter 44 Joseph's motivation is to test his brothers. They have proved their *'emet*/truthfulness by producing Benjamin. Now he wants to learn whether they have grown and changed—whether there is the possibility of reestablishing brotherhood with them. (Paradoxically, as the brothers pass the test, Joseph will learn more than he had expected. Judah's speech will give him the key for interpreting the mystery of his *own* life. We will return to this later.)

The first dream has been fulfilled in 43:26, but the blessing of reconciliation among the brothers has not been realized. In this story a wise, human response is required to complement and complete the divine activity. Thus, structurally, the divining cup incident is to the fulfillment of Joseph's first dream what the construction of store-cities was to Pharaoh's dreams. The store-cities will contain the blessing of the harvest; the divining cup is the final test of *'emet*/faithfulness that, if passed, may bring the blessing of reconciliation among brothers.

Although the dominant theme of this story may be the providential care of the family of Israel through Joseph's career, reconciliation among brothers is a strong and closely related sub-theme: family survival involves both escape from famine and reconciliation among brothers. In chapter 37 the brothers were angry at Joseph when he tattled and jealous when he received the special garment—"they hated him, and could not *speak peaceably* to him" (37:4). These feelings were intensified by Joseph's dreams (37:5, 8, 11). The narrator reports no word spoken to Joseph as they cast him into the pit. In fact, when the brothers recall that incident in 42:21-22, they describe it as not listening to his entreaties.

The alienation theme is continued on Joseph's part as he *"speaks harshly"** to his brothers when they first come down to Egypt (42:7); and in their first four encounters they are separated by an interpreter. The descriptions of Joseph's weeping indicate a gradual change in his attitude toward his brothers as he perceives that they have changed. But even in the banquet scene, which might have made a fitting climax, the narrator stresses the physical separation of Joseph from his brothers (43:32). They sat "before him." The language suggests a royal court in which the brothers are placed in subservient positions to the ruler. Even the phrase "They drank and became drunken with him *[ʿimmô]"** suggests the same court background.[12] The brothers are together, but they are not a family. Only after they have passed the test in chapter 44 does reconciliation begin: "And he kissed all his brothers, and he wept upon them. And after that his brothers *spoke with* him" (45:15).[13]

It had been Joseph's reports of his dreams that exacerbated the brothers' ill will toward the youth. They had interpreted the dreams as both a claim to divine favor and a sign of an overweening pride that was nurtured by Jacob's special love for Joseph. They naturally refused to see anything providential in a plan that would cast them down before any brother. There was a strong antimonarchical strand in early Israelite history, shaped by centuries of oppression at the hands of rulers who claimed to be benevolent shepherds of their people.[14] The last thing that Joseph can do, if he wants to reestablish his place as brother in the family, is to overwhelm his brothers with his power. Conversely, the brothers must pass the divining-cup test so that Joseph can again become a brother and part of the family.

The theme of favoritism producing conflict runs throughout the book of Genesis. At the human level it begins in the rivalry between Sarah and Hagar, forcing Abraham to favor Isaac and drive out Ishmael. It continues in the rivalry between Isaac's sons, Jacob and Esau—each favored by one parent. The struggle between brothers continues in the next generation, caused in large part by Jacob's special love for Rachel and her offspring over Leah and hers. In all these stories the younger son wins out over the older, and geographical separation helps resolve the conflict. Ishmael becomes a wilderness dweller as he and Hagar disappear from the story. Jacob flees to Haran, at Rebekah's behest, so that Esau will have time to forget what was done to him. When the brothers again meet twenty years later, Esau has indeed forgotten. He falls upon Jacob's neck and kisses him. Then each brother departs to his own special country.

The Joseph story continues these themes and brings them to a new resolution. Favoritism and deception play crucial roles in chapter 37. Like Sarah and Isaac, Rachel and her sons are the husband/father's favorites. As with the three earlier sets of brothers, parental favoritism sets up serious sibling rivalries. As with favoritism, so with deception. Just as Isaac had been unable to recognize *(nkr)* the disguised son he was blessing, Jacob, who had deceived his father and won that blessing, was himself deceived by his sons when he recognized *(nkr)* Joseph's bloodied garment and drew the wrong conclusions. Joseph also lived separated from his brothers for twenty years and finally had forgotten all his hardship and all his father's house (41:51). But at the crucial time of confrontation Joseph remembers his dreams and undertakes a series of actions that eventually results in reconciliation among the brothers. This reconciliation, however, will not be an uneasy peace best preserved by geographical separation. It is a reconciliation that results in the geographical reunification of the family of Israel.

It is a commonplace that Genesis 1–11 provides the prologue to inintroducedthe story of Israel by depicting the ever-increasing alienation within the human community. Humankind had been created to live in Eden, in close proximity to God. Genesis 11 ends with a fragmented humanity—scattered and no longer able to understand one another's tongue.

One might assume that when Abraham is introduced, the story will describe how God begins to overcome the alienation among humans through the covenant community of Israel. But strangely the rivalry and hatred among brothers that had begun with Cain and Abel are continued within the family of Abraham. In fact, these themes that were present but muted in the generation of Isaac and Ishmael become increasingly intensified, culminating when the sons of Jacob behold the approaching "master dreamer" and determine that he shall die.

Paradoxically, divine favor has played a crucial role from the beginning in catalyzing the conflict among the brothers. We first note its appearance as God prefers Abel's sacrifice to Cain's. In the story of Israel divine favor is carried out through a parent. Abraham is driven to heed Sarah's words and turn against Ishmael when he learns that Isaac will be the child of promise. Rebekah's special love for Jacob may be traced directly to God's decree, given to her alone, that the second-born will ultimately prevail over the first-born. Divinely inspired dreams, given to a younger son who wears a special garment, continue and intensify the theme of divine and parental favoritism that produces conflict.

In Genesis 45 the conflict of brothers begins to be resolved. The brothers, through Judah's bold action in Genesis 44, have passed the crucial test. When they discover Joseph's true identity, he is no longer a vengeful sovereign for them but a brother; more important, he is not a vengeful brother but a forgiving brother. They have earned forgiveness for their crime against their brother.

Full reconciliation, however, cannot take place until they can resolve the issue that had partially instigated that crime: divine favoritism. Only when Joseph explains that the dreams indicated a specially ordained family role rather than a personally privileged divine love are the brothers able to approach him. Only when they perceive that Joseph's suffering and survival had played a key role in continued life for the family of Jacob-Israel are they able to "speak with him." The survival of the family had been the key issue in Judah's entreaty to Jacob to send Benjamin with them to Egypt. And the survival of Jacob-Israel had been the key theme in Judah's desperate plea before the Egyptian lord. The brothers have come in the course of the story to choose unity over separation, even if it means a shared slavery that could easily be avoided. They have also changed from a hatred that wills death for a favored one to an urgent concern for the life of the entire family. In fact, it is Judah's stress on the survival of "the little ones"—the next generation—that finally moves Jacob to risk the death of his last beloved son, Benjamin.

I have tried to show how the divining-cup incident in Genesis 44 is the culmination of the plot-doubling device begun in chapter 42. It places the brothers in a position of having to choose whether or not to repeat their crime of Genesis 37. Will yet another favored brother be sacrificed, escalating the danger to the life of Jacob-Israel—both as father and as symbol of family cohesion? Their action indicates that they now prefer the life and survival of all over the death/cutting off of any. The long history of the sibling rivalry motif that began with Cain and Abel was introduced into the Joseph story by 37:4 ("but when his brothers saw that their father loved him more than all his brothers, they hated him . . ."). It now moves toward resolution as they fall on one anothers' necks and kiss one another. The Babel motif of alienation resulting in a breakdown of communication, also introduced into the Joseph story in 37:4 ("and [they] could not speak peaceably to him"*) and intensified by the role of the court interpreter, moves toward resolution as "after this his brothers spoke with him"* (45:15).

The remainder of this paper will discuss another key doubling in the Joseph story: Reuben/Judah. Many scholars see both playing the "good brother" role in Genesis 37. In the original version there was one good brother, they claim, and the present confusion in the text results from a conflation of sources.[15] Redford goes on to say, in fact, that Judah's role is not only a secondary intrusion into the narrative, but it also represents a diminution of the story's overall literary artistry.[16] There may indeed be a conflation of sources, but I will argue that the redactor displays great artistry. In the final redaction Reuben and Judah play contrasting roles. Whereas Reuben will gradually weaken and disappear as the story unfolds, Judah will undergo the most important change of any of the characters so that he will play *the* key role in catalyzing the reconciliation. To what extent has the narrative prepared us for Judah's dramatic rise in Genesis 43–44?

Reuben, the firstborn, is described as the good son in chapter 37. When the brothers see Joseph coming in the distance and plan to kill him, it is Reuben who seeks to foil the plan. Whereas the brothers plot a violent death for Joseph, Reuben sets limits: "let us not smite a life."* Acceding to part of the brothers' plan, he suggests that Joseph be thrown into a nearby pit alive rather than dead. The basis for his request is the prohibition against shedding blood. But the text makes clear that Reuben's interest is to rescue Joseph and restore him to his father. When the unexpected intervention of Midianites foils Reuben's plan, he bursts out in lamentation for himself: "and I, where shall I go?" (37:30). This may mean merely, "How can I face my father?" But might he see himself as banned fugitive, unable to return to his father because he has not lived up to the responsibility of firstborn in protecting his brother?

Judah, the fourth-born of Leah, plays a role that sets him in contrast with Reuben. The text makes no mention that Judah's interest is to rescue Joseph. Instead Judah piously speaks of not laying a hand on a brother; but the effect of his suggestion is not so different from murder: Joseph will be removed from their midst and reduced to slavery. In many ways biblical law equates selling a person into slavery with murder.[17] Judah wants the same results as his other brothers, but he seeks profit from the deed (37:26-27).

Both plans—Reuben's to save and Judah's to profit—are foiled. Out of nowhere come the Midianites, and in a half verse they carry out the action contemplated by the brothers. Like the nameless stranger who met Joseph at Shechem and told him his brothers had moved on to Dothan, the Midianites are mere agents of the plot. They appear suddenly in the story to foil the opposing machinations of Reuben and Judah and disappear after they have served their function.

N. Leibowitz, backed by midrashic interpretation, sees Joseph's nameless stranger as a divine emissary.[18] Given the normal economy in biblical narrative style, there seems to be no need to tell us that Joseph was sent first to Shechem but then redirected to Dothan. Like the Midianites, the stranger appears from nowhere. He engages Joseph in a conversation that could easily have been omitted, and then he disappears from the story. Leibowitz infers that the narrator is going out of his way to emphasize the divine intent behind Joseph's fateful encounter with his brothers. I would argue the same thing for the role of the Midianites. They frustrate the plans of Reuben and Judah, but their sudden intervention into and disappearance from the story may cause us to anticipate that a larger plan, not yet revealed to characters or reader, is being carried out.

One must examine the larger context of the Joseph story to determine why Reuben and Judah play these opposing roles. Deriving his line of argument from midrashic interpretation, J. Goldin points us in a fruitful direction by referring to Genesis 34–35.[19] In 35:22 we learn that Reuben had sexual relations with his father's concubine, Bilhah. He may have been attempting to assert the rights of primogeniture and assume the role of the father,[20] but we learn from Genesis 49:3-4 that in fact his premature action had caused him to lose this status in his father's eyes. Goldin suggests that, besides fulfilling his special responsibility as firstborn, Reuben may have been desperately attempting to regain his lost/threatened status by saving Joseph's life.[21] When Reuben finds the pit empty, his response, as translated by Goldin, is "what now is left me" (37:30*b*).[22] This alternate translation, like the conventional translation used above, leaves Reuben bemoaning his own fate as a response to Joseph's tragedy.

What about Judah, the fourth-born? His star may be on the rise. Levi and Simeon, the second- and third-born sons, had fallen from favor through their deceitful destruction of the city of Shechem (Genesis 34). Jacob rebukes them for their recklessness (34:30) and refers to it again in Genesis 49:5-7 in declaring their reduced status. Judah is next in line. If he stays out of trouble, and if Reuben does not regain favor, the special status of family leadership may fall to him. The only remaining rival is Joseph, the son favored by his father. Thus not only does the larger context of

Genesis 37 show us how important it is for Reuben to save Joseph and return him to his father; it also reveals how much Judah stands to gain by being rid of the only other rival for special status among his brothers.[23]

When the harsh-speaking Egyptian lord begins to test the brothers in chapter 42, Reuben still appears to be the "good brother." But there are now further ambiguities: his goodness has even more self-centeredness than before. The brothers speak with one accord in remembering and repenting their guilt; they admit that they did not heed Joseph's appeals for mercy. Only Reuben breaks the brothers' eloquent solidarity. Shrilly he turns on them with an "I told you so," refusing to accept the guilt while recognizing that he must share the judgment. The brothers remember not heeding Joseph. Reuben attempts to identify himself with the innocent, wronged younger brother—reminding them that they also did not heed him earlier. But they had indeed followed his lead in chapter 37. It was Reuben's advice to throw Joseph into the pit, as part of his plan to save the lad and return him to his father. Reuben's goodness was ineffective. His plan did not work, and we learn later that if it had worked, Jacob's family would not have survived the famine. As chapter 37 concluded, we found Reuben proclaiming his tragic isolation. The brothers did not heed his words, probably because of their irrelevance to the problem of explaining Joseph's disappearance to their father.

Reuben's goodness is similarly ineffective in chapter 42. The threatening situation before the Egyptian lord did not require a querulous expression of innocence that resulted in division and recrimination. The true firstborn should provide leadership that assumed at least a shared responsibility for the situation. He should be the spokesman, coming up with an imaginative response to the Egyptian lord's accusation that would enhance the unity of the family and deliver the brothers from their peril. His lack of leadership here is a foil for the later doubling situation. Chapter 44 will portray another brother taking action before the Egyptian lord in even more threatening circumstances with vastly different results; and the reader is forced to compare the two spokesmen in these analogous situations.

When the brothers return to Jacob and describe their Egyptian adventures, they try to soften the severity of their position.

Simeon is not a hostage bound over into prison, but simply a brother left to stay with the Egyptian. There was no threat of death to Simeon for failure to bring Benjamin to Egypt—only the promise to hand over Simeon and to allow the brothers to purchase grain in Egypt. The aged Jacob's response to this news is full of self-pitying, ineffective recrimination. After twenty years he still grieves for Joseph. Because he fears for Benjamin's life, he is incapable of an imaginative response. Here Reuben steps forward, making a statement more reckless than Jephthah's, offering the life of two sons as pledge for Benjamin's.

Reuben's language reminds readers of his earlier intent "to *bring him* [Joseph] *unto* his father"* (37:22). In chapter 42 the same words are used to express Reuben's promise regarding Benjamin: "two of my sons you may kill if I do not *bring him unto you*"* (42:37). We know that Reuben tried and failed before. If Reuben fails again, his suggested resolution will wreak further death in Jacob's family. Many years ago Jacob had jumped to secure the birthright of Esau—the foolish, impulsive firstborn. Now as a father he must be haunted to see Esau's traits reappear in his firstborn, Reuben—so desperate to win favor that he will risk cutting off his own descendants. Jacob's impulse is to refuse, to cut his losses and take no further risk of lives in the family. Simeon's fate remains in abeyance until the grain sacks are emptied as the famine continues.

When the famine had first hit, Jacob had been quick to seize the initiative in preserving life among the family (42:1-2). The key words here are "so that we might live and not die."* The brothers, on the other hand, are depicted as "staring at each other," helpless and paralyzed, incapable of taking productive measures. Now in chapter 43 we see a feeble, pitiful old man, unwilling to risk Benjamin's life, begging his sons to "return, bring for us a little food."* With the wisdom of the senile, he does not mention Benjamin, hoping that his sons have forgotten the awful terms. Perhaps they can secure a few scraps without risking Benjamin's life. At this point Judah intervenes to make things clear to his father. Joseph had told the brothers that if they did not bring Benjamin with them they would die (42:20). He knew that the famine would continue and that the brothers would be forced to return to Egypt to survive. Judah had understood Joseph's meaning precisely, and he twice repeats that if they do not bring Benjamin they will not have access to the Egyptian who is the sole dispenser of the grain.

Judah has become the spokesman and leader. The main turning point is reached, however, when Judah offers to assume personal responsibility for Benjamin's life in verses 8-10. Just as chapter 37 forced us to contrast the two brothers' attempts to deliver Joseph from death, the analogy between the offers of Reuben and Judah to be responsible for Benjamin forces us to contrast their words in order to see why Reuben's offer hardened Jacob's resolve not to send Benjamin, whereas Judah's words won him over. Unlike Reuben, Judah is successful because he sets Jacob's decision in a larger context. He sees clearly that the continuation of the whole family is at stake, and he is able to get this insight through to his father by picking up and building on the same phrase Jacob had used in 42:2 to respond to the famine: "*so that we might live and not die*—also we, also you, also our offspring."* Whereas Reuben offered to destroy part of the next generation if he could not return Benjamin to his father, Judah emphasizes the necessity that the next generation must continue. He shows Jacob that Jacob's efforts to save the life of the younger, favored son are threatening the continuation of the entire line. How was Judah led to that conclusion?

Although the midrashic tradition was aware of many of the parallels between Genesis 37 and 38, Robert Alter has demonstrated how these parallels create a new literary unity, integrating the themes of the Judah-Tamar story into the Joseph narrative.[24] Alter concentrates primarily on the integration between chapter 38 and chapters 37–39 of *Leitwörter,* images, and themes: Judah goes down from his brothers and Joseph is brought down to Egypt; Jacob mourns for "dead" Joseph, and Judah mourns for his dead sons; the brothers send the bloodied garment—"Please recognize . . ."*—to unmask deception; a garment is dipped in kid's blood, and a pledge is taken by Tamar for a kid; Tamar's successful seduction is deemed righteous, but Potiphar's wife's attempted seduction is a sin against God.

Earlier I tried to show how many of these themes, especially deception and recognition, go back to Jacob's early struggle with

Esau for the blessing and at the same time look forward to Joseph's recognizing his brothers while they were unable to recognize him. Just as Jacob had put kidskins on his arms and neck to deceive Isaac and as Tamar had changed her garb from widow to harlot to deceive Judah, so Joseph's royal garb, given much attention in the narrative, effectively prevents the brothers from recognizing him.

Another key thematic relationship between Genesis 38 and the Joseph narrative has not been pointed out by other scholars. It is introduced in Judah's interior speech in 38:11. After losing Er and Onan, Judah sends Tamar back to her father's house until his younger son shall grow up. Readers learn instantly what only gradually becomes apparent to Tamar: Judah's action is a ruse to protect the life of his youngest son, "for he thought 'lest he die also like his brothers.'"* Marriage to Tamar seemed to invite death. Chapter 38 proceeds to describe the desperate risk that Tamar takes so that she may bear a child—and the family of Judah will continue. She deceives the deceiver. Tamar becomes pregnant by Judah; and when the patriarch recognizes the pledge tokens and realizes the meaning of her action, he says, "She is more righteous than I, because I did not give her to Shelah, my son."* Thus we see Judah's growth in Genesis 38 as he moves from an understandable desire to protect his youngest son, given in interior speech, to a public proclamation of his wrong. The episode ends with a description of Judah's line continuing—not through Shelah, who remains outside this story—but through the twin offspring of Tamar.

As Seybold has pointed out, Onan's selfish refusal to continue the family of his dead brother through Tamar establishes a thematic parallel with the action of the brothers in Genesis 37, who become callous wasters of life through their hatred of Joseph.[25] The real point of Genesis 38, however, is that Judah is at first also a waster. Ironically he becomes a waster by trying to safeguard the life of Shelah, his youngest son.

By now it should be clear why it is Judah who can step forward to convince Jacob to send Benjamin. We have noted that Jacob has changed from the bold initiator of chapter 42 who saves his family from famine to the pathetic pleader in chapter 43, shriveled into paralysis because he has put Benjamin's safety above all other

considerations. In chapter 38 Judah learned the crucial importance of the continuation of the family. He is able to bring Jacob
back to his senses by demonstrating that his protective favoritism
for Benjamin will destroy the future generation of the family of
Israel. Judah demonstates to Jacob that Israel must live into the
future. Whereas he left personal items in pledge *('rbn)* to Tamar
until the kid be brought, he now pledges himself *('rbn)* to Jacob
until Benjamin be returned home safely. If not, says Judah, he
(not his sons, the next generation) will bear the guilt all his days.
That is, Judah is now willing to risk giving up the firstborn/favored
status he's schemed to win in chapter 37.

After the divining-cup incident Judah again emerges as the
brothers' spokesman before the Egyptian lord. Whereas Reuben
turned against his brothers and proclaimed his innocence in a
similar setting (42:22), Judah admits to Joseph that God has
"found out the guilt of your servants" just as surely as the cup had
been "found" in Benjamin's sack.

Judah's speech before the Egyptian lord also takes a different
direction from his speech to Jacob. Whereas he stressed the
preservation and continuation of the family in confronting his
father, Judah now focuses on the preservation of the father in
addressing the Egyptian lord. As he summarizes the past (once
more tying past crime to present predicament), Judah highlights
the old man's fragility, his total attachment to the one remaining
son of Rachel, and the threat that if harm befall Benjamin the
brothers will "bring down . . . my father, mourning, to Sheol."*
Whereas he had told Jacob that not risking the life of the son will
be the death of Israel as a continuing family, Judah now tells the
supposed Egyptian that the life of the father is bound to the life of
the youngest son, and that the loss of Benjamin will be the death of
Israel, the family's progenitor. True, Judah is himself the pledge
for Benjamin's safety, but his speech shows that his father's life is
more important to him. Thus he offers to remain in Egypt as slave
so that Benjamin may go up with his brothers and so that Israel
may live.

Joseph's dreams were partially interpreted by his brothers and
father in chapter 37, but not until Judah's speech are we (and
Joseph) given sufficient narrative perspective to reach a more

complete interpretation. Judah's speech shows what the brothers have learned—that the loss of a brother would be the death of Jacob-Israel. Perhaps Joseph did not realize what additional grief to his father his test of the brothers would cause. Paradoxically, there is something more important that *Joseph* must learn from *Judah:* the risking / offering up / suffering / descent of a brother can mean life for the family of Israel.

Judah twice alludes to the Sheol descent motif in his speech before Joseph. As Seybold and others have pointed out, the pattern of the opening chapters of the Joseph story is a threefold descent: into the pit, into Egypt, and into prison.[26] Both in the narrative structure and in the mind of Joseph, the hero who had dreamed of dominion was descending. The brothers see Joseph coming and ambiguously refer to him as "ba'al of the dreams." This means something like "hot shot dreamer"; but the allusion to Baal—the Canaanite vegetation god who annually descends into the pit and then arises—underscores the mythic descent pattern of the hero. This pattern is further underlined by Jacob's outburst upon learning of Joseph's death: "I will go down *[yrd]* unto my son, mourning, to Sheol"* (37:35). Meanwhile, we learn, Joseph was "brought down" *(yrd)* to Egypt (39:1). In 40:15 Joseph comments to the butler and banker on his innocent suffering, designating the prison in which he remains as "the pit"—a term synonymous with Sheol in biblical tradition and used only one other time in the Hebrew Bible for a prison.[27]

When Judah offers to remain enslaved in Egypt so that Israel will not enter Sheol and "the lad might go up with his brothers," Joseph is finally able to perceive the full meaning of his life. In chapter 45 he correlates his dreams of ascendancy with his past suffering: "You sold me here [descent] . . . but God . . . has made me a father to Pharaoh [ascendancy]" (45:5, 8). And the purpose of it all, Joseph now sees, is "God *sent* me before you to *preserve life* . . . to *keep alive* for you numerous survivors"* (45:5, 7).

Judah did not realize that, in offering to remain enslaved so that Benjamin could return, he was helping this strange Egyptian understand the meaning of his own life. In fact, however, Joseph was learning the same lesson that Judah had taught Jacob. The narrator underscores this by developing the symmetry between what Joseph claims that God has done with him and what Judah had earlier insisted that Jacob must do with Benjamin: "*Send* the lad with me . . . that we may *live* and not die . . . also our offspring."* That is, the favored one must descend/be offered up/be risked so that "Israel" (referring both to the father and to the clan) might not perish.

Joseph's speech before his brothers in chapter 45 suggests analogies with Abraham, Judah, Jacob, and God in the Genesis story: what Abraham had done willingly with Isaac, what Judah could not do with Shelah, and what Jacob had done grudgingly with Benjamin, God did with Joseph. As the brothers learn that the divine favoritism they had once hated involved the risking/ descent of the chosen one so that Israel might live, they can now perceive Joseph's dreams of ascendancy in a new light. But reconciliation among the brothers—a major theme in the Genesis tradition—can begin only as the brothers realize that they have passed the test. They have affirmed their solidarity with Benjamin by returning with him to Joseph's city. And one of their number has gone even further, offering up not his son but himself so that Israel would not enter Sheol and "the lad might go up with his brothers."

Joseph's self-revelation to his brothers in chapter 45 prepares for the larger family reunion involving Jacob that will fulfill Joseph's second dream. The Joseph story has reached its climax and is winding down, but we should remember that it is an episode within the larger story of Jacob. As the second dream unfolds toward its unusual fulfillment, the ancient patriarch again assumes center stage, and the brothers move off to the wings. In the preceding chapters Jacob the heel-grabber had become Jacob the son-grabber—unwilling to risk Benjamin's descent so that the family might live on. When he hears that Joseph is alive, Jacob impulsively determines to go down to see him before dying. The father who once moaned that he would go down, mourning, to Sheol to seek out his dead son Joseph now prepares to go down to Egypt to meet a living ruler. But as he reaches the border, he hesitates, offering "sacrifices to the God of his father Isaac" (46:1). Sheol and Egypt have become analogous in the story. Jacob is about to leave the land of promise, about to enter Egypt. Jacob and the reader must recall earlier episodes involving the ancestors and Egypt in the context of famine: Sarai and Abram go down in 12:10-20 with ambiguous results: was it an act of foolishness or faith? More recently, Isaac was commanded by God not to go down to Egypt when famine again struck the land (26:2ff). Small wonder that Jacob holds back. Is he risking the promise through this descent into Egypt? Will "the God of his father Isaac" sanction this going down?

The descent-ascent motif continues as God addresses Jacob in a night vision. Here the patriarch must appreciate the lesson his sons have learned—he should not fear descent, for "I will go down with you" (46:4). As God's presence prospered Joseph in Potiphar's household and in prison (39:3-5, 21-23), so God's presence will prosper Jacob in his descent, making Israel a thriving nation down in Egypt. "And I will also bring you up again." As God caused Joseph's ascendancy in Egypt, delivering the family and land from famine, so Jacob will be brought up again to Canaan—his body returned amidst the pomp and circumstance of an Egyptian ceremony.

Any reader should now know that the experience of father and son will continue in the descendants: Israel will "go down" as she enters bondage in Egypt. But she also will prosper in her bondage (Exod. 1:5), and finally God will say to Moses: "I have *come down* to deliver [Israel] . . . and to *bring them up* . . . [to] a land flowing with milk and honey" (Exod. 3:8). The belly of Sheol is transformed into a nurturing womb. Although evil was feared or intended at every stage, God has intended it for good (cf. 50:20).

The second dream is nearing fulfillment. In 46:29, as father and lost son finally meet, the text says "and he [Joseph] *appeared* unto him (Jacob)"*—using a Hebrew word that consistently describes a theophany in the Bible. The narrator metaphorically suggests Joseph's royal splendor, but the reader is also asked to remember the cosmic dreams of the sun, moon, and stars. After Joseph has settled the family in Goshen, Jacob prepares for death. His primary concern is that he be buried in Canaan. When Joseph vows that he will carry out the proper burial, Jacob "bowed down *[vayyištaḥû]* on the head of the bed"* (47:31). The dream has been fulfilled in its own way, with the object of the verb left ambiguously unstated. When Joseph agrees to be the agent through whom the divine promises made to Jacob in 46:4 are to be carried out, the patriarch "bows down"—in gratitude to the son, but, more important, acknowledging and accepting the mysterious arrangements of providence.

In the following episode, with Jacob hovering near death, Joseph brings his Egyptian-born sons for a blessing and possibly for adoption. Surprisingly, Jacob states that Ephraim and Manasseh are "as Reuben and Simeon." That is, Joseph's offspring are to assume the role of firstborn in Israel. Paternal choice and special roles continue. The narrator stresses Jacob-Israel's dim vision "so that he could not see" (48:10). But, says the patriarch, "God has caused me to see your seed"* (48:11). Jacob-Israel will see not as man sees, but as God causes to see.

Jacob continues the motif of divine favoritism—of Ephraim, the younger, over Manasseh. Joseph protests, but Jacob answers "I know, my son, I know" (48:19). We remember the blind Isaac, who gave the blessing to the right son, though unwittingly. Unlike his father, Jacob sees truly. God has shown him through his experience that although brothers may be reconciled, divine favoritism remains. The offspring of Joseph will play out that drama in Israel's future. Through his ordeal with Joseph and Benjamin, and through his final vision of the deity upon leaving Canaan, Jacob has acquired a new perspective. He is now content to accept a mysterious providence that has brought and will continue to bring blessing and tempered reconciliation out of favoritism and conflict. Jacob sees—that his god has firm and knowable purposes that are nevertheless brought to fruition in paradoxical and surprising ways.

Scholars have generally regarded Genesis 49, in which Jacob gives final blessings to his sons, as an example of early Israelite poetry that reflects the political prominence of the tribes of Joseph and Judah in the early monarchical period. Others see the blessing of Judah as eschatological-messianic, pointing to a distant age beyond the time of the writer. It has rarely been noted how well the song dovetails into the larger story of Jacob, with *Leitwörter* and motifs that link the song to earlier episodes in his life. Now at the point of death, Jacob assumes an almost omniscient point of view, as he sees the future emerging from the past. At no point is the playful wonder of his retrospective vision into the future more evident than here: "it started out or looked like X, but lo, it became Y" is a recurring motif. Reuben—the first of Jacob's procreative strength—is no longer first because he "went up" to his father's bed in a premature attempt to assume the rights of primogeniture and the role of the father (cf. 35:22). Simeon and Levi are strong in anger, with implements of violence (their "cutters/cutting" perhaps punning on the cutting of covenant by cutting of foreskins in 34:13-31) that resulted in the slaying of Shechem and Hamor (the man and the ox of 49:6?) with the "edge of the sword." Like the people of Babel who were scattered *(pûṣ)* for building a city, Simeon and Levi will be scattered *(pûṣ)* for conquering Shechem.

We have seen that Judah is a main character in the Joseph story, and that he and Joseph are the two people whose development is most clearly documented. Judah played a leading role in selling his brother into bondage; yet he becomes the key to a positive resolution of the plot. He convinces Jacob to send Benjamin to Egypt and then helps Joseph understand the meaning of his dreams when he describes Jacob's distress and offers to remain in Egypt in Benjamin's stead. I have tried to argue that the incident that changed Judah's perspective was his encounter with Tamar in chapter 38. Is it possible that, in his last words on Judah, Jacob is playfully pondering a son's foibles that led to blessing?[28]

Many of Jacob's final blessings in chapter 49 contain words that play on the names of the sons. In the case of his fourth-born, "Judah" *(yᵉhûdâ)* is closely followed by "praise you" *(yôdûkā)* and "your hand" *(yādᵉkā)*. The end result, for Judah, will be domination over his enemies, with his brothers *bowing down* before him—precisely the role he may have been aiming at by getting rid of Joseph.

"From the prey *[ṭeref]*, my son, you have gone up." Are we being invited to compare and contrast Reuben's "going up" to his father's couch with Judah's "going up" from "the prey"? In 37:33 Jacob had exclaimed, upon seeing Joseph's bloody garment: *ṭārôf ṭōraf yôsēf* ("Joseph has surely become a prey"*). Jacob had assumed it was a wild beast that had killed his son, and in Genesis 49 he refers to Judah as a lion's whelp that had gone up from the prey. Is the father identifying the guilty son? A further ambiguity appears when Jacob says, "From the prey, *my son,* you have gone up." Is he referring to Joseph or to Judah when he says "my son"?

Jacob shifts from the image of the brothers bowing before Judah to Judah as a bowing/couching, stretched-out lion. The first term can have a sexual connotation,[29] especially when reinforced in the first half of verse 10 by the reference to the ruler's staff "between his feet" (a sexual euphemism). In this sexual context when Jacob speaks of the "staff not departing from Judah," we are reminded of Judah's sexual encounter with Tamar in which he left his staff with the woman in pledge of payment.[30]

Judah had met Tamar on the road to Timnah, which is located in the valley of Sorek ("vineyard"). This may be the reason that the poet shifts to vineyard imagery *(gefen/śōrēkâ).* Judah had tarried, binding his ass to the vine (49:11). The two words for "ass" *(ᶜir/ᵃtōn)* may recall the names of Judah's oldest sons *ᶜēr* and *'ônān.*[31] Vines will break; they are not strong enough to hold a tethered ass. The actions and fate of Judah, Er, and Onan threatened the life of the family vine. Whereas Judah earlier participted in the deception of his father by dipping Joseph's cloak in kid's blood, he must now wash his own garments in the blood of the grape flowing from the broken stock, as he experiences the death of Er and Onan.[32]

While smiling grimly over his son's shady past, perhaps seeing analogies to his own youthful days, Jacob ponders its relationship to Judah's blessed future. The son who had schemed mightily to assume the role of the firstborn and had then been willing to give it all up in Egypt will indeed have his brothers bow down before him in days to come. The son who had let his staff depart from him—given to Tamar because he had been unwilling to send Sheleh to her—will indeed not lose his staff/scepter of rule again "until Shiloh [Shelah?] comes."*[33] Judah's folly had resulted in the near breaking of the family vine, as Joseph was sold into Egypt, as Er and Onan both perished. Tamar turned the tables, however; and the end result of the rule of Judah's line will be a paradisiacal abundance with grapes and milk in such great supply that clothes can be washed, wine can be drunk, and asses can be tethered without concern for the waste of broken vines.

In most cultures of the ancient Near East, cosmic unity and stability could not be assumed. The world order reflected an ongoing conflict between deities whose power and mood were in constant flux. There was an ever-present threat that the precarious order of creation could slip back into the chaos whence it had come. The primary goal of each culture's myth and ritual was to reestablish and preserve the cosmic order. In later times the pre-Socratics, while scorning mythology, would attempt to reach the same goal through philosophical constructs. Although Israel had her origins among the peoples of the ancient Near East, she reached a different world view at a relatively early stage of her history. The deity who spoke to Moses and the patriarchs could not be fully fathomed, but a unified, stable order underlying the cosmos could be assumed. Israel's covenant ritual affirmed and celebrated the new order that had been manifested in her early history.

Writing of the "revolution of consciousness" sparked by monotheism, R. Alter describes the effect that the Israelite world view had on biblical narrative.[34] He aptly suggests "prose fiction" as the most appropriate category for understanding biblical narrative, calling it a "mode of knowledge" and "form of play" that gives the writer freedom to explore, shape, and order the close-up nuances and panoramic vistas of human experience.[35] A unified cosmos is presupposed, liberating the writer to focus on the foibles and often mundane quality of human activity. The narrator assumes an omniscient voice, but the reader receives only fleeting glimpses of perfect knowledge.[36]

In concurring with Alter, I am not denying the presence of tribal etiologies, Egyptian background, or conflated sources in the Joseph story. I am maintaining, however, that all these elements have been subsumed in a powerful work of imagination that depicts human beings deciding and acting, both foolishly and wisely, in a world where mortals shape their destiny within a divine plan. The story's conclusion was not predetermined. Dreams may envision what is divinely determined, but they do not delineate the appropriate human response. Joseph could have rejected his brothers when he first saw them in Egypt; Jacob could have refused to send Benjamin; Judah could have allowed Benjamin to remain enslaved in Egypt. The characters brought the story to its fitting conclusion. But the narrator makes it clear that the characters were able to learn and grow only because they were placed in a cosmos that, given proper cooperation from its supporting cast, brings life out of death and transforms evil into good.

7. AN EQUIVOCAL READING OF THE SALE OF JOSEPH[1]

Edward L. Greenstein

Introduction

The story of Joseph and his brothers (Genesis 37–50) poses a particular sort of challenge to the modern reader. Especially in the early episode concerning the sale of Joseph into slavery (37:18-36 with 39:1), the text becomes almost consistently inconsistent. It wavers back and forth between conflicting narrative sequences, or "versions" of the story's action. According to one version, the brothers throw Joseph into the pit with the original intention of letting him die. But then, at the behest of Judah, they sell Joseph to a passing caravan of Ishmaelites, who in turn sell Joseph in Egypt. According to the second version, the brothers throw Joseph in the pit, but Reuben plans to deceive the others and return Joseph surreptitiously to their father Jacob/Israel.[2] Then, unexpectedly, a passing group of Midianite traders removes Joseph from the pit and thereby confounds Reuben.

Such narrative style, in which inconsistent lines of action are interlaced through the text, may have been both familiar and acceptable to an ancient or preliterate audience,[3] but it has rubbed against the sensibility of modern, Western readers. One scholar, in a valuable book-length study of the Joseph narrative, declares that "chapter 37 contains one of the most blatant discrepancies in the entire Pentateuch, viz., the contradiction surrounding Joseph's sale into Egypt."[4] Typically, scholars have not read the text for what it is. Rather, modern analyses of the text tend to fall within three categories, none of which allows for a narrative unity in which inconsistencies may make up part of the narrative structure itself.

In the first category are readings of the text that express embarrassment at the inner contradictions and excuse them by attributing them to different authors[5] or folk-traditions[6] that have been ineptly combined. It is assumed, therefore, that divergent versions of the story were spliced together by an editor (or redactor) who was unsuccessful at eliminating the inconsistencies among his sources.[7] As one notable commentator puts it, "The work of a competent writer surely presupposes an inner consistency of theme and details. Yet vv. 21-30, as they now read, are marked by inconsistency, duplication, and discrepancies."[8]

Such an approach does point out the existence of irreconcilable aspects of the story, but it fails to proceed beyond this observation, resigning itself merely to tolerate the inconsistencies as unfortunate. It projects a "scientific" bias for inner consistency onto a work of literature as though it were scientific discourse and not narrative.[9] Moreover, it analyzes the text in terms of its alleged historical components rather than in terms of the interaction of these components within the text. A literary approach must occupy itself with the integration of the two "versions" of the story within the text, without exclusive regard for logical consistency or the independent historical development of the divergent versions themselves.

The second category comprises readings that attend to one version of the story and ignore the other. Thus, some read only the version in which Joseph's brothers sell him to the Ishmaelite caravanners.[10] Others read only the version in which the Midianites pull Joseph out of the pit and thereby frustrate Reuben's plan.[11] Such readings refuse to respect the text by failing to acknowledge twofold sequences of action.

In the third category are readings that attempt to smooth—or skip—over the various discrepancies between the two versions and harmonize them into a single narrative sequence. Several such readings thus identify the Ishmaelites with the Midianites, interpreting "Ishmaelites" as a generic term for "traders" on the basis of Judges 8:24.[12] A careful reading of the text, however, must acknowledge that the Ishmaelites and the Midianites are distinguished from each other.[13] For example, the former are described collectively as a "caravan," while the latter are depicted as "men." Furthermore, such readings overlook the fact that, according to one reading of verse 28 (see below), the Midianites sell Joseph to the Ishmaelites, who are said to have taken Joseph to Egypt (compare 39:1);[14] but according to verse 36 it is the Midianites (Medanites) who convey Joseph into Egypt.[15] This, together with our remarks above and more subtle ambiguities that will be discussed below, militates against a conflation of the two accounts in a paraphrase such as the following: "Seeing the Ishmaelite caravan coming along, the brothers decide instead to sell the boy into slavery, [but] it appears that the Midianites beat them to it."[16]

In my view it is the proper role of literary study to enable the reader to experience the text thoroughly—not to *explain* the text, but to *expose* it.[17] Taking a cue from Martin Buber, the reader must experience the text not as an objectified "It" to be analyzed, but as a subjectified "Thou" to be encountered.[18] Our approach will follow from the premise that a work of art is a systematic whole in which every part functions within the system. The reader of the text must be able to see each meaning-producing element in the text and to explain how these components interact to form a whole. With respect to our two versions of the sale of Joseph, our analysis will endeavor to expose the double narrative sequences and describe their interrelation and points of contact. It will then be revealed that there is in our text an artful correlation of sequences of action and structural arrangement.

Our approach has been facilitated considerably by the structural analysis of narratives by the late Roland Barthes.[19] Barthes has applied his method to the analysis of another biblical narrative in which readers sense the presence of discrepancies—the story of Jacob's struggle with the angel (Gen. 32:23-33).[20] There Barthes embraces the narrative's ambiguity, which may have come about through the "tangling" of two "versions" of the story. He then goes on to show how the narrative proceeds not according to what we would regard as a logical sequence, but rather according to a *"metonymic montage":* "The themes . . . are *combined,* not *'developed.'* . . . Metonymic logic is that of the unconscious."[21]

Such a view is mandated by the presence in the text of a "friction between two intelligibilities"[22] in the narrative sequence. We may observe a similar "montage" of narrative sequences in the story of how Joseph was taken to Egypt. Here, too, the reader is manipulated to vacillate "between two intelligibilities." This effect may have been precisely the redactor's intention.[23]

As we said above, biblical scholars generally assume that a redactor has woven together a text from various preexisting sources or traditions. Many then attempt to isolate these sources and traditions in order to reconstruct them in their earlier, more "original" state. It might then be possible to study the ideology of the author(s) of the sources, who represent diverse traditions or schools of Israelite thought. This, in fact, continues to be a major preoccupation of contemporary biblical scholarship. In a literary study, however, we are interested in the final product of the redactional process in the text as we have received it.[24] If the text that we accept as the final product contains discernible discrepancies between one verse and another, we do not presume that the redactor had attempted to remove them but failed. Rather, we allow that the redactor may have been well aware of the inconsistencies and desired to leave them in the text.[25]

These remarks would not warrant reiteration were it not that even literary analyses of biblical literature that commit themselves to dealing with the text in its present form break down when they must face a text rife with discrepancy and duplication. In such cases they resort to source criticism.[26] But it behooves the student of biblical literature to acquire a method for reading biblical narratives *as they are told,* or as they "tell themselves."[27] In the analysis that follows, I shall attempt to remain sensitive to the narrative's own style and try not to impose our cultural expectations upon the text.

The Reading

We enter the Joseph narrative at the point where the brothers, already resentful of Joseph and his vision, spy him on his way to find them (37:18).[28] In unison ("They said one man to his brother") they decide to kill him. But the text becomes ambiguous

117

when the brothers say, "Now come, let us kill him, let us throw him into one of the pits."[29] It is not yet clear whether they intend to murder Joseph and throw his corpse into a pit or murder him by means of throwing him into a pit and leaving him to the elements. Then, either way, they plan to deceive their father by telling him that "an evil beast has eaten him." At this point Reuben intercedes, urging his brothers not to take Joseph's life with their own hands. The scrupulous reader, however, will observe that verse 21 also bears the seeds of ambiguity. First, it states that "Reuben heard" (of the brothers' plan), which might imply that he had somehow been absent from the brothers' deliberation. Second, it relates that Reuben "rescued him [Joseph] from their hand," which could mean that the brothers had already laid hands on Joseph.

The ambiguity becomes a contradiction when Reuben exhorts his brothers to throw Joseph into a pit instead of "spilling [his] blood." But the brothers had planned to cast Joseph into the pit anyway: Reuben's substitute plan assumes that the brothers had not planned to abandon Joseph (dead or alive) in the pit. Moreover, verse 22 implies that the brothers had originally intended to slay Joseph with their own hands but acquiesced to Reuben's plea to let him die from deprivation in the pit. This turn of the story does not remove the contradiction but serves to oppose the alternative reading of verse 20, according to which the brothers conspire to murder Joseph by abandoning him alive in the pit. Of course, as the continuation of verse 22 informs us, it was Reuben's intention to deceive the brothers by removing Joseph from the pit surreptitiously. The intended deception of the brothers by Reuben thus stands as a foil to the brothers' intended (and successful) deception of their father.

By this point the reader should perceive a bifurcation in the narrative between two overlapping sequences of action: (a) the brothers decide to do away with Joseph by throwing him in the pit (alive or dead); (b) the brothers, heeding Reuben's advice, abandon a plan to slay Joseph themselves and throw him into the pit. The subsequent action—stripping Joseph of his robe, throwing him into the pit, and sitting down to dine—appears to be shared by both sequences. Thus, the bifurcated sequence converses from this point until verse 28, when a narrative sequence opens that becomes incompatible with the action of the preceding three verses. Those verses note that the brothers sight a caravan of Ishmaelites and plan to sell Joseph to them instead of letting him die in the pit. This sequence corresponds closely to the characterization of the brothers in sequence (a) above. Namely, the brothers abandon one plan in which they are more directly responsible for Joseph's death for another plan (there Reuben's, here Judah's) in which they are less directly culpable. In fact, the language of the text reinforces such a reading. The brothers introduce their first plan with the word *lekhu wenahargehu*— "Come, let-us-slay-him"—(verse 20). Judah's plan, the last one adopted by the brothers, parallels the language of the first, *lekhu wenimkerennu*—"Come, let-us-sell-him—(verse 27). In addition, Judah's rationale, "Let not our hand be upon him," echoes Reuben's earlier exhortation, "Extend not a hand upon him," Reuben thinking he might rescue Joseph "from their hand." In addition, the formulation of the first and last schemes follows upon a *sighting* by the brothers (there of Joseph, here of the caravan).

But in verse 28 it is related that "Midianite trading men pass by, they pull and they raise Joseph out of the pit, and they sell Joseph to the Ishmaelites for twenty [units of] silver." A close reading of this verse reveals that it is ambiguous. Two readings converge on one clause, or, to put it differently, one clause is open to two readings. The clause in question is *wayyimkeru 'et-yoseph layyishmecelim*—"they-sold Joseph to-the-Ishmaelites." According to the syntax of the verse, the verb *wayyimkeru*, "they sold," follows as the fourth in a sequence of verbs of which "Midianite trading men" is the explicit subject. Therefore, the syntactic reading is: the Midianites sold Joseph to the Ishmaelites. However, the attentive reader is aware of another reading, which I call the "allusive" reading. The phrase *wayyimkeru 'et-yoseph layyishmecelim*, "they-sold Joseph to-the Ishmaelites," only alludes to the words of Judah to his brothers: *lekhu wenimkerennu layyishmecelim*—"Come, let-us-sell-him to-the-Ishmaelites" (verse 27). With this association in mind, the reader can disregard the syntactic sequence and understand the subject of *wayyimkeru*, "they-sold," in verse 28 to be Joseph's brothers.

In fact, various readers of our text have chosen between these two readings and selected one or the other. Those with a more literary bent, seeking unity, have generally opted for the "syntactic" reading. Compare the following rendering by a contemporary novelist: "But Midianite traders passed, hauled and lifted Joseph up from the pit and sold Joseph to the Ishmaelites for twenty pieces of silver."[30] Bible scholars, seeking sources, have more often preferred the "allusive" reading. Compare, for example, this translation (a slash indicates a boundary between hypothetical sources): "Meanwhile, Midianite traders passed by, and they pulled Joseph up from the pit. / They [the understood subject is the brothers] sold Joseph to the Ishmaelites for twenty pieces of silver."[31]

In a faithful reading, the reader must be sensitive to both messages, leaving them both open. It can then be observed that the two simultaneous readings of "they-sold Joseph to-the-Ishmaelites" correspond to the two sequences that we have identified above and are now prepared to identify here. The "allusive" reading, according to which the brothers sold Joseph to the Ishmaelites, follows the (a) sequence: The brothers carry out the second substitute plan and sell Joseph to the Ishmaelites, who in turn sell Joseph in Egypt (37:28-36; 39:1). In a subordinated sequence, the brothers plan to deceive Jacob/Israel and then carry out their deception (37:32-34).

The "syntactic" reading, according to which the Midianites pull Joseph out of the pit, follows the (b) sequence: Reuben influences the brothers to leave Joseph in the pit, planning to remove Joseph and return him to Jacob/Israel; but the Midianites remove Joseph first, thereby frustrating Reuben's plan; the Midianites then sell Joseph in Egypt. The two sequences are summarized on the diagram on pages 124-25.

The final action in sequence (b) compels the reader to return to the ambiguous reading of "they-sold Joseph to-the-Ishmaelites" (verse 28) and select the "allusive" reading for the clause. This may require the reader to re-analyze the narrative sequence at that point,[32] since the "syntactic" reading may have been assigned by the reader to the (b) sequence by default, while the "allusive" reading conforms to the (a) sequence. In any event, the clause "they-sold Joseph to-the-Ishmaelites" is equivocal in its context, that is, at that point in the narrative's self-disclosure to us. The equivocation in this clause is merely a miscrocosm for the equivocal effect created for the surrounding narrative of the sale of Joseph as a whole by the twofold sequence of action.

It should now be evident that within the narrative concerning the sale of Joseph there are two narrative sequences. At points the two sequences coincide, and at points they present incompatibilities in conflict with each other. Each, alternately, reaches for the reader's acceptance. The effect may be likened to an experience such as would be produced by viewing two films, partly different and partly the same, superimposed on a single screen.[33] Where the films are similar, a clear image would be seen as the frames from both films correspond. But where the films are divergent, the images would be confused and unintelligible; one film would obstruct the perception of the other. The chief difference between the two analogous experiences is that in viewing two superimposed films the blur is perceived immediately, while in reading two clear but contradictory narrative accounts, the "blur" is perceived upon reading the second account in trying to make sense of it in light of the preceding account.

Yet, a structure that is similar to the one that we find in the sale of Joseph episode may be found in the classic film *Rashomon* (1951), by the Japanese director Akira Kurosawa. In its core section the film presents the audience with five conflicting accounts of a crime of passion as told by five characters, three of them directly involved and two of them witnesses. The audience is never given the means by which to determine what had "objectively" occurred.[34]

In our text, sequences (a) and (b) are conflicting or competing intelligibilities. The structure of the narrative, which juxtaposes components of sequence (a) with components of sequence (b), produces the very sense of ambiguity and conflict that is conveyed by the actions delineated within the two sequences. The two sequences are thus played off against each other in terms of narrative arrangement and action-sequence.

In sequence (a) the brothers are master of their machinations, selecting a plan for doing away with Joseph and ultimately attaining their end. In the subordinated sequence, they plan to deceive their father, and again they achieve the object of their designs. The degree of their attainment is signified in the text through the language of Jacob/Israel's reaction to seeing the bloodied robe in verse 33. He duplicates verbatim the words that Joseph's brothers had construed in order to deceive their father (verse 20): "An evil beast has eaten him."

But sequence (b) provides an antithesis to sequence (a). Reuben sways his brothers from their original scheme, planning to rescue Joseph himself and deceive the brothers. But the Midianites catch them all unawares and foil Reuben and stymie the brothers by taking Joseph. (Since the continuation of the story requires that Joseph go down to Egypt, it is necessary that the brothers succeed to some degree and that Reuben fail.)

The effect of this juxtaposition is to produce an ongoing dialectic between the machinations of the brothers and the countermeasures of Reuben. The actions of each sequence are thereby blurred in the reader's *ultimate* perception. In terms of the narrative's action, the brothers' success in achieving their end in sequence (a) is compromised and delayed by the efforts of Reuben and the surprise appearance of the Midianites in sequence (b). The only actions that appear without obfuscation are those in which both sequences converge: The brothers plan to do away with Joseph . . . Joseph is thrown into a pit . . . Joseph is taken to Egypt by passing traders (of ambiguous identity) . . . (Jacob/Israel is led to believe that Joseph was killed by a wild animal).

In the larger context of the entire Joseph story, later references in the text continue to reinforce the equivocal reading of the sale of Joseph. When Joseph is imprisoned in Egypt, he tells his fellow inmates that he was "stolen from the land of the Hebrews" (40:15), which seems to correspond to the message in 37:28 that the Midianites "pulled and raised Joseph out of the pit." But when Joseph discloses his true identity to his brothers, he announces: "I am Joseph, your brother, whom you sold to Egypt" (45:4; cf. verse 5). This seems to conform to the "allusive" reading of 37:28, in which we understand that the brothers sold Joseph to the Ishmaelites. The two sequences, when visualized, vie with each other in their respective claims to intelligibility—like the conflicting testimonies in *Rashomon*—and have the effect of blurring our image of what happened. In the end, the reader cannot be certain of what human events actually took Joseph down to Egypt.

But the story's ambiguity concerning the natural or human chain of events that led to Joseph's servitude in Egypt throws into bolder relief the actual "cause" of Joseph's fate. As Joseph himself explains to his brothers—and via the narrative to the reader—"Now it was not you who sent me here, but God" (45:8; cf. verses 5, 7). By blurring the human factors leading to the enslavement of Joseph, the narrative sharpens our image of the divine factor in bringing it about.

The brothers, who had denied divine providence by belittling Joseph's dreams (which in the ancient Near East in general and in our narrative in particular have the status of revelations), learn that Joseph's descent to Egypt was part of God's larger design.[35] An equivocal reading of the sale of Joseph leads to the realization that, in the view of our narrative, it is not crucial to our understanding of the story whether the brothers sold Joseph to the Ishmaelites or the Midianites kidnapped him. It is important, rather, to perceive that the descent of Joseph to Egypt and his subsequent rise to power there reveal divine providence in history. This, of course, is the single most pervasive theme in the Bible. But in our text the theme is evinced not only by the action of the narrative, but also, as I have tried to show, by the structural arrangement of the narrative. Somewhat simplified, one sequence of human action rivals the other, leaving only the divine manipulation of events clear and intelligible.

Epilogue

At first blush, it might seem that our reading of Genesis 37 discovers too sophisticated a narrative arrangement for the ancient Hebrews to have contrived. One may question whether our interpretation conforms to the stylistics of biblical storytelling or whether the redactor(s) of the Bible intended to convey the meaning we have found. In all honesty, we must plead agnosticism concerning the conscious, and certainly the unconscious, intentions of the biblical or any other author. Nevertheless, our reading receives strong support from the fact that a structure similar to the one we have analyzed in Genesis 37, producing a nearly identical effect and "message," can be recognized in Numbers 16. That chapter combines into an overlapping sequence the stories of two rebellions against Moses, one by Korah and his followers and one by Dathan and Abiram. Verses 1-11 concern only the insurrection of Korah, and verses 12-14 mention only Dathan and Abiram. Moses' angry reaction in verse 15 seems to be directed against the latter pair, but in the following verse Moses addresses the former. In verse 23 the two groups are combined. The thrust of the story is to vindicate Moses as the sole legitimate leader of the Israelites, and toward that end Moses bids the earth to "open its mouth" and devour the rebels. The text then relates that the earth swallowed them up (verses 31-32), but "them" seems to refer to Dathan and Abiram as antecedents (see Verse 25). As the debacle is being narrated, the reader is often confused about precisely who is involved in what. But, as in Genesis 37, the ambiguity serves to blur our image of the rebels and focus on Moses, who stands triumphant when the dust clears.

In the foregoing I have not endeavored to present a complete, proper "close reading," structural analysis, or thematic interpretation of Genesis 37, although I have enlisted these methods where I felt them to be profitable. What I have tried to do is fundamental to such study: to expose the multiplicity of readings within the text and the design of the literary arrangement. My analysis begins to suggest a collaboration in the narrative between action and structure, which in their interaction help to produce "meaning." I also hope that the example of my analysis may help advance the development of methodologies for the literary reading of "composite," inconsistent texts, of which there are several in the Bible.[36]

A

They said each man to his brother, "Look! the ol' master of dreams is coming. Now, come, let us slay him, let us throw him in one of the pits, and we shall see what becomes of him.' [Then] we shall see what becomes of his dreams" (37:19-20).

B

CONFLICT

Reuben heard and rescued him from their hands. He said, "Let us not strike a living thing!" Reuben said to them, "Do not spill blood, throw him into this pit which is in the wilderness, and extend not a hand upon him," so that he might rescue him from their hand to return him to his father (37:21-22).

A

It was when Joseph came to his brothers, they stripped Joseph of his

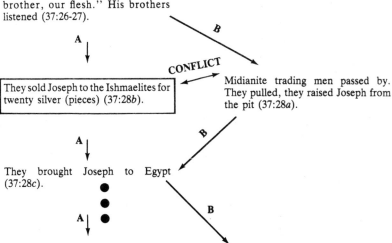

robe. . . . They threw him into the pit, the pit being empty, there was no water in it. They sat down to eat food, they lifted their eyes and saw, and look! a caravan of Ishmaelites was coming from Gilead . . . (37:23-25).

A | B

Judah said to his brothers, "What profit is there if we slay our brother and cover over his blood. *Come, let us sell him to the Ishmaelites,* and let not our hand be upon him, for he is our brother, our flesh." His brothers listened (37:26-27).

A

B

CONFLICT

They sold Joseph to the Ishmaelites for twenty silver (pieces) (37:28*b*).

Midianite trading men passed by. They pulled, they raised Joseph from the pit (37:28*a*).

A

B

They brought Joseph to Egypt (37:28*c*).

A

B

Joseph was brought down to Egypt. Potiphar, Pharaoh's major domo, the chief steward, an Egyptian man, bought him from the hand of the Ishmaelites who brought him down there (39:1).

I am Joseph your brother whom you sold to Egypt (45:4).

The Midianites sold him to Egypt, to Potiphar, Pharaoh's major domo, the chief steward (37:36).

For I was stolen, stolen from the land of the Hebrews (40:15).

8. THE UNITY OF GENESIS

Bruce T. Dahlberg

It is the contention of this essay[1] that the book of Genesis, taken as a whole and by itself, offers us a unified work of literary art. It is a unitary composition as it now stands—thematically developed and integrated from beginning to end. I do not mean for a moment that certain widely recognized phenomena of literary heterogenity in Genesis are to be ignored; yet, except for a brief recognition of them, I shall have to take these features of the book, related to the history of its composition, more or less for granted.[2]

We have to be reminded that behind the book of Genesis there stands a period of perhaps centuries during which the book was taking its present shape, receiving its form in a developing tradition—no doubt both oral and written. The "word of God," to use the classic theological expression, apparently comes to us not through any one single author. More than a few anonymous individuals and groups shared in its composition. Genesis as we have inherited it consists of at least two major narrative strands. The first and "primary" strand, as I shall call it, begins with the Eden story in chapters 2 and 3 and continues through much of the narrative, including the final story of Joseph. A second narrative strand, which appears to begin with the creation story of 1:1–2:4*a*, seems to be intertwined with the primary strand and is commonly referred to among students of the Bible as the "Priestly" strand because of its frequent attention to formal religious observance and ritual. The Priestly strand's attention to the Sabbath day

(2:2-3) and to the rite of circumcision (17:9-14) are examples of this distinctive interest in rite and ritual. Conflated with these two major narrative strands are one or two others, less easy to trace, but their degree of prominence in Genesis is not such as to require attention in this essay.[3]

It is not necessary or proper to rehearse here the scholarly investigations that have led to these observations about Genesis; they are summarized in many introductions to the book. However, awareness of the collective or communal character of the origins of Genesis can help us assess more accurately and appreciate more sensitively the nature of its art.

Certain features of the thematic structure of Genesis that tend to unify the whole work are well known and relatively easy to recognize. It is commonly observed, for example, that in the "primary" narrative strand, which gives the basic shape to Genesis, the stories of the patriarchs (chapters 12–50), beginning with Abraham's obedience to the divine command to migrate to Canaan, reverse the theme of recurrent expulsion, alienation, and scattering abroad that marks the human experience posited in the first eleven chapters of Genesis. The particularity implied in the "election" (God's choosing) of the patriarchs (and thus of Israel) is also universal, meaningful to the whole human race, which is portrayed as "fallen" in chapters 1 through 11.

In this respect, it is not a new thing to say that all of Genesis holds together thematically. Nevertheless, the patriarchal narratives tend to be seen by most interpreters mainly as a first stage leading into the events of the Exodus and after. Thematically and aesthetically, in terms of the narrative's plot, Genesis is thus considered incomplete in itself. In his otherwise authoritative commentary on Genesis, Gerhard von Rad states, "Genesis is not an independent book that can be interpreted by itself," and goes on to observe that Genesis is merely the first of what he calls the "intelligible sections of the Hexateuch" (the first six books of the Bible, concluding with the conquest of Canaan under Joshua).[4] What I wish to suggest is that, although it is not inappropriate to speak of Genesis as "prologue" to the rest of the Hexateuch, that term does not adequately and fully describe a composition that aesthetically and, in terms of theological statement, is complete in itself.

Let me draw attention, first, to the long concluding section of Genesis, namely, the story of Joseph (chapters 37–50). Recognized by nearly everyone as a complete and self-contained narrative, the Joseph story occupies a disproportionately large space compared to any of the other patriarchal stories in Genesis. Further, it is longer than the entire eleven chapters of primeval history that precede the patriarchal narratives.

The Joseph story is often seen as a sort of *bridge* between the patriarchal legends and the Exodus narrative, and is thought to have been included in the present book especially to serve that purpose, as well as for its inherent religious interest. However, the Joseph story seems to exceed the requirements of a mere bridge. In its sheer length, and in the heroic dimensions of its subject, its story of deliverance *in* Egypt competes with and very nearly overshadows the Exodus story of the deliverance *from* Egypt. In a careful study of the Joseph narrative, George W. Coats, though he accepts its bridge or transition function, also notes that whether or not the anonymous Yahwist (biblical scholarship's designation for the author of what we have termed the "primary" strand in Genesis) was the artist who created the story of Joseph (a moot point in Coats' view), the Joseph story does indeed suit that strand's literary construct and fits well into its theology.[5] It is precisely here that I believe we may see a more intimate relationship between the Joseph story and the rest of the primary strand of stories that come before it in Genesis. True, the Joseph story does provide, *de facto,* a transition from the patriarchal narratives to the Exodus. But, more important, it functions as a completion to and consummation of everything in the book of Genesis that precedes it.

Specifically, I suggest that the story of Joseph, taken together with the "primeval" narratives that are comprised in chapters 1 through 11 in Genesis, forms with them rhetorically an *inclusio* for the primary narrative strand of the whole of Genesis. That is to say, the Joseph story at the end of Genesis and the primeval history at the beginning provide together a literary bracketing—a beginning and an ending, a frame—to the Genesis narrative; and this is of major significance to interpretations of the book.

First, we may remind ourselves of the Eden story's subtle exploration of the mystery of human sin and guilt. Following an account of God's prohibition against eating of the fruit of the tree of the knowledge of good and evil, the serpent and the woman engage in their famous colloquy. The serpent says to the woman, "You will not die. For God knows that when you eat of it your eyes will be opened, and you will be like God, knowing good and evil" (3:4-5). It cannot be coincidence that in the concluding chapter of Genesis we first hear Joseph's brothers appealing to him in these words: "Forgive the transgression of the servants of the God of your father" (50:17), and then we hear Joseph responding "Fear not, for am I in the place of God? As for you, you meant evil against me; but God meant it for good, to bring it about that many people should be kept alive, as they are today" (50:19-20).

A correspondence exists between the beginning and ending stories in Genesis. The serpent had declared, "You will be like God. . . ." Joseph exclaims, "Am I in the place of God?" The serpent had promised, ". . . knowing good and evil." Joseph declares, "You meant evil against me, but God meant it for good." The serpent had said, "You will not die. . . ." Joseph perceives life saved from death: "God meant . . . to bring it about that many people should be kept alive as they are today." It seems that the use of these specific words in Joseph's conversation with his brothers, a conversation in which he in effect responds to the serpent's lines (3:4-5) point for point, serves and is intended to serve dramatically and theologically as a reversal of the scene portrayed earlier in Eden, and as a resolution of the problem exposed there.

Such correspondence between the beginning and ending of Genesis is by no means limited to this example, although it is the most obvious and arresting. There are a number of affinities of like nature which, taken singly, might reasonably be attributed to coincidence but which, taken collectively, support the initial perception that the Joseph story is intended as the climactic outworking of the problems of humanity posed in the first eleven chapters of Genesis.

In a number of ways Joseph appears to have been drawn intentionally as an "antitype" to Adam and, for that matter, to other main representatives of humanity who figure in chapters 1 through 11. In his study of the Joseph story, Coats concludes that the story's plot has two principal goals: "to describe reconciliation in a broken family despite lack of merit among any of its members" and "to depict the characteristics of an ideal administrator."[6] We can say that this is also a description—in reverse, so to speak—of the humanity portrayed in the first eleven chapters of Genesis: of those alienated from one another and unreconciled and of those failing the "administrative" responsibilities demanded of them. For the Priestly strand of narrative, humankind is intended to "have dominion" over everything (1:28), while for the "Yahwist" (or primary) narrative strand, man is to "till [the garden] and keep it" (2:15). Turning to the story of Joseph in Egypt, we see that he achieves on a grand scale what Adam was charged with but did not achieve, back in the beginning.

Again, Adam and Eve, expelled from Eden, are shut off from the tree of life (3:22-24); Joseph, disclosed as alive to his brothers, who had to leave Canaan for Egypt because of famine, tells them, "God sent me before you to preserve life. . . . God sent me before you to preserve for you a remnant on earth, and to keep alive for you many survivors" (45:5, 7). The expulsion from Eden is echoed, but the movement away from life is reversed.

Further, the famine in the Joseph story threatens the survival not only of Egypt and of Israel, but of the inhabited world: "All the earth came to Egypt to Joseph to buy grain, because the famine was severe over all the earth" (41:57). Thus, the universal famine in the Joseph story reminds us of the universal deluge in Genesis 6–9 of the primeval history, except that Noah's earth is destroyed whereas Joseph's, because of his fidelity and virtue, is spared. In this respect, again, Joseph is what I have called an "antitype" to the protagonists of the primeval history—in this instance especially to Noah. By this I mean that the later figure (Joseph) fulfills in his person and accomplishments what the earlier figure (Noah) only suggested or showed the need for. The storehouses built by Joseph against famine can be viewed an antitypes to the ark built by Noah against flood. All these details support the suggestion made earlier that the story of Joseph together with the primeval history of chapters 1 through 11 form an *inclusio* for the primary narrative strand of the whole of Genesis. Joseph recovers what the primeval ancestors of humanity lost.

In a number of other ways the story of Joseph seems to resonate thematically with the rest of Genesis. The strife between Joseph and his brothers, and its resolution in reconciliation, is explored with both insight into human psychology and the recognition that this is, paradoxically, and simultaneously, the outworking of Providence (45:5-8; 50:20). Hence, in this way, the Joseph story forms a concluding and conclusive word in Genesis on the conflict between brothers portrayed initially in the Cain and Abel narrative and resurfacing in the stories of Isaac and Ishmael and of Jacob and Esau.

Even the brothers' deception of their father Israel (Jacob) by the false evidence of Joseph's coat dipped in goat's blood has been seen by several commentators as a subtle and ironic recollection of Jacob's own youthful deception of Isaac (27:15-23; 37:29-35). Also relevant, in this connection, is the Hebrew term *kethoneth passim* used to designate the "long robe with sleeves" (37:3, etc.) that Jacob made for Joseph, because "Israel loved Joseph more than any other of his children." The noun *kuttoneth* ("tunic" or "robe") occurs in Genesis only one other time—in the plural—to describe the "garments of skins" *(kothnoth 'or)* that "the Lord God made for Adam and for his wife" (3:21). The occurrence of such allusions suggests again that the narrative does indeed point to Joseph as a counterpart to Adam.

Concerning the Joseph story and its relation to the rest of Genesis, one is reminded that the election of the patriarchs, seen in its universal aspect as a blessing to all the peoples of the earth ("By you all the families of the earth shall bless themselves"— 12:3; 18:18; 22:18; 28:14, etc.) is, for Abraham, Isaac, and Jacob, a promise for the future. In the Joseph story this promise is, for the first time, fulfilled: "The Lord blessed the Egyptian's house for Joseph's sake; the blessing of the Lord was upon all that he had, in house and field" (39:5).

Taking all these considerations into account (and other readers can surely add more examples to those given here), I am led to conclude that although the Joseph story does indeed bring the patriarchs down into Egypt and thus sets the stage for the Exodus event and in that sense may be seen as a bridge between the patriarchs and Moses, the Joseph story is nevertheless integrated intimately and functionally with the events and the theological motifs of the preceding Genesis material and serves as its artistic and theological culmination. The book of Genesis begins its narrative with the dilemma caused by humankind's betrayal of the Spirit by which it was created, a dilemma to which God responds with his call to Abraham. It finds its *telos* or end in the Joseph story: Joseph is an ideal for Israel and for the human race, and it is toward the incarnation of this ideal in Joseph that the whole Genesis narrative moves. Pharaoh sums it up as he exclaims rhetorically: "Can we find such a man as this, in whom is the Spirit of God?" (41:38).

Most of what has been said here draws on observations concerning the "Yahwist" or "primary" narrative strand in Genesis or to material closely related to it. But certain additional observations relevant to the unity and integrity of Genesis can be made about the elaborative "Priestly" narrative strand, which often seems to function as a form of *commentary* on the primary strand, or seems to enter into a dialogue with the thought of the primary (and presumably the earliest) strand of Genesis.

For example, it seems to me scarcely an accident that the Priestly strand, presumably with the primary narrative's account of the temptation of humankind in Eden to become "like God" (3:5) in mind, is at pains in its own version of the creation tradition to express the theological irony that humanity was, after all, created in the likeness of God (1:26; 5:1). And one can further suggest that the preoccupation of man with gaining the knowledge of good and evil in the primary strand (chapters 2–3) is not seen as a problem in the Priestly strand, given the latter's conviction, reiterated throughout the creation story of 1:1–2:4*a,* that the whole creation and all the creatures are unqualifiedly good as God made them. Indeed, the speculation seems justified that the Priestly strand may be calling attention in its own way to the primary strand's ultimate resolution of that problem: "You meant . . . evil, but God meant it for good" (50:20).

It is certainly the case that the Genesis narratives foresee that the descendants of Israel will return to Canaan from Egypt. Subsequent events as Israel remembered or understood them requires this element in the story. Nevertheless—and this is the point—the book of Genesis celebrates a divine deliverance that takes place *in* Egypt and *before* the Exodus in a narrative that is meaningful and self-contained. One might compare the book of Genesis as a whole to an orchestral overture to a dramatic opera:

an introduction, yes, but also a work of art complete in itself—a sort of overview of what is to take place, a survey in prospect of all the great themes. God already does in Genesis what he will do again in the deliverance from Egypt. Readers faced in life with the experience of Exodus can "take heart," so to speak, from Genesis.

III. LITERARY APPROACHES
TO SELECTED BIBLICAL NARRATIVES

9. BALAAM'S ASS: SUTURE OR STRUCTURE?

Ira Clark

The story of the mage, Balaam, who blesses rather than curses the triumphant campaign of the chosen people poised to invade Moab, is notorious among biblical scholars on the lookout for factual narratives of actual events. There seems little doubt that the tale-teller spliced two separate introductory accounts of Balaam's bowing to God's will instead of to King Balak's. Judged as history, the two are inconsistent. Why would God give Balaam permission to go from Mesopotamia to Moab on condition of obedience to divine will and then get mad at the soothsayer for making the journey, so that the angel has to make a couple of initial appearances to the ass and a final revelation to Balaam? And why would the storyteller have Balaam ride the ass impossibly fast and improbably far on his forced march?

One frequently invoked principle of literary, if not of historical or source studies, is first to assume that a work possesses an essential integrity and then to focus on apparent illogicalities, such as the incident of Balaam's ass, in order to illuminate that integrity. Although this procedure is not always successful (some works simply lack unity), and though it is logically circular, it does compel audiences to consider more encompassing interpretations. So, I suspect that the story of Balaam's ass, that funny folktale seemingly at odds with God's previous grant, is not the crude suture of a bumbling redactor; instead, it is a tale-teller's entertaining structural emphasis on the main issue of a three-part story with a single impact. God's jokes, no less than his potent commands or his sublime visions, inevitably display his all-powerful providence.

The narrator of Balaam's story presents a series of three sections—two episodes and a longer concluding narrative. The first (Numbers 22:1-20) sets the scene and establishes the almightiness of God's actions in a straightforward fable. The second (Numbers 22:21-40) repeats the lesson, reinforcing and extending the impact through a seriocomic beast tale. The last (Numbers 22:41–24:25) begins as another joke supporting the lesson but then incrementally soars into a prophetic vision imbued with the awesome might of God ordering history through his chosen people.

The story opens with the people of Moab in dread of the multitudes of Israel camped on their border at the end of a victorious campaign against the Amorites. Moabite terror is so great that their king, Balak, sends a delegation of emissaries from both his own counselors and the leadership of their allies, the Midianites, to engage the ultimate defense system. These nobles are to persuade the eminent soothsayer, Balaam, from Babylonia, center of great magicians, to charge back with a powerful curse against the Israelites. Such a curse, its potent word magic enforced by the powers of the universe, is to halt the Israelite march. After the elders have made their offer, Balaam needs a night of consultation with the Hebrew God, who refuses to allow a curse against the chosen people. But when they return to Moab weaponless, Balak sends another mission to Balaam, this time a larger group of advisers of greater stature to promise more substantial rewards. When Balaam consults God the night of this second visit, he is granted permission to return with the delegation, but with a proviso: "Only what I bid you, that shall you do."

In the opening episode the narrator sets out two essential axioms and one principle of construction. First, he assumes the Israelite point of view; that is, the Israelites are a unique people, apart from all other nations because God has chosen them to carry out his design for history. Second, he entertains no doubt about who rules the universe and humanity. Even a powerful magician and prophet from an alien religion is subject to God; he is an instrument under God's control, even though he does not belong to the unique chosen nation. As Balaam warns the emissaries the second night, he must seek God's grant before he can go with them: "Though Balak were to give me his house full of silver and gold, I could not go beyond the command of the Lord my God, to do less or more."

The narrator also establishes a repetitive incremental pattern by which he reinforces his Israelite point of view that God completely rules the universe and has chosen a particular people to carry out his design. The first sequence is built on a double request, both by the emissaries to Balaam and by Balaam to God. Furthermore, the second request of the emissaries gains magnitude and force over the first in both elaboration and length: the political status of the delegation, the terms of the offer, and the wording of the request and reply all increase markedly. A formal pattern of increasing sizes and intensities has been fixed. This pattern in the second and third sections enforces a sense of God's all-powerful providence and his designation of the escapees from Egypt as his instruments for civilization.

The narrator links the first section to the third through the laughter in the second. His primary axiom is made memorable through the comedy of Balaam's ass. But his comic point requires acceptance of his secondary axiom, that of the Israelite point of view. This perspective establishes the basis for ridicule first of Balaam, then of Balak and the Moabites, and finally the ridicule of all ungodly nations; for our sarcastic laughter at Balaam now and of the others later depends on the assumption that God's children can see God and his angelic messengers. Those who cannot, Balaam for now and the rest later, become the butts of God's, and the narrator's, didactic jokes. It further seems to me that the derogatory view of Balaam in later biblical passages (except for Micah 6:4-5) derives from the Israelite point of view, thus reinforcing my notion that the ridiculing episode about Balaam's ass, whatever its origins, is integral to Balaam's tale.

Past editorial concern over God's wrath, in spite of his previous permission to Balaam to proceed, strikes me as a misinterpretation brought on by a lack of proper perspective on those scenes in which the angel of the Lord repeatedly blocks the movement of Balaam's ass. To focus on that concern is to evade the critical question at this juncture: Can Balaam see the angel and understand God's plan for him, or not? The hyperbolic cumulative joke on Balaam is that not only readers, but even the ass that bears Balaam, can see God's purpose manifested in his angel, while the preeminent seer—who has just declared his dependence on God for his auguries—has yet to see or to understand his own declaration. He needs to be taught a lesson: one cannot look and listen for God's commands just at crises, but must be constantly alert to them.

To teach Balaam about God's providence (and to entertain and teach audiences over centuries), the narrator returns to the pattern of augmented repetition. The sarcastic laughter of our recognition increases over the triple blockading of Balaam's journey to Moab, a journey that also serves as a metaphor for his passage through life. The first time, God's angel with drawn sword forces the ass off an apparently broad road into a field, for which Balaam beats the ass. The second time, the angel blocks a narrow path between walled vineyards, and when the ass swerves it crushes Balaam's foot, for which Balaam beats it again. The third time, the angel stands "in a narrow place, where there was no way to turn either to the right or to the left." The ass can only lie down, so now Balaam, in a rage, strikes it "with his staff." When the Lord opens the mouth of the beast to protest the beating, ridicule increases because of Balaam's failure to notice the miracle; he does not hear and understand God, but goes right on to threaten the ass, wishing for a sword. At the same time, from the Israelite vantage, the audience watches the ass watch the angel brandish a sword over the spiritually blind and deaf seer, the alien prophet who has promised to look and listen for God's commands. Thus, when the ass turns to interrogate Balaam, we too are asking: Who's the ass? And, isn't God's wrath more than justified when it is directed against someone's refusal to see and to hear what he has just promised to follow?

The design of the episode is cumulatively organized. Balaam's journey from the Euphrates to Moab is ordained to teach Balaam to understad the essential belief established in the first episode. Manifestations of God's providence are structurally increased. A doubled episode is tripled, and Balaam's greater and greater blindness, deafness, and rage incur graver and graver danger.

Most of all, God's providence is structurally manifested to channel Balaam's journey until God compels Balaam to *understand* what the soothsayer has before merely *affirmed,* thereby reinforcing the audience's understanding as well. The journey moves from the highway of choice, to a restricting narrow path, to a place of decision so straitened as to compel Balaam either to see and hear God from an Israelite more than a pagan viewpoint, or to perish. Only then does the Lord open the eyes of the seer so that he understands the eminent danger of refusal. Now he bows and abases himself. The angel's accusation and acknowledgment of the punishment designed for Balaam only confirm an audience's earlier ridicule and condemnation. What is left but for Balaam to confess, "I have sinned, for I did not know that thou didst stand in the road against me"? The viewpoint and structure of the second episode have compelled assent to God's all-encompassing providence, which Balaam at last begins to understand. When his offer to return home rather than proceed to Moab is rejected in favor of his, and God's, original purpose, the repetition of God's command takes on new meaning: "Go with the men; but only the word which I bid you, that shall you speak."

Balaam's arrival in Moab and his brief welcoming talk with Balak conclude the second episode with a summary of the central theme established in the first episode and reinforced in the second. When Balak questions Balaam's reluctance to come, asking if Balaam does not appreciate the honors and rewards available from Moab, Balaam recalls his opening statement to the second mission: "Have I now any power at all to speak anything? The word that God puts in my mouth, that must I speak." But now he recalls the confirming experience of the second episode.

While this capping scene recalls the first episode through the hindsight provided by the second, it also provides transition to the third section. As Balak goes off with Balaam to the sacrifice, the Israelite audience watches with a considerable sense of *déjà vu.* Balak is another alien who is initially warned that all power resides in God, when Balaam, the very power Balak himself has summoned and rested his faith in, tells him. Nevertheless, Balak cannot hear, see, or understand God's active providence. It is his turn, that of the Moabites, and of the rest of the hostile nations, to be the butts of recurring didactic ridicule.

In opening the third part of his story, the narrator no longer has to depend on straightforward reiteration of the principle but can now rely on structural elaborations to carry the joke. Using the equation of sight with knowledge, he simply recalls the Israelite perspective: the next morning a company go up a bare height of Baal from which Balaam "saw the nearest of the people." Scornful laughter depends on the concluding upset of each of the three formulaic, elaborating repetitions of a solemn ceremony. Each time, Balak climbs to a vantage point, then prepares for Balaam's divination the mysterious seven altars, and sacrifices on each a bull and a ram; next, Balaam receives God's message and returns to Balak and his noble retinue anxiously awaiting the curse that will halt the Israelite juggernaut; when Balaam blesses rather than curses God's people, Balak and Moab are nonplussed but remain deaf and blind to God's message, even though at each of their protests Balaam elaborates that he can say only what God allows. Their ridiculous stance is increasingly absurd with each stupidly unresponsive reaction of the pagan leaders: let's try again.

Augmentation of the joke is primarily based on the principle of perspective. The pagans believe that if they change the height and the religious ambience of the vantage point for launching the curse, they can change the results; if only the proper military position can be established, they can win the spiritual battle. Therefore, from the bare height of the first failure, Balak hustles Balaam up to the field of watchers on the commanding top of Mount Pisgah, from which the chosen people do not appear to be so numerous; but the climb causes Balaam to increase the terms of the Israelite blessing and to predict disaster for the Moabites. So Balak angrily ascends once more, now to the top of Peor, which, apparently higher, overlooks the whole desert; but this third ascent leads Balaam to expand the previous rejections and prophecies. His simpler prophecies ascend to oracular vision so frustrating to Balak and the Moabites that Balak is reduced to pounding his palms. What, of course, has so stymied the Moabites is that they cannot see, cannot understand that all perspectives rise to the perspective of the chosen people and of God. As Balaam has ascended and soared into vision, ironically they have ascended in body but descended into what from the Israelite perspective would be called blindness of the soul.

When Balaam now prophesies the glorious victory of God's chosen people over all the pagan nations, the pattern of three merges into one of four so that the doublet of the first episode that evolved into a triplet in the next has become a quadruplet in the last. Here another splice needs to be considered. Textual scholars generally agree that the repetitiousness and the names for God in Balaam's four oracles result from the first two oracles belonging to the E redaction and the third and fourth being part of J. But I wonder if the narrator is not using these repetitions, as he seems to have used his other splice, not just to save duplicate renditions for posterity or for intrinsic interest, but more as effective structure. The incremental repetitions indicate to me that the teller is systematically and artistically augmenting his oracles to show that all power derives from God's providence, and that those who believe, particularly those delivered from Egypt, have been chosen by God to wield it.

When Balak called Balaam, he was negotiating to obtain the most potent weapon available, Balaam's curse. His alliance had the intent that his finger would point that weapon against the tribe of Israel. But when Balaam returns the first time from examining the sacrifice, he first acknowledges Balak's request and then refutes it: "How can I curse whom God has not cursed? How can I denounce whom the Lord has not denounced?" Then he acknowledges God's blessing on his chosen people and celebrates their magnitude. Finally he wishes to be guided by God as a righteous man, thereby implying an alliance with the Israelites. When Balaam returns the second time, he expands by initially contrasting God's power with man's and by announcing the power of the chosen people in the similes of the horns of the wild ox and the voracious lioness.

At the beginning of the third oracle Balaam sees, hears, and understands, so this time he ignores ceremony and does not bother to look for omens in the sacrifice. He announces at once his new, direct, visionary and prophetic mode: "The oracle of Balaam the son of Beor, the oracle of the man whose eye is opened, the oracle of him who hears the words of God, who sees the vision of the Almighty, falling down, but having his eyes uncovered." This oracle announces a power dependent directly on the Spirit of God without any form of mediation; thus it is unimaginable to the

Moabites. In this inspired state Balaam describes more eloquently than before the beauty of the chosen, who are like living vegetation in the desert, life-giving waters in an arid land. And he expands his previous similes; the wild ox will crush bones and pierce with arrows. When Balak realizes that he has no control over the power just demonstrated, he tries to shut Balaam up, without success. Balaam continues the inspired oration of one who "knows the knowledge of the Most High": the symbolic star and scepter shall rise to crush not only Moab, but also the other neighboring pagan nations. Balak must understand that God alone controls the universe; God's finger appoints everything.

After the humiliation of Balak, Moab, and their neighbors, along with the exaltation of God's providence and chosen people, the narrator concludes that "Balaam rose, and went back to his place; and Balak also went his way." The narrator is parting as well with his audience, having imparted a new understanding of providential guidance on the way to God's place. For however inaccurate the tale of Balaam and his ass appears to be as a history, and even if the last redaction appears to be two separate accounts of Balaam's oracles as a text, it is no botch as a story. Both the famous central episode and all four prophecies in the last section are integral to the incremental form of a story so designed as to celebrate, from the viewpoint of the unique chosen people of God, God's omnipotent control of human events.

Biblical authors who later condemned Balaam in their writings, medieval audiences who chortled at the ass in liturgical and miracle plays, and modern readers who recall little other than the inset oriental beast fable, have been responding to the craft of a storyteller. His first episode lays down the central Israelite point of view as God's chosen people, which sees, through the repetitive incremental elaboration of a doublet, the principle of God's active guidance of the universe. The second episode reinforces the principle in the laughing ridicule of a triplet which guides the audience from the same viewpoint to a renewed understanding of the principle along the horizontal plane of a directed journey through life. The third episode ascends vertically with the elaboration of the joke on three higher vistas for four prophecies, which soar from ceremony into visionary praise of God and his chosen.

10. SAMSON'S DRY BONES
A Structural Reading of Judges 13–16

James A. Freeman

For some three thousand years, Samson has held readers in
awe. Sir Thomas Browne summed up the wonder of Judges
13–16 for his age as well as for ours when he observed, "Search
all the Legends of times past, and the fabulous conceits of those
present, and 'twill bee hard to find one that deserves to carry the
buckler unto *Sampson*."[1] However, the same narrative that
captivates also perplexes. Critics from many eras and schools
have tried to squeeze Samson's bulk into their particular mold.
Excepting only the Song of Solomon, I can think of no other
short section of Scripture that has so vexed readers into exegesis.
Literal, typological, tropological, anagogical, rationalist, and
mythological techniques have been employed to translate the
Danite's birth, adventures, and death into other modes of
sequential discourse.[2] But, if I am typical of modern readers,
then I often find these methods turn me into a latter-day Samson.
Not, I hasten to add, the inspired hero who tears apart lions of
ambiguity, but rather the blind slave to other men's words who
trudges wearily in circles.

A structural examination of the Samson tale helps to make sense
of both text and context, however, and frees those who accept such
a reading from the nonliterary concerns that would be necessitated
by some other critical techniques. After mentioning general rules
about pattern in narrative and after offering reasons to expect

organization in Judges, I will present a four-part paradigm that I find in the story and spell out the consequences of such a taut framework. An analysis couched in the idiom of modern structuralism has the advantage of not demanding many extraliterary assumptions from general readers. They need no longer be religious believers, for example, or students of archaeology, ethics, or comparative mythology: they can deal with the text itself. Most important, perhaps, is the resolution of incongruous elements that structuralism accomplishes. The Lord's promise and Samson's profligacy can now exist in the same literary environment—without recourse to previous belief or to piecemeal rationalization.

I

The events of Samson's life are recited sequentially. Listeners as diverse as Aristotle, Lessing, and children at bedtime know that stories are articulated in time. Like trains emerging from tunnels, they proceed in a certain order: beginning is followed by middle is followed by end. We falsify this characteristic human expectation of first / next / finally if we begin an examination of Samson by untimely ripping certain deeds or motifs from the series in which they appear. Only after we determine the order of particular events may we remove them for analysis.

With this truth of narrative propriety in mind, let us recall how episodes in Judges 13–16 are arranged. Presented first are those supernatural happenings which advise readers to expect a religious hero who will somehow free the oppressed Israelites. Surprisingly, this prefatory section leads not to a history of national liberation but to a résumé of Samson's dangerous liaisons with three women, two of whom are Philistine and the third at least in the Philistines' pay. Finally, the amorous, roaring boy who lusts and rampages in this middle section, the apparent contradiction of chapter 13's divine promises, is sheared, blinded, and self-killed. His defeat and death do little to clarify beginning, middle, and end and leave us with the uncomfortable feeling that he may be no more than a hero of ballad songs and snatches unfit for academic regulations concerning probability in narrative.

There certainly does seem to be reason for us to accuse the tale of being disjointed and unpremeditated. The author encourages us in chapter 13 to expect a pious, patriotic hero. The unnamed champion has his entrance delayed, much like that of Odysseus or Hamlet, so we may be conditioned by certain conventional preliminaries: the delayed birth resembles those of traditional leaders like Isaac, Joseph, Samuel, and John the Baptist. A supernatural messenger comes not once but twice, commanding that the child will be ritually devoted to Yahweh. The parents dare not refuse since more than one-third of this chapter (9 English verses of 25) emphasizes the angel's awesome mien. Having reflected on this first chapter, a perceptive reader must feel that the author has taken pains to prepare the way for a virtuous and socially conscious judge.

The subsequent chapters, however, violate such expectations. Although announced as the champion of the Lord, a deity who lacks female consorts, Samson indulges in reckless carnality. Although a Hebrew, he disobeys general rules about honoring parents and avoiding mixed marriages, all the while violating specific Nazirite taboos. Quite unlike God, who regularly defeats alien deities, Samson allows himself to be betrayed. Perhaps, as most commentaries insist, the entire biography is no more than crude folklore with little artistic coherence beyond the hero's herculean personality.

But I find such literary despair unwarranted. There are at least five reasons to suspect that a tale that has attracted such a wide variety of commentators, each of whom senses implicit significance, is in fact a finished art object and has a rational distribution of narrative quanta. All human beings appreciate echoic regularity and normally seek patterns in disciplines such as music, where exposition and recapitulation are common; visual art, which is distinguished by gesture and parallel gesture; and literature, in which restatement pleases as much as statement.

Consider the context: The Samson data are incorporated in Judges, a highly patterned book that exemplifies a concept of history in which events repeat themselves. As indicated in chapter 2, Judges records a tripartite sequence of crime ("And the people of Israel did what was evil in the sight of the Lord"), punishment ("he gave them over to plunderers"), and redemption ("The Lord raised up judges"). Throughout the book, this orderly system happens in an inflexible series of apostasy, invasion, and deliverance. It is only when readers learn to value predictable replication, to agree that time moves in ordered patterns, and to anticipate the same actions in the same order that they can understand Judges.

My second reason for suspecting structure in the Samson story also springs from a paradigm that is found through the whole book. The activities of twelve *shofetim* are commemorated. Not eleven judges, or thirteen, but precisely twelve. Individually they are as dissimilar as Jacob's twelve sons or the twelve Greek Olympians. They may pass in review before us collectively, however, since they are disciplined by the magic numeral. The full significance of the holy dodecad to ancient Hebrews has been lost, but we can say that its presence in a story is presumptive evidence of intelligent control.

A third reason to assume that the Samson legend has a coherent structure is suggested by a recent writer who reminds us how often the story deliberately builds up our expectations and then dashes them. Samson's mother is barren, yet she has a child; Samson is a Nazirite, yet he associates with wine, corpses, and Philistines; his first father-in-law does not expect him to return, yet he does; and so forth.[3] This simple device of frustrating our preconceptions occurs so frequently that we have greater corroboration of the existence of organizing principle beneath the superficially disjointed material.

Related to this foiling of our anticipations is yet another technique, that of referring to different kinds of an object or action. For example, fire allusions are common. The "flame" that "ascended" from Manoah's altar not only parallels the upward flight of the Lord's messenger (13:20) but also prepares us for the fiery jackals' tails (15:4-5), the ropes falling from Samson's arms "as flax that has caught on fire" (15:14), and the cords snapping like scorched tow (16:9). The number three recurs (three women, thirty wedding "friends," three hundred jackals, three thousand Philistine victims). There are variations upon wet/green versus dry when the author opposes honey to a carcass, a fresh jawbone to a brittle one, "Spring of the Caller" (15:19) to arid land, and seven pieces of undried gut to seven dessicated thongs. Another pair of references concerns binding, the first as a result of Samson's agreement with his own people (15:13), the second because of a perfidious contract with Delilah (16:21). Samson's two prayers also illustrate the author's characteristic interest in varying a referent. The hero first prays for water so that he may outlive his enemies (15:18) and then so that he may "die with the Philistines" (16:30). A final example of permutation, this one brilliantly expanded by Milton in *Samson Agonistes,* is the idea that sensory pleasure as well as its opposites, betrayal and punishment, lurk in enclosed places (lion's body, wedding chamber, prison, Philistine building). Each of these variations gains its effect by awakening our memory of an exemplar and should alert us to the author's efficient premeditation.

My fifth reason to posit a rhythmic distribution of events in the Samson episode is the careful arrangement of speeches. One critic is so struck by it that he points to "the basic ternary pattern: A speaks, B answers, and then A caps it."[4] Samson's first exchange with his parents (16:2-3) demonstrates the order: Samson demands that his father and mother get the Philistine woman for his wife; they ask whether he cannot marry an Israelite; he rudely ends the conversation by commanding, "Get her for me." Samson again shows this brusqueness to his Timnite father (15:1-3), and the author reminds us that in order for stories to be effective, they must balance the predictable with the unforeseen. Here Samson's unexpected nastiness to his natural father and to his father-in-law is conveyed by the familiar A-B-A sequence.

Even before we excavate the orderly bones of a rational structure, then, the other repetitions that surround Samson— the historical pattern, the holy numeral twelve, the narrative tactics of reversing expectation or restating motifs, and the position of speeches—all cooperate with standard exegetical assumptions about some buried design and meaning in the tale. Let us now turn to these bare bones and their significance.

II

Here is the structure of Judges 13–16 as I see it:

INITIAL PARADOX: BIRTH FROM BARREN WIFE (CHAPTER 13)

A. Manoah and wife without issue: line will die (verse 2)
B. Messenger from the Lord with information:
   a. Human: They will bear son (3)

> Samson will be consecrated (4-5*a*)

> Son will initiate movement of national liberation from Philistine domination (5*b*. 3-5 repeated to Manoah in 6-14)

   2. Divine: Messenger will not eat food (15-16*a*)

> The Lord will accept sacrifice (16*b*)

C. Messenger says name is wonderful; his ascent is mysterious (17-20*a*)
D. Manoah and wife fall to ground, fear death because they have "seen God." False fear of betrayal by God (20*b*-22)

I. WOMAN OF TIMNAH: SEEN AND REQUESTED (14:1-4)

A. Samson kills lion (5-6)
B. Samson eats honey (8-9)
C. Samson asks riddle (10-14)

A'. Philistines threaten, "We will burn you" (15*a*)
C'. Philistines ask, "Have you invited us here to impoverish us?" (15*b*)

D. Samson betrayed by wife (16-18)

II. CONSEQUENCES OF TIMNAH (14:19–15:2)

A. Samson kills thirty Philistines (14:19*a*)
B. Samson returns to possess wife (14:19*b*–15:1)
C. Father-in-law asks, "Isn't her younger sister better?" (2)
C. Apparent betrayal by father-in-law

III. CONSEQUENCES OF TIMNAH, CONTINUED (15:3-6)

B. Samson enjoys guilt-free revenge. "This time I shall be blameless in regard to the Philistines when I do them mischief" (3)

A. Samson uses 300 jackals to destroy Philistine grain (4-5)

C'. "The Philistines said, 'Who did this?'" (6a)

D'/A'. Philistines betray kinsmen, kill bride and father (6b)

Philistine interlude

IV. SLAUGHTER (15:7-13)

A. Samson creates "a great slaughter" (7-8a)

B. Samson retreats to cave at Etam (8b)

C'. Frightened by Philistines who wish "to bind Samson" (A'), Hebrews ask Samson, "What, then, is this that you have done to us?" (9-11)

Hebrew interlude

D. Apparent betrayal by own countrymen (12-13)

V. CONSEQUENCES OF SLAUGHTER (15:14-19)

A. Samson kills entire Philistine group (14-15)

B. Samson celebrates victory with chant (16)

C. Samson asks the Lord, "Shall I now die of thirst?" (18)

D. Failure of betrayal by death. Having drunk water at Lehi, "he revived" (19)

VI. TRANSITION (15:20)

Samson judges Israel for twenty years (20)

VII. WHORE OF GAZA: SEEN AND BOUGHT (16:1)

A. Ambushers plot to "kill" Samson (2)

B. Samson dallies until midnight (3a)

C. Samson puts city gates on hilltop (3b)

D. Ambush fails

VIII. DELILAH: LOVED, BUT BOUGHT BY PHILISTINES (16:4-21)

A. Tyrants desire to tie up Samson and torture him (4-5)

B. Samson successfully preserves secret of strength

C. Samson gives three plausible but false answers to foil wife's quizzing:

C 1 - gut	D 1 - snaps (7-9)
C 2 - rope	D 2 - snaps (10-12)
C 3 - loom	D 3 - breaks (13-14)

D. Samson finally betrayed by Delilah:

C 4 - hair	D 4 - cut (15-21)

IX. TRANSITION (16:22)

Samson's hair begins to grow (22)

FINAL PARADOX: DEATH FROM DISABLED WARRIOR (16:23-31)

D. Apparent betrayal by promise of the Lord
1. Divine: Philistine sacrifice with joy to Dagon (23-24)
2. Human: Dagon's followers' "hearts were merry" (presumably with wine and unclean food) (25a)

   Philistine messenger summons Samson, disabled hero of Hebrew movement for national liberation (25)

   Samson performs before uncircumcised

C. Samson asks the Lord to "remember" him (28a)
B. Samson has lost sight and desires death (28-30a)
A. Samson kills self, Philistines, as all fall to ground: Manoah's heroic line dies (30b-31)

There is a total of eleven major sections: one initial, one final, two transitional, and seven intervening. By far the longest part is that which details the consequences of Samson's first liaison (five sections). His other two liaisons occupy one section apiece.

Each individual section is to be read top to bottom.

The entire sequence is to be read left to right.

Events recur in a relatively rigid order. The alphabetical key is:

A = a threat or an act of destruction. Usually the killing of human beings, either planned or accomplished, this ruin extends to the (apparent) extinction of Manoah's line due to his wife's infertility. Also, A covers the burning of Philistine crops since, quite obviously, life ends without food. *Note:* After Samson is said to have judged Israel for twenty years, the aggressive impulse is initiated by Philistines *against* Samson. Thus episodes VII and VIII begin with a reversal of direction so far as destructive urges are concerned.

B = an act of personal pleasure. The simplest examples are largely narcissistic: eating honey alone, dallying with a woman, emitting a "barbaric yawp" over fallen enemies. While the end sections are more complicated, they too involve the gratification of some physical need: for a son, food, or sacrifice in the initial section; for the return of strength and sight that have been lost; and for revenge in the final section. Samson's retreat to a cave, like his three defenses against Delilah's wheedling, preserves him in agreeable isolation.

C = a question. Whether unanswered (name of God's messenger) or answered (wedding riddle), inquiries regularly punctuate the narrative. I take two incidents as C since they strongly imply puzzles. The setting of Gaza's gates on some hill (16:3) is a visual enigma, which leads one to ask, "What are *they* doing *there*?" Similarly, Samson's final prayer (16:28) is as problematical as any petition to deity: will it be granted? Also, his prayer involves a central problem of the whole tale: has Yahweh forgotten Samson?

D = an act of betrayal. The act may be real (Delilah) or apparent (Hebrews giving Samson to Philistines). The agent may be anyone: God, wives, father-in-law, countrymen (both Philistine and Hebrew).

Four final notes about the sequence. I try to apportion major blocks of action. There is a temptation, quite understandable when one has a useful pattern, to see the ABCD sequence in minor blocks also. For example, Samson's final betrayal by Delilah might be patterned in the same way as his longer deeds have been.

A   Delilah cuts hair, destroys his strength. (16:19)

B   Samson responds to her warning with accustomed but false egotism: "I will go out as at other times—and shake myself free!" (16:20)

C   Samson ignorant that God "had turned away." (I.e., "Where is my strength?") (16:20)

D   Samson's status as hero and potentiality as liberator (apparently) betrayed: he is blinded and bound. (16:21)

Next, is there any defensible reason for ABCD? Why not ACBD, ADCB, ACDB, or ADBC? As I will soon suggest, this order may represent a progression from crude muscular display in A to a more specialized sensory activity (B) to an even more sophisticated act of mind (C), all of which prompt betrayal (D). The one exception to this sequence (15:3-5) strikes me as an artful variation rather than a denial. Samson here gloats over his curious fire-jackal revenge before executing it, surely a permissible irregularity in the narrative.

Liekwise, why does the Gaza incident not precede the one at Timnah? At this point, I can only surmise that the order of the three affairs is a donnée impervious to rational justification. While destroying / enjoying / quizzing / betraying have a certain arguable development, the placement of the liaisons does not suggest much to me. It may be based on historical fact (the Timnah episode *was* first) or it may be based upon the same benign arbitrariness we accept in fairy tales ("Once upon a time there was a man who loved three women . . .") or in mathematical demonstrations ("Let A equal . . .").

Finally, what of the interludes (14:15; 15:6; 15:9-11)? Although the tale's pattern impresses me more than these irregularities, they should be mentioned. Certainly they introduce no unfamiliar gestures. In addition, the one verse 14:15 egregiously alters the ABCD routine. But there are rough analogies to these anomalies in other works. For instance, who speaks the final lines of Milton's "Lycidas" or of Gray's "Elegy"? I can only conclude that literature, like life, displays occasional resistance to even the most benign programs.

III

This analysis of the structure of Judges 13–16 furnishes five major insights, which have to do with (1) the reader, (2) God's connection to the reader, (3) Samson's connection to the reader, and the story's message to the reader concerning (4) individuality, and (5) marriage.

To begin, the predictable pattern we have outlined allows a reader to enjoy Samson's berserk escapades without fearing they will require him to abandon his own moral balance. The structure denies any superficial impression he may have that Samson is merely a Semitic Rob Roy or Hebrew Paul Bunyan, an assertion frequently found in commentaries. If there was a historical Samson—and we need not deny the possibility—his life was probably as fragmented as our own lives are. Yet his biography skillfully diminishes picaresque elements. His deeds may resemble scalps on a warrior's belt, but they are carefully arranged. There is some irony in that the story's most notable gestures—slaughter, selfish pleasure, asking, and snaring—seem incapable of rational control. This portion of Judges nonetheless imposes a grid upon the Danite's exuberance. Much like other hagiographies or like Augustine, who organizes his confession of thieving, lust, and misbelief into an artful sequence of sin / meditation / sin / meditation / etc., this story moderates its subject's rage by means of its own rage for esthetic order, thus protecting a reader from ungovernable emotions.

Second, if the pattern protects a reader from fear in the presence of otherwise unrestrained fury, then it also comforts him by showing how Yahweh operates, mysteriously but surely. For this structural approach mirrors in miniature that large anxiety of biblical Jews: how can a person be sure of being in contact with deity? During each period of their history, Old Testament Jews seem to fail in their attempts to internalize God's control. No matter how worthy the human or how urgent the need for discipline, breakdowns regularly occur. Those slaves who flee Egypt soon murmur against Moses, and their successors regularly murmur against his descendants. The law codes, the debate about kingship, the words of the prophets, the cries of fearful men in Psalms—all express the anguish of a people who feel they are falling through time without the support of their creator.

In Samson's tale, the set of four repeated acts confirms our hope that no one, not even a rogue male who habitually operates in Philistine lands and licentiously bullies his way into bizarre relationships, is outside the governance of Yahweh. The story pointedly reminds us four times that Yahweh's spirit moves Samson (14:4, 6, 19; 15:14), and the tale ends with praise for the successful annihilation of so many heathen. No matter how reprobate his deeds seem, the pattern underlying them reassures us that they are directed, that they are not just detached acts of an isolated man. Whether Samson feels himself to be part of a system is doubtful—as one of my colleagues says, he is usually a "dumb Palooka." But others who are not comprehending agents—an exploited factory worker, for example, or a neurotic—still fit models in *Das Kapital* or *The Psycho-pathology of Everyday Life*. By extension, our own lonely lives may very well be part of the same plan that embraces Samson.

Third, our pattern suggests that Samson is meant to be a gigantic Everyman. He exercises three faculties that we all possess: muscular strength, sensory apparatus, and intellectual capacity. It is true he uses these common resources to keep others at bay: his muscles crush the life from enemies, his senses deny the need for community by titillating him in bouts of private pleasure, and his mind propounds riddles that exclude those who do not know the answers. But others who live with him in this world of triple faculties also plot annihilation and ask questions. It is not necessarily the tripartite divison of human talents that distin-guishes Samson as our surrogate. Plato and Dante have also separated our common powers into three components, but this story connects the qualities with a wide range of vehicles. Bare hands, jackals' tails, or a donkey's jawbone are tools of muscle; taste buds, genitals, or an encapsulating cave satisfy the senses; riddles or egregiously misplaced city gates are instruments of mind. Samson uses all he, and we, possess.

The fourth insight that our pattern furnishes concerns our capacity for independence and may be called minatory. Although every human being can impose imaginative control over his aggressive acts, although we are all governed by God, and although we all share physical, sensory, and mental equipment, only Samson is routinely betrayed. Seven of the nine treasons center on Samson. Actual betrayals by his wife at Timnah and by Delilah show how he might have suffered if the other apparent betrayals had happened at the instigation of the father-in-law at Timnah, his own countrymen, thirst at Lehi, the ambushers at

Gaza, and the proud worshipers of Dagon. Thus I conclude that the "moral" of his life runs like this: man has many gifts. But they are dangerous. Strength, sense, and mind, like Pandora's curiosity, are divinely infused but hazardous. Each trait is Janus-faced in that it is simultaneously a means to achieve independence from some group and, frighteningly, a reason for the group to destroy an escapee. The lesson I receive concerns the perennial tension between desire for autonomy and fear of exclusion. Samson demonstrated that the very talents that authenticate an individual, that enable him to stand alone, are the same that prompt a community to seek and destroy him. Quite clearly, Samson disregards the values of togetherness. He is the hypostasized id within each of us, that liberal rebel which craves personal satisfaction despite the needs of state, religion, or family. His thrilling aloneness is possible only for a time; at his end, he pays debts by killing enemies of his nation, opponents of his god, and scorners of burial rights. Having strayed temporarily, he returns to the group. His gifts were, as the story says, always for the greater glory of God.

There is an important final insight: Samson explores one possible way by which individuals may choose to mitigate their aloneness. He arranges unions with three women. All the marriages are exogamous—except, perhaps, that with Delilah, who may originally have been Hebrew in lineage although not, during her affair with Samson, Israelite in loyalty. Each alien union is associated with a different space: the patrilocal habitation of the Timnite girl contrasts to the neutral dwelling of the Gazite whore, while both domiciles differ from Delilah's virilocal home. Taken together, these three residences exhaust the major permutations of married quarters. Likewise, the degree to which Samson owns each woman illustrates three ways to allocate families: the Timnite belongs to her husband when he is present and to other men during his absence; a prostitute belongs to no one (or to everyone—the distinction is slight); a wife should be the exclusive possession of her husband whether he is present or away. In the amounts of connubial monopoly as in the places of marital abode, Samson may be said to experience all that marriage can offer to human beings.

Indeed he does more than participate in a series of theoretical variations. Although his first and last women differ in place and degree of proprietorship, they both wheedle a secret from him and let outsiders diminish him. The conclusion we must draw from these dank examples of alien wives who betray their Israelite groom is inescapable: only marriages within a group can support and protect. The man who rejects parental advice and crosses tribal boundaries to fetch a foreign wife cannot expect security. Whatever independence he has displayed by marrying exogamously will be punished.

Since Manoah and his wife are the first couple whom we meet, they necessarily provide a model for any later marital relationships. Their union is, surprisingly unlike that of their son, endogamous and fruitful. The way in which this Israelite wife augments Manoah's selfhood by dispelling his fear contrasts sharply to the way in which alien women behave toward Samson. The foreign wives compromise two mechanisms by which he had thought to enrich and protect himself, the riddle of the eater and the mystery of his strength. Whatever lure may lie in a mixed marriage, the author of Judges persuades us that it cannot gain us a helpmeet for our private expression. No reshuffling of place or proprietary arrangements can metamorphose some foreign woman into a facilitating partner.

IV

Up to this point I have argued that the Samson story has a repeated four-part structure and that this pattern makes available certain truths about people in relation to narrative, to the Lord, to their faculties, to individuality, and to marriage. Despite such mathematical certainty, I must end by asking two open-ended questions.

The first requires us to juxtapose the ABCD sequence to those concerns about separating from a group and marrying outside the *mishpacha,* or family unit. If our strongest impressions often arise at the end of a narrative, why does the final section neglect marriage entirely and, more important for our particular topic, why does it invert the order of events? Death / gratification / petition / betrayal are present, but reversed, and they refer to a solitary hero. If the anxieties about individuating and mating really are important to the story, why does it not clarify their effects at the conclusion?

We dodge this first problem if we say there are precedents for chiastic arrangement. God, after all, interrogates Adam, Eve, and the serpent after their trespass. Then he chastizes them in reverse order: the snake will crawl, Eve will experience the spectrum of sexuality, and Adam will delve and die. However, I find that our *commutatio* neither satisfies a plain sense of justice nor leads to some epiphany. It certainly ends a sequence of expected gestures and lets us know, rather bleakly, that Samson's adventure is finished. He dies with no son to preserve his image, no wife to bewail him, no band of forty-seven ronin to avenge him, no hope of personal revivification, nor any explanation from a whirlwind. Furthermore, the commutation places together two D incidents and thus emphasizes them. It seems to make victors of Delilah, the Philistine agent, and Dagon, the Philistine deity. Not only does the end apparently invalidate any significance that has accrued to Samson's earlier deeds, but, since no women are now involved, it prompts us to remember the initial section. That original complex of God / messenger / faithful parents-to-be / saving son is cruelly parodied now. The major figures are Dagon, Dagon's messenger, Dagon's adherents—all of whom torment God's failed savior, who is blind, barren, and banished from his people. In something of the same way that Jeremiah (4:23-28) envisions the Day of the Lord as a rolling backward of our world to its primordial chaos, so Samson's narrative denies all the magnificent potentiality that had been predicted in chapter 13.

One tentative solution to this riddle of reversal may spring from the Old Testament's perennial difficulty in describing a hero. Few characters survive its hard-eyed histories. Joseph, perhaps, and Joshua, Gideon, and a few others emerge relatively unscathed at the end of their tales. But unwarted portraits are unusual in the Old Testament. Thus when Samson loses his eyes, he is effectively *hors de combat*. Unlike Dandolo, Doge of Venice, or Jan Ziska of Bohemia, he is only a blind individual, not a blind leader. His survival has depended upon the degree to which his three faculties have cooperated. Once he reveals his secret, he loses the power of muscle and negates the values of sense and mind. In yet another way, then, this reversal emphasizes our complete dependence upon Yahweh. No matter how able or how crippled we may be, no matter how independent or how conventional, our talents do not mold time but rather are held inexorably in its grasp.

The last question raised by the four-step pattern involves more than Samson's tale. How widespread is such patterning in the Bible? Students of Matthew have long recognized its careful organization. More recently, a few readers have claimed to discern patterns in parts of Genesis. Is there some innate urge that prompts writers to shape their material in particular ways? Certainly the scholars who detect carefully articulated structure in the *Iliad,* Catullus, Virgil, *Beowulf,* and Milton should give us reassurance that the Bible, too, may combine inexplicable literary originality with formal organization.[5]

11. A HUMAN COMEDY: THE BOOK OF RUTH

Phyllis Trible

A man's world tells a woman's story.[1] With consummate artistry, the book of Ruth presents the aged Noami and the youthful Ruth as they struggle for survival in a patriarchal environment. These women bear their own burdens. They know hardship, danger, insecurity, and death. No God promises them blessing; no man rushes to their rescue. They themselves risk bold decisions and shocking acts to work out their own salvation in the midst of the alien, the hostile, and the unknown.

Four scenes mark the contours of this story.[2] These scenes form a circular pattern whereby the third and fourth return to the concerns of the second and first. Variations of this design appear within each scene so that the parts shape the whole and the whole molds the parts. This total symmetry lends integrity to the story; it sets it apart as an aesthetic object; and it embraces meaning as inseparable from form and content.

Underlying this surface design are the deep structures of relations that generate it.[3] On the human level, females and males move between life an death. On the divine level, God works between blessing and curse. The human movements are open and deliberate, while the divine activity is hidden and fortuitous. In many forms, these basic opposites produce tension in the narrative even as they converge to effect transformation and resolution.

Death Abounding

Scene One: Chapter 1

A. Introduction: vv. 1-7. (1) The story begins in the tension of grammar (vv. 1-5). Third-person narration names the characters, specifies their relationships, and describes their plight, but it does not allow them to emerge as human beings. Subjects of verbs, they are objects of discourse; spoken about, they do not speak. Accordingly, they hover between person and nonperson. This grammatical tension is their existential tension. Confronted with famine, four characters hover between life (person) and death (nonperson). Thus the form of the introduction mirrors content, and its content mirrors form.

A famine in the land of Judah motivates a sojourn in the country of Moab. While native soil offers death, foreign soil offers life. Hence, a healthy family departs a sick land. True to patriarchal custom, Elimelech the father leads this journey. Accompanying him are Naomi, his devoted and traditional wife, and *his*—thus the text reads—his two sons, Mahlon and Chilion. The fullness of this family corresponds to fertility in the land of Moab. Yet recovered harmony between land and family shatters soon, this time not from the natural but from the human side. Elimelech dies. Naomi becomes a widow, though not without hope, since the narrator transfers the parental claim from the dead father to the living mother. Noami is "left with *her* two children" (v. 3).[4] Furthermore, the storyteller moves swiftly to overcome the incompleteness of the family by reporting that the sons take Moabite wives, Orpah and Ruth. These marriages contrast with that of Elimelech and Naomi. Exogamy opposes endogamy.[5] But the opposition is complementary. The foreign land of Moab, which has already given to a Judahite family food (life) in the face of famine (death), now restores that depleted family to a transformed whole and provides it with a possible future (life) through the continuation of the family line.

The comfort of this news is short-lived. In four Hebrew words, ten years pass without the arrival of a third generation. Mahlon and Chilion die. With death again canceling life, a whole family shrinks to a solitary figure. Naomi stands alone. The narration focuses entirely upon her, but it avoids her name. "The woman," it says, "was bereft of her two children and her husband" (v. 5). From wife to widow, from mother to no-mother, this female is stripped of all identity. The security of husband and children, which a male-dominated culture affords its women, is hers no longer. The definition of worth, by which it values the female, applies to her no more. The blessings of old age, which it gives through progeny, are there no longer. Stranger in a foreign land, this woman is a victim of death—and of life.

(2) The extremities of Naomi's predicament signal change, which both grammar and content confirm (vv. 6-7). For the first time, she becomes the subject of active verbs. A nonperson inches toward personhood. Still the storyteller is cautious. She or he continues to withhold the name of this woman while speaking about her. Thus it is the pronoun *she* who "started with her daughters-in-law to return from the country of Moab" (RSV). It is *she* who heard "that the Lord had visited his people and given them food" (RSV). It is *she* who then "set out from the place where *she* was" (RSV).

These words of change belong to a transitional passage that carries a double function: to complete the introduction and to prepare for the dialogue. It accomplishes the first function through inclusion. The introduction begins with an exodus from Judah (v. 1); now it ends with the announcement of a return to that land (v. 7). It begins with the problem of famine; now it answers with the promise of food. It begins with a man choosing a future for his family; now it ends with a woman—the sole survivor of that family—choosing her own future. Within this ring structure, the themes of land, food, and family have contrasted, crisscrossed, and coalesced as they alternate between life and death. In these ways the conclusion of the introduction completes the beginning, yet with differences.

The differences aid the second function of the passage: to prepare for dialogue. First, by making Naomi the subject of verbs, the third-person narration anticipates her active role. Second, by twice using the verb *return,* it heralds a central emphasis. Third, by reporting twice that the two daughters-in-law accompany the aged widow, it points to major tension. Thus by the structure of grammar, by the use of key words, and by the release of information, verses 6-7 lead the hearers from introduction to dialogue. This double function of completion and continuation resolves the grammatical-existential tension between person and nonperson, between life and death. Resolution comes along sexual lines. The males die; they are nonpersons; their presence in the story ceases (though their absence continues). The females live; they are persons; their presence in the story continues. Indeed, their life is the life of the story. One set of opposites has worked its ways to a resolution that in turn generates other sets of opposites.

B. Body: vv. 8-21. (1) Precisely at the point where third-person narration yields to dialogue, where introduction leads to action, women take over the story (vv. 8-14). In this entire first episode, no men are present; women alone speak and act. And furthermore, that solitary widow, who has been stripped of all identity, is now, at the place of poetic speech, given back her name.[6] *Naomi* speaks to her daughters-in-law:

> A   Go, return <u>each of you to her mother's house.</u>
>
>   B   May the Lord deal kindly with you,
>   C   as you have dealt with the dead and with me.
>
>   B'   The Lord grant that you may find a home,
> A'   <u>each of you in the house of her husband.</u>
>
>   (1:8 RSV)

Age commands youth; a Judahite advises Moabites; one counters two. Yet as childless widows, these three are one.

Unexpected in a patriarchal culture is the phrase "mother's house."[7] Yet the words are singularly appropriate here. Mother-in-law opposes mother. In addition, this phrase emphasizes the radical separation of these females from all males. It juxtaposes present reality with past and future. Once these women were wives of husbands, and that status would be desirable again. Meanwhile, however, they are women without men. Hence, "to her mother's house" each young woman is urged to return (RSV).[8]

In this speech, Naomi invokes the *ḥesed* ("kindness") of Yahweh.[9] Now the basis for her invocation is not a past action by Yahweh to which Noami can point as insurance for future goodness, because the past has meant only famine, dislocation, and death. It offers no intimations of divine blessing. Strikingly, the basis upon which Naomi invokes Yahweh's *ḥesed* is the gracious hospitality of her daughters-in-law: May the Lord deal kindly with you, *as you have [already] dealt with the dead and with me*" (RSV). At the heart of Naomi's poem, both in structure and in meaning, these female foreigners become models for Yahweh. They show the deity a more excellent way. Once again, levels of opposites meet and crisscross: the past loyalty of human beings (foreign women, at that) is a paradigm for the future kindness of the divine being.

After her first speech, Naomi kisses her two daughters-in-law in an act of farewell. They lift up their voices and weep. But the scene is not over. Naomi has ordered, "Return each of you to her mother's house" (v. 8 RSV). The young widows reply by returning these words to their mother-in-law: "No, we will return with you to your people" (v. 10 RSV). The vocabulary of return, by which Naomi herself emerged as a person in the narrative now functions similarly for Orpah and Ruth.[10] In using it, they seize the initiative and potential for a new direction that breaks with custom and with common sense.

Naomi does not understand. Her way cannot be their way. "Turn back, my daughers, why will you go with me? . . . Have I more sons in my womb *[mē'ay]* who could become husbands for you? . . . If I were to bear sons, would you wait until they were grown?" (vv. 11-13*a*). Rhetorical questions bring Naomi full circle. She returns to Yahweh, whose *ḥesed* she has invoked earlier for her daughters-in-law. That invocation was the irony of implied judgment. Now implication becomes explication. Yahweh is indeed found wanting: "No, my daughters, for it is exceedingly more bitter for me than for you that the hand of Yahweh has gone forth against me" (v. 13*c*). From seeking the kindness of Yahweh for the future, Naomi returns to citing the cruelty of Yahweh in the past and the present. These two disparate references to deity frame her consistent advice to Orpah and Ruth. Nowhere in the scene does God intervene in a direct way. Human speech alone interprets divine activity, and that speech is ambivalent: "May God deal kindly with you—that God who has dealt harshly with me."

Three times Naomi commands that the women turn back, and each time she cites the necessity for them to find husbands (vv. 9, 11, 12-13). If their lives are to be fulfilled, then they must remarry, because their male-structured society offers no other possibility. Moreover, their chances for remarriage are far greater in the native land of Moab than in the foreign land of Judah. Naomi herself is powerless to help. Throughout the exchange, her counsel is customary, her motive altruistic, and her theology tinged with irony.

As on the first occasion, a narrative report follows Naomi's second speech. The relationship between these two reports (v. 9*b* and v. 14) is chiastic in part and in whole:

	a b c		
A	Then she kissed them,	B'	Then they lifted up their voices and wept again.
			c' b'
B	and they lifted up their	A'	And Orpah kissed her
			a'
B	voices and wept.		mother-in-law, but
	(RSV)		c' b' a'
			Ruth clung to her.
			(RSV)

Besides being a mnemonic device, the similarities in both structure and content suggest consistency in the characters of all three women. But the differences give the crucial meaning, that meaning which enables the story to move forward. It comes with the reversal of subjects and objects in A and A'. Though intended as a farewell (A), Naomi's kiss lacks that power, for these young women are not objects at the control of their mother-in-law. They themselves choose their individual responses (A'). Perhaps this point needs elaboration with particular reference to Orpah. Although following the advice of Naomi, Orpah is nevertheless in charge. She does not submit; she decides. *Her* kiss of farewell—not Naomi's—signals her future. Thus the reversal of subject and object in A and A' allows Orpah to appear in the story, if only for one brief moment, as a whole human being, one who chooses her destiny. This structural change performs a similar function for Ruth, and there the break is even sharper. Not only does Ruth decide; she decides contrary to Naomi's orders.

In taking the initiative as subjects of verbs, these young women differentiate themselves from their mother-in-law. In choosing different responses to her, they differentiate themselves from each other. Once they spoke (v. 10); now they act (v. 14). Orpah does the expected, Ruth the unexpected. As a result, both emerge as persons. Use of their names, for the first time since the introduction (v. 4), clinches this point.

Two women of common age, country, and experience have faced together a crisis in life. At first responding identically, they have at last chosen differently. If there must be reasons for this divergence, the storyteller considers them superfluous. Evaluation is likewise unnecessary so that the decisions are recounted without praise or blame. Similarly, the young women neither explain nor evaluate. By contrast, Naomi herself speaks both reason and judgment. Having already cited the need to find husbands as the reason that these widows should return home, Naomi praises next the decision of Orpah and urges Ruth to emulate it: "See, your sister-in-law has returned to her people and to her god; return after your sister-in-law" (v. 15). Orpah is a paradigm of the sane and reasonable; she acts according to the structures and customs of society. Her decision is sound, sensible, and secure. Nevertheless, Orpah dies to the story. However commendable her way, it is not the dynamic of the tale.[11] Ironically, her alliance with Naomi means separation from that mother-in-law.

(2) The movement of life is with Ruth and Naomi (vv. 15-18). At the same time, however, Naomi has isolated Ruth by making Orpah the acceptable model. If Naomi stands alone by the force of circumstances, Ruth stands alone by the force of decision. Her choice makes no sense. It forsakes the security of a mother's house for insecurity abroad. It forfeits possible fullness in Moab for certain emptiness in Judah. It relinquishes the familiar for the strange. Naomi rejects this radical decision. Hence, the two women begin their lives together in separation. Ironically, Ruth's opposition to Naomi means unity with the mother-in-law:

> Entreat me not to abandon you,
> to return from following you;
>
> For where you go, I will go;
> where you lodge I will lodge.

Your people are my people
and your god my god.

Where you die, I will die
and there I shall be buried.

Thus may Yahweh do to me
and thus may he add,

If even death separates
me from you.

(1:16-17)

From a cultural perspective, Ruth has chosen death over life. She has disavowed the solidarity of family; she has abandoned national identity; and she has renounced religious affiliation.[12] In the entire epic of Israel, only Abraham matches this radicality, but then he had a call from God (Gen. 12:1-5). Divine promise motivated and sustained his leap of faith. Besides, Abraham was a man, with a wife and other possessions to accompany him. Ruth stands alone; she possesses nothing. No God has called her; no deity has promised her blessing; no human being has come to her aid. She lives and chooses without a support group, and she knows that the fruit of her decision may well be the emptiness of rejection, indeed of death. Consequently, not even Abraham's leap of faith surpasses this decision of Ruth's. And there is more. Not only has Ruth broken with family, country, and faith, but she has also reversed sexual allegiance. A young woman has commited herself to the life of an old woman rather than to the search for a husband, and she has made this commitment not "until death us do part" but beyond death. One female has chosen another female in a world where life depends upon men. There is no more radical decision in all the memories of Israel. Naomi is silenced by it (v. 18). She does not speak again to Ruth in this scene, nor does she speak about her. Ruth's commitment to Naomi is Naomi's withdrawal from Ruth.

(3) "So the two of them went on until they came to Bethlehem" (vv. 19-21 RSV). Of their journey from the plateau of Moab across the Jordan River to the hills of Bethlehem, we know nothing. Instead, the narrator rushes the story to Bethlehem, where "a whole town was excited because of these women." Interestingly, the town speaks through its women, another sign of the exclusively

female character of the first scene. "Is this Naomi!" the women exclaim. Then that emptiness which has continued to triumph overwhelms in Naomi's response: "Do not call me Naomi" (sweet one), she says; "call me Mara" (bitter one).[13] The opposites of life and death are present within one person. Furthermore, Naomi, woman of reason and of judgment, pursues her suffering. True to her earlier portrayal, she speaks a chiastic language to explain the power of death in her life as divine curse:

A for <u>Shadday</u> has dealt very bitterly with me.

　　B I went away full but <u>Yahweh</u> has brought me back empty.
　　　　　　　▪▪▪▪▪▪▪▪
　　B' Why call me Noami when <u>Yahweh</u> has afflicted me
　　　　　　　　　▪▪▪▪▪▪▪▪
A' and <u>Shadday</u> has brought calamity upon me?

(1:20c-21 RSV*)

Her words begin and end with Shadday, who has wronged her. The two middle lines reiterate this calamity as they contrast fullness and sweetness with emptiness and affliction. These contrasts are variations of the underlying opposite, life/death. For Naomi, the divine is the author of death who has destroyed life on the human side. Overpowered by it all, this aged widow fails to acknowledge that Ruth is with her. Life is utter, total, complete emptiness—from famine on a physical level to famine on a familial level to famine at the very core of her being. "I went away full, but Yahweh has brought me back empty."[14] Yet Naomi does not have the final word; that word belongs to the storyteller.

C. Conclusion: v. 22. Having given the story to women after the introduction, the narrator takes it back for the conclusion. This ending mitigates the emptiness of Naomi. She is not alone. "Ruth the Moabite her daughter-in-law is with her." Every word counts in this corrective. Ruth is the name of radical decision and total commitment to Naomi. Ruth the Moabite has chosen Naomi the Judahite. Ruth the daughter-in-law has chosen Naomi the mother-in-law. Moreover, these two people have come to Bethlehem at the beginning of the barley harvest. The possibility of fullness in the harvest tempers the threat of famine. Accordingly, scene one closes not in the deep anguish that Naomi has sounded but in a cautious movement toward well-being. Ruth

169

and the barley harvest are two signs of life opposing the death statements of Naomi.

This Day Our Daily Bread

Scene Two: Chapter 2

A. *Introduction: v. 1.* In scene two the narrator continues to affirm fullness over emptiness. Boaz is the third sign, though his name is given only at the close of the introduction (cf. v. 19c). Three brief phrases identify him, and all three contest the power of death in Naomi's life. First, Naomi has "a kinsman." To be sure, this person is "a kinsman of her husband's," but in the extended families of Israel that identity relates him to Naomi, so that in Bethlehem she is not completely bereft of family. Second, this kinsman is "a man of substance" *'îš gibbôr ḥayil).* [15] The phrase opposes Naomi's emptiness, poverty, and powerlessness. Third, this man is "of the clan of Elimelech." Although the description may appear redundant, it carries a nuance. At the beginning of scene one, the family of Elimelech is equated with death. Elimelech and his two sons speak not at all, and they die quickly. Scene two begins by contrast. There is in the clan of Elimelech a male identified with life. He will speak and he will endure. His name is Boaz, and his appearance begins to restore a balance between female and male as creatures of life. By introducing him prematurely, while withholding his name until the end, the narrator arouses interest, creates suspense, and suggests importance.

B. *Body: vv. 2-22.* (1) After the introduction, the storyteller steps back and the women speak (v. 2). This structural pattern corresponds to scene one, but at the same time it reverses the order of speakers. Here Ruth leads. She informs Naomi of her decision to "glean among the ears of grain after him in whose sight I shall find favor" (RSV). [16] If these women live in social and familial famine, they need not yield to physical hunger. The young foreigner sees an opportunity for survival and acts upon it. Naomi assents, now with an intimacy of language absent since Ruth defied her advice. "Go, my daughter," she says.

(2) Ruth goes then by her own choice, and yet another

dimension shapes the occasion (vv. 3-17). Since that dimension exists independently of the characters, the narrator reenters to describe it: "she happened to come to the part of the field belonging to Boaz, who was of the family of Elimelech" (v. 3 RSV), It is a felicitous expression, "she happened to come," reporting chance and accident while hinting that chance is caused.[17] Within human luck is divine intentionality. In addition, the latter part of this report stresses again the presence of male life in the family of Elimelech.

Almost immediately Boaz himself appears (v. 4). A man of power and prestige, he surveys the scene, speaking divine amenities to his reapers, and spots the female stranger. He does not know her. "Whose maiden is this?" he asks (v. 5 RSV). Truly a patriarchal question. After all, a young woman must belong to someone; she is possession, not person. Thus Boaz does not ask *her* name but rather the identity of her owner. His question fits his culture, but it does not fit this woman, who is in tension with that culture. Accordingly, the servant cannot answer in the traditional way. He cannot identify Ruth by a (male) lord; she has none. So the servant describes her as the foreign woman "who came back with Naomi from the country of Moab" (v. 6 RSV). Her name he does not give. Her identity he derives from her own strangeness and from another woman.

With that information, Boaz speaks to Ruth (vv. 8-9). He grants her permission to glean; he directs her to the young women in his fields;[18] and he protects her from the young men. Boaz, man of power, assists Ruth, woman of poverty: the male lord grants privileges to the female foreigner; and the older man protects the younger woman. In this last instance, then, he appears as a senior adult, a male counterpart to Naomi.

Ruth's response is appropriately deferential: "Why have I found favor in your eyes, that you should take notice of me, when I am a foreigner?" (v. 10 RSV). It is also ironically subtle. This inferior foreigner, now speaking to a superior, has by choice (and by chance) created this situation. Her deference results from her daring; it is derivative, not determinative. Ruth herself suggests this distinction when to Boaz she repeats a phrase that she as used with her mother-in-law: "to find favor." In other words, Ruth has accomplished here what she set out to do. The favor that Boaz gives her is the favor that she has sought. Therefore, she, not he, is shaping her destiny. That a patriarchal culture restricts her options makes her initiative all the more remarkable. Her decision to "glean among the ears of grain after someone in whose sight I shall find favor" (v. 2 RSV) gives her independence as a human being in the midst of dependence as a needy case.

Boaz himself acknowledges that Ruth is no ordinary individual. Concern for this foreign woman marks him as a true child of Israel, who understands that Israel itself lives as a stranger and sojourner in the world. After all, Israel had its beginning in the foreigners Abraham and Sarah, who journeyed to an alien land to become channels of blessing for all the families of the earth (Gen. 12:1-5). These ancient memories echo now as Boaz speaks to Ruth. He describes her as the one who left her father and her mother and her native land to come to a people whom she did not know (v. 11). This description validates the analogy between Abraham and Ruth that her earlier words to Naomi implied. Moreover, Boaz adds an ingredient—which was both clearly present in the call of Abraham and noticeably absent in the choice of Ruth—the ingredient of divine blessing: "May Yahweh grant your action due recompense, and may your payment be full from Yahweh the God of Israel under whose wings you have come to seek refuge" (2:12 *AB*). Boaz's language envelops Ruth within the Abrahamic paradigm of the foreigner who breaks with the past and receives the promise of blessing for the future. But differences remain. Ruth herself chose to abandon the past without call or blessing. The divine blessing extended to her now comes not directly from God but through a human being. Though its content is not specified here, Boaz shall have occasion to remember and make good his prayer. Meanwhile, Ruth responds to him with characteristic deference (v. 13).

If the repeated deference of Ruth results from her own decisions, then the actions of Boaz in her behalf mean reaction and not initiative. Things are once again not what they seem. Deference is initiative; initiative is reaction. The first meeting of these two people happens because of a choice and a chance, neither of which Boaz directs. This powerful male has not rushed to the rescue of a destitute female. His graciousness has not sought her out, even though in response it now extends to her. In truth,

Boaz's own words (v. 11) show that he knew already of the plight of Naomi and Ruth; yet until now he, Naomi's kin, has done nothing to help these women. Again, although he has been fully told all that Ruth has done for Naomi, he does not even know Ruth when he sees her in his field (v. 5). Now the story does not censure Boaz for dereliction of duty, but it does subordinate him to the women. He has patriarchal power, but he does not have narrative power. He has authority within the story but not control over it. The story belongs to Ruth and Naomi—and to chance, that code for the divine.[19]

Mealtime arrives. Boaz continues to show kindness, offering Ruth more bread and wine than she is able to eat. As she returns to the field, he instructs his young men to "let her glean even among the sheaves" and to "pull out some from the bundles for her" (vv. 15-16 RSV). In this setting, the young men who are harvesting have their opposites in the young women who are reaping (vv. 8-9).[20] Ruth has been told to keep close to the young women; the young men have been told not to molest her. Thereby an earlier pattern repeats itself. The women signal life; the men, death. At the same time, however, these young men draw water for Ruth to drink (v. 9), and they provide sheaves for her to glean (v. 15). As males opposing females, they threaten death. As males helping a female, they promise life. Hence, they mediate opposites.

This episode ends, as it began, with a narrative report: "So she set forth and went and gleaned in the field after the reapers" (v. 3a RSV); "so she gleaned in the field until evening" (v. 17a RSV). What Ruth determined to do, she has done.

(3) At evening Ruth returns to her mother-in-law with food for the hungry (vv. 18-22). From the dangers of the field, she finds security in the city. Naomi is eager to know what happened, even as she invokes blessing upon the one who has helped her daughter-in-law. Their conversation builds on incongruities. Naomi does not know in whose field Ruth has gleaned.[21] Though Ruth knows the name Boaz, she herself does not know in whose field she has gleaned. Each woman has both more and less information than the other. The hearers of the story await full disclosure. A periodic sentence, compounded by redundancy, delays that disclosure: "So she told her mother-in-law with whom she had worked, and said, 'The man's name with whom I worked

today is Boaz'" (v. 19*e* RSV). When the narrator first introduced Boaz, he or she supplied the name only at the end (v. 1). Similarly now, Ruth withholds the name until the close of her sentence. The suspense of the sentence structure, then, is the emphasis of its revelation. Naomi's reply follows a comparable pattern by delaying the crucial information until last. It commences with a blessing for Yahweh, "whose kindness *[ḥesed]* has not forsaken the living or the dead," and it concludes with the news that Boaz "is a relative of ours, one of our redeemers" (v. 20 RSV*).[22] Slowly the bitterness of an old woman is being transformed.

Yet how very strange is her disclosure. Naomi knows that Boaz is a close relative, but she has not sought his help. Why we do not know. Is it that emptiness has so overpowered her that she forgot his existence, even as earlier she failed to understand that Ruth was with her? Or is it that calamity paralyzed her will to act? Or is Naomi in this instance a woman of her culture who waits for the man to act first? Whatever the reason, she has not sought out Boaz. By the same token, Boaz has not approached her, even though he knew of her plight. Only through the choice of Ruth and through the chance of cause have male relative and female relative acknowledged each other. And with this acknowledgment Naomi now includes Ruth in the family: "The man is a relative of *ours,* one of *our* redeemers." Relinquishing isolation, the mother-in-law embraces the daughter-in-law who has already embraced her.

Immediately after these words of familial inclusion, the narrator juxtaposes the national exclusion of Ruth by calling her a Moabite: "And Ruth the Moabite said, 'Besides, he said to me, "You shall keep close *[dbq]* by my servants, till they have finished all my harvest"'" (v. 21 RSV*). This narrative statement, followed by Ruth's concern for providing food, parallels the verse that introduced the entire scene: "And Ruth the Moabite said to Naomi, 'I shall go to the field and glean among the ears of grain . . .'" (v. 2). In both instances the storyteller stresses the alien status of Ruth. On the one hand, how difficult and courageous for a foreign woman to glean in the field (v. 2); on the other, how healing and fulfilling for the empty Naomi to embrace Ruth the Moabite in the language of kinship (v. 20).

Naomi's identification of Boaz as "one of our redeemers" hints at the use that she will make of this relationship later. Certainly she wants Ruth to remarry (cf. 1:9, 11-13), although Ruth herself has not shown a corresponding interest. Her concerns have been loyalty to Naomi and food for the two of them, and her responses here to Naomi's statement bear that out. She does not comment on Boaz as redeemer; after all, she came to his field by chance. She does not comment on herself as relative; long ago she made that decision. Instead, she assures her mother-in-law that, thanks to Boaz, food will be available throughout the harvest. Her first act upon returning home at evening was to give Noami food (v. 18; now her last words in this encounter return to that act (v. 21). Ruth is faithful to Naomi, and she can provide for the two of them. In other words, Ruth is not looking for a husband.

Noami answers with words akin to Boaz's: "It is well, my daughter, that you go out with his young women, lest in another field you be molested" (v. 22 RSV*). Boaz and Naomi unite as an older generation concerned for the safety of a young woman in an environment of young men. Male and female mediate life and death.

Ruth began this day by speaking to Naomi (v. 2); now Naomi has concluded it by speaking to Ruth (v. 22). Thus the movement of their day (v. 2 and vv. 18-22) surrounds the movement in the field (v. 3 and v. 17), and this circular design bespeaks a feminist content: the women surround the episode with Boaz. Moreover, design and content yield a feminist interpretation: in their own right the women shape their story. They plan (v. 2); they execute (vv. 3-17); and they evaluate (vv. 18-22). But this symmetry is also asymmetrical. Whereas the young woman takes command at first, the old woman outstrips—not matches—her at last. Much longer than the dialogic introduction, the conclusion moves back and forth between these two females until it stops, where it started, with Naomi.

The structure of this ending parallels the dialogic conclusion of scene one, though its content differs significantly. In both dialogues Naomi has the last word (1:20-21 and 2:10, 22). The first time she perceives herself all alone in bitterness and sorrow. This time she begins to move out of isolation and despair, because Ruth and Boaz have reached her. Accordingly, Naomi hints at a reinterpretation of her past. Shadday, who brought calamity (1:21), is now Yahweh, "whose kindness has not forsaken the living or the dead" (2:20 RSV). Self-centered sorrow yields to divine blessing through human agents.

175

C. Conclusion: v. 23. Naomi's speeches are not, however, the final word of scenes one and two; that word belongs to the storyteller. Although he or she struck a note of well-being in scene one with the phrase "the beginning of the barley harvest," here the narrator reverses that sentiment with the phrase "until the end of the barley and wheat harvests" (RSV): "So she [Ruth] kept close *[dbq]* to the women of Boaz, gleaning until the end of the barley and wheat harvests; and she lived with her mother-in-law" (RSV*). The phrase is a warning, since the end of the barley season may mean the return of famine and emptiness. If present kindness has softened past harshness for Ruth and Noami, their future is still uncertain. At the end of scene one, then, Naomi speaks death; the narrator suggests life. At the end of scene two, Naomi affirms life; the narrator cautions death. And at the conclusion of each scene narration opposes dialogue; the storyteller is in tension with the characters; and the hearers wait in suspense.

Salvation by Courage Alone

Scene Three: Chapter 3

A. Introduction: vv. 1-5. As the last and first to speak, Naomi is the verbal link between scenes two and three. These two scenes are designed similarly, with conversations between the women surrounding a meeting of Ruth and Boaz. Moreover, they share parallel themes: in scene two, women struggle to survive physically, and in scene three, they struggle to survive culturally.

Unlike both preceding scenes, however, scene three has no narrative introduction. From the beginning the characters are in charge, and they dispel any caution of the narrator about their future. Naomi takes over. Aware of the kindness of Boaz, she begins to act upon it. She does not wait for matters to take their course or for God to intervene with a miracle. Instead, she herself moves from being the receiver of calamity to becoming the agent of change and challenge. Once in the land of Moab she urged each of her widowed daughters-in-law to return to her mother's house, with the hope that each of them might find a home in the house of a husband (1:18). On that occasion, Naomi knew their need, as dictated by their culture, but she was powerless to help. Now she returns to that need with the power of a plan: "My daughter, should I not seek a home for you, that it may be well with you?" (3:1*b* RSV).

This rhetorical question introduces an outrageous scheme, dangerous and delicate. Ruth is to dress in her finest clothes and go alone at night to the threshing floor where the men are eating and drinking in celebration of the harvest. After Boaz has satisfied himself with food and drink and has lain down to sleep, Ruth will approach him, uncover the lower part of his body, and lie down. Just how much of the lower part of his body she is to uncover remains tantalizingly uncertain in the text.[23] That sexual overtones are present is, however, patently certain. "When you have done this," Naomi concludes, "then Boaz himself will tell you what to do" (v. 4*c*). Surely at this point the man will take over; that is the least one expects.

Ruth agrees to the plan: "All that you say I will do" (v. 5 RSV). This reply differs from her earlier responses to the topic of a husband. In scene one Ruth's allegiance to Naomi superseded that need; in scene two Ruth's struggle for their physical survival submerged that need; here in scene three Ruth's allegiance to Naomi accords with that need. Loyalty to self and to mother-in-law signifies for Ruth a movement from dissent to perseverance to consent. Her willingness to obey Naomi now means a second meeting between her and Boaz. It contrasts with the first encounter in that circumstances, place, and time reverse. The first meeting was by chance; the second is by choice. The first was in the fields; the second at the threshing floor. The first was public; the second private. The first was work; the second play. The first was by day; the second by night. Yet both of them hold the potential for life and death.

B. Body: vv. 6-15. The narrator emphasizes the obedience of Ruth by reporting and repeating the events that Naomi has forecast. Repetition impedes the progress of the story as it heightens suspense. In addition, it both confirms and contradicts the accuracy of Naomi's calculations. "So she [Ruth] went down to the threshing floor and did just as her mother-in-law had told her. And when Boaz had eaten and drunk, and his heart was merry, he went to lie down at the end of the heap of grain" (vv. 6-7*a* RSV).

"At the end of the heap of grain": a minor detail, yet important for the execution of the plan. The phrase suggests an area separate from the other sleepers and accessible to the waiting woman. Is this detail another hint of that blessed chance which aids these women in their struggles for life? Earlier Ruth happened to come to the field of Boaz (2:3). Does Boaz happen now to lie at the corner of the threshing floor? We cannot be sure. At any rate, Ruth "came quietly and uncovered his lower body and lay down" (v. 7*de*).[24] How will a patriarch of Israel respond to this bold action by a woman from Moab?

Midnight comes. The man stirs in his sleep, no doubt feeling the chill of the night air upon his exposed body. Groping about in the dark, he discovers the woman lying next to him. "Who are you?" he asks (v. 9 RSV). If their first meeting elicited a question of ownership—"Whose maiden is this?" (2:5 RSV)—the second evokes a question of personal identity: "Who are you?" In both instances, a woman has surprised a man; she has taken initiative to seek life under threat of death.

Thus far the script for this second meeting has happened as Noami planned. Indeed, the narrator has already said that Ruth "did just as her mother-in-law had told her" (v. 6*b* RSV). But now, when Ruth answers the question of this startled man, she changes that script. "I am Ruth, your maidservant," she replies (v. 9 RSV). At this point Naomi said that Boaz would take charge: "He will tell you what to do" (v. 4*c* RSV). That is not the case, however. Ruth herself is in charge; she tells Boaz what to do. "Spread your *wing [kānāp]* over your maidservant, for you are a redeemer" (v. 9*c*; cf. *AB*). By a word play Ruth calls upon Boaz to make good on his prayer for her blessing. In the field he wished that a full reward be given her by Yahweh, the God of Israel, "under whose *wings [kānāp]* you have come to take refuge" (2:12 RSV). Now at the threshing floor, Ruth recalls and appropriates that language as she challenges Boaz to be the occasion of divine blessing in her life. Marriage is that blessing. And the man who asked it for Ruth is himself capable of fulfilling it. Besides, as redeemer he has an obligation to perform.[25] A foreign woman has called an Israelite man to responsibility.

Ruth's utterance conforms to her portrayal throughout the story as the defier of custom, the maker of decisions, and the worker of salvation. It puts her in tension with her mother-in-law and with the narrator. Furthermore, it confirms the posture of Boaz as re-actor to the initiative of this woman. The suspense of this entire episode—from its conception by Naomi through its description by the narrator, to its altered consummation by Ruth—subsides as Boaz replies (vv. 10-12 RSV). His words are characteristically gracious, recalling his earlier response to Ruth. There is the theme of divine blessing: "May you be blessed by the Lord, my daughter" (RSV; cf. 2:12). Through comparison, there is the theme of *ḥesed* to Naomi: "You have made this last kindness greater than the first" (RSV; cf. 2:11). Through contrast, there is the theme of young men as foils to Boaz: "in that you have not gone after young men, whether poor or rich" (RSV; cf. 2:9*b*, 15). Finally, there is the theme of assurance and of praise: "And now, my daughter, do not fear, I will do for you all that you ask, for all my fellow townsmen know that you are a woman of worth" (RSV; cf. 2:8, 9, 11, 12). "A woman of worth" (*'ēšet ḥayil*): that description matches precisely the narrator's depiction of Boaz as "a man of worth" (*'îš gibbôr ḥayil;* 2:1). Female and male; foreigner and native; youth and age; poor and wealthy—all these opposites are mediated by human worth. The audience breathes a sigh of relief. A dangerous and delicate scheme on the part of two women has resulted in kindness and blessing from a man. Not one word of censure does Boaz utter or intimate.[26]

But this patriarch has not finished speaking; the audience relaxed too soon. "And now it is true that I am a redeemer," he continues; "yet there is redeemer nearer than I" (v. 12; cf. *AB*). This distinction in the order of male redeemers disturbs the progress of the story. At the same time, it may account for the failure of Boaz to act thus far, since responsibility belongs to another man and custom decrees that the proper order be followed. Now that the women have forced the issue, however, Boaz will respond. His words to Ruth continue in a chiastic pattern. Night surrounds morning; the immediate situation encircles the coming resolution; instruction encompasses condition and promises:

A Remain this night, and in the morning,
    B   if he will do <u>the redeemer's part,</u>
       well and good; let him redeem;

B' but if he is not willing to do <u>the redeemer's part</u> for you,
    then, as Yahweh lives, I will redeem you.

A   Lie down until the morning.
    ▪▪▪▪▪▪▪▪▪▪▪▪▪▪▪▪▪▪▪▪▪▪▪▪▪▪▪
                                            (3:18; cf. *AB*)

"To do the redeemer's part" means to marry Ruth. At the beginning of this scene Naomi herself linked redeemer with marriage (vv. 1-2). Later Ruth makes this same connection when she tells Boaz to spread his wing over her because he is a redeemr (v. 9). Boaz understands, but his reply wavers between promise and postponement. From relief his words return to suspense as opposites press in and tension mounts. Females and males—Ruth, who is present, and Naomi, who is absent; Boaz, who is present, and the unnamed redeemer, who is absent—hover between life and death. Future mediator between Ruth and the nearer redeemer, Boaz is present intimate of Ruth on the threshing floor. A compromising position occasions a command performance. Consequently, deeds of night both precipitate and threaten the resolution of morning.

Ruth lies at the "feet" of Boaz, but she rises before daylight in order that their encounter might remain in the secrecy of the dark (v. 14*a*). Boaz also wishes to preserve the privacy of the occasion. Speaking through an impersonal construction, he distances Ruth from himself and calls her "the woman":[27] "Let it not be known that the woman came to the threshing floor" (v. 14*b* RSV). What Boaz's words say, they are. Content and form merge to signal the dissolution of intimacy and the departure of Ruth—yet, not immediately. Just before she leaves, Boaz addresses her directly: "Bring the mantle you are wearing and hold it out" (v. 15 RSV). Into it he measures barley. Once again, then, his action assures fullness over famine to parallel the conclusion of their first meeting (2:14-16). A second parallel is Ruth's success. Potential for life has overcome potential for death. And a third parallel is her return home. From the danger of the threshing floor, she returns to the security of the city.

C. Conclusion: vv. 16-18. Alone the two women talk. Naomi asks, "How did you fare, my daughter?" (v. 16 RSV). The answer is an odd mixture of third-person narration and direct discourse, a combination that hides the extraordinary acts of Ruth and highlights the ordinary acts of Boaz. Although Naomi's question is explicitly about Ruth and only implicitly about Boaz, both answers are explicitly about Boaz and only implicitly about Ruth. First the narrator reports: "The she told her all that the man had done for her" (RSV). Omitted is any report of what Ruth had done, especially of her forthright instructions to Boaz. And yet it was precisely her request that called Boaz to a duty that he did not voluntarily assume. By failing to report specifically, is the narrator covering for Ruth? Would a disclosure of what she said be too much for Naomi to bear? After all, Naomi had expected Boaz to tell Ruth what to do (v. 4*c*). Or has the radicalness of Ruth's performance escaped the awareness of the narrator? Earlier she or he maintained that at the threshing floor Ruth "did just as her mother-in-law had told her" (v. 6 RSV), when in fact she did more and other than her mother-in-law had told her. Be that as it may, the narrator's reply diverges from Naomi's question.

Ruth's reply does the same. Characteristically, it concentrates upon Naomi and upon food: "These six measures of barley he gave to me, for he said, 'You must not go back empty-handed to your mother-in-law'" (v. 17 RSV). The reply says nothing about marriage and the redeemer's responsibility. Is Ruth reticent to speak openly about this matter? Does she prefer to leave the details of her radical behavior where they occurred—in the darkness of night, at the corner of a grain heap, in whispers between female and male? At any rate, her bold actions for the sake of survival and for the hope of blessing move toward fulfillment. She need say nothing more. And indeed, these are her last words in the entire story. Appropriately, they focus upon the mother-in-law to whom Ruth committed herself for better or for worse, even beyond death.

If Ruth mediates life for Naomi, Naomi mirrors that activity. Her last words advise Ruth: "Wait, my daughter, until you learn how the matter turns out, for the man will not rest, but will settle the matter today" (v. 18 RSV). Ruth is to wait because Boaz will not wait. Thus, opposite actions converge to yield the resolution. "How the matter turns out"—the vagueness of this phrase contrasts with the specificity of its parallel, "the man . . . will settle the matter today." Vagueness invites speculation. Plan is replacing change, but whose plan? Naomi's? Ruth's? Boaz's?

They have all participated, but is there something more? Has not Boaz in this very scene both derived blessing from Yahweh (v. 10) and rooted his own resolution in a Yahwistic vow (v. 13)? "How the matter turns out" may be divine plan in, through, and by human agents.[28]

Having introduced scene three by plotting a dangerous mission, Naomi concludes it by counseling a patient wait. Thereby she too completes her speeches in the story; her function is fulfilled. That Ruth may now find a husband satisfies Naomi's original concern. Furthermore, this woman who began as the voice of sorrow and sadness, of bitterness and suffering, of famine and emptiness approaches now the threshold of fulfillment and joy. Through transformation her circle is closing; death is becoming life. So Naomi's voice fades; like Ruth, she steps aside. At this juncture, the drama ceases to be their story and becomes the story about them.

Scene three provides yet another sign of well-being. Unlike the preceding scenes, it has no concluding statement by the narrator. Eliminated is the tension between author and characters, between narration and dialogue. All in all, the story is moving toward its resolution.

All's Well That Ends Well

Scene Four: Chapter 4

A. Vv. 1-12. The fourth scene begins with a public gathering at the gate of the city where business and legal transactions take place (vv. 1-12). Its setting compares and contrasts with the first meeting of Ruth and Boaz (scene two). Their meeting was a family affair. Although it happened in public, it was not a public happening, since the workers in the field formed only the backdrop. Now that family affair is no longer a chance encounter. Through the insistence of Naomi and Ruth, it has become a public matter that the elders of the city must witness as participants.

This public gathering is entirely a man's world. No women are present, even though their actions alone have made the occasion mandatory. Boaz takes charge. At the gate he meets the redeemer and invites him to sit down. Strikingly, Boaz does not call this man by name: "Turn aside, so-and-so,"[29] he says; "sit down here." Next Boaz summons ten men of the elders of the city to sit down so that he might present the case. Speaking directly to the redeemer (whom the narrator does not name either), Boaz reports:

<pre>
         A   B
The portion of the field which belonged to our kinsman Elimelech
      B'   A'
Naomi is selling, she who returned from the field of Moab.
</pre>

(v. 3)

Structured chiastically, these words recall early opposites. The native soil of Judah and the foreign soil of Moab surround a dead husband and his living wife. Whereas the husband led in the journey from Judah to Moab, the wife manages the return. If these words echo the past, they surprise the present. Boaz is giving new information. We did not know that Naomi was selling land. Why, we are surprised that she even has land to sell.[30] That fact is itself an incongruity of life and death. Rights over a parcel of land (life) belong to a woman of emptiness (death). Again, the suggestion of direct communication between Boaz and Naomi is surprising, since nowhere do these two meet and talk. Finally, there is the surprise of diversion and suspense. Boaz' statement appears to sidetrack the journey of the tale. Thus he continues speaking: "So I thought I would tell you of it, and say, Buy it in the presence of those sitting here, and in the presence of the elders of my people. If you will redeem it, redeem it; and if you will not redeem it, tell me and then I will know, for there is no one except you to redeem it and I come after you" (v. 4 RSV*).

This I-you language highlights tension between two males. Both living members of the family of Elimelech, one instructs the other. The reply is immediate and firm. "I will redeem," says the unnamed one. Only then does Boaz come to the subject, albeit in a twisted way:

<pre>
              A   B
The day you buy the field from the hand of Naomi,
     B'   A'
   then Ruth the Moabite, widow of the dead, you "buy"[31] to restore
the name of the dead to his inheritance.
</pre>

(v. 5 RSV*)

183

Once more, a chiastic structure presents opposites (see 4:3). Patriarchal duty surrounds two females, and that duty means the revival of life over against death: "to restore the name of the dead to his inheritance." By delaying this information about Ruth until after the redeemer has agreed to redeem the land, Boaz exposes the motive and character of this man. "Then the redeemer said,

> 'I am not able to redeem it
>   lest I impair my own inheritance.
> *You* take on my redemption-responsibility
>   for I am not able to redeem it.'"
>
> (v. 6; cf. AB)

It appears that originally this man agreed to redemption for personal gain, the acquisition of property, rather than for familial restoration. Opposing *I* and *you,* his own words show that selfish interest, while they show no interest at all in Ruth. Since he refuses, then, to do the part of a redeemer, the outcome is assured for Ruth and Boaz.

A chance meeting in the fields, followed by a daring meeting on the threshing floor, has worked its way to denouement through proper and customary channels of patriarchy. Thereupon ensues an ancient ceremony in which the giving of one's sandal signifies a redemption and exchange transaction. So remote is this custom that the narrator interrupts to explain it (4:7-8).[32] Upon completion of the ceremony, the redeemer fades from the story. As a foil to Boaz, he is finished, and he finishes, as he began, without a name. Now the story provides ample reason for his anonymity. Since he refused to "restore the name of the dead to his inheritance," he himself has no name. Anonymity implies judgment. Moreover, this judgment portrays the redeemer as the opposite of Elimelech, with Boaz as their mediator. Unlike Elimelech, the redeemer speaks; unlike the redeemer, Elimelech has a name. As a result, both men hover between person (life) and nonperson (death). For Elimelech this conflict is resolved, on the one hand, by physical death and, on the other, by narrative life. His name continues to appear in the story (2:1, 3; 4:3, 9) so that his absence is presence, his death is life. For the redeemer this conflict is resolved, on the one hand, by physical life and, on the other, by narrative death. The redeemer dies to the story in order to live to his own inheritance. Between these two males is Boaz with both name and speech. He speaks to the redeemer, and he restores the name of Elimelech. He is totally the life that they are partially.

Next Boaz addresses the elders and all the people:

Witnesses are you this day that

I have bought
  all which belonged to Elimelech and to Chilion
    and to Mahlon from the hand of Naomi
    and also Ruth, the Moabite, the widow of Mahlon,

I have bought
  to be my wife
    to restore the name of the dead in his inheritance
      that the name of the dead may not be cut off from among his brothers
      and from the gate of his native place.

Witnesses are you this day.

(vv. 9-10 RSV*)

For the first time since the introduction to scene one (1:2), the entire family that sojourned from Judah to Moab is named. The story begins to complete itself as the dead live in the living. Ruth is named also—and in a special way. The order of verb followed by the object ("I have bought all that belonged to Elimelech," etc.) reverses to emphasize her: "and also Ruth, the Moabite, the widow of Mahlon, I have bought." Of all the characters in scene one, only Orpah is missing. While obvious, the omission is also subtle. Orpah's place at the beginning belongs at the end to the unnamed redeemer. But substitution means dissimilarity. Orpah had both name and speech (1:10). She decided to die to the story by returning to her own people, and the judgment upon her is favorable (1:15). The unnamed redeemer chooses to die to the story by returning to his own inheritance, and the judgment upon him is adverse. After all, he is not a foreign woman but the nearest male kin. Thus he passes away with the infamy of anonymity.

The public meeting concludes with words of the people and the elders. Addressed to Boaz, these words begin and end with Yahweh and Ruth (though the men do not call her by name). This witness statement stresses fertility, the restoration of a male name, and the continuation of a male line for both the dead and the living.[33]

May Yahweh make the woman, who is coming into your house *[beth]*
  like Rachel and Leah who between them built the house of Israel.

May you show fertility in Ephrathah
  and bestow a name in Bethlehem.

And may your house be like the house of Perez, whom Tamar bore to Judah
    because of the children Yahweh will give you from this young woman.
                                        (vv. 11-12 RSV*; cf. *AB*)

Comparison of Ruth to the ancient mothers Rachel, Leah, and Tamar recalls the parallel between Ruth and Abraham, yet with differences. Although the analogy with Abraham exalted Ruth, as a model of the radicality of faith, comparison with these women views her in the traditional role of bearer of children. An exclusively female episode suggests the first comparison (1:8-21); an exclusively male occasion asserts the second (4:1-12). Nevertheless, both analogies locate Ruth the foreigner solidly within the traditions of Israel. Recognition of her worth climaxes here a public gathering.

This episode is unique in the story because of its heavy patriarchal cast. Men alone decide the future of women. In addition, Boaz presents the situation of these women quite differently from their own understanding of it. He subordinates both of them to male prerogatives: the buying of land and the restoration of the name of the dead to his inheritance. While the first of these matters does have a feminist slant in that the widow, Naomi, has inherited land which she has the right to sell, that slant is hardly the concern of Boaz. He talks about keeping that land within the family of Elimelech.

The second issue reinforces this male perspective: "to restore the name of the dead to his inheritance" (RSV*). Before the elders, Boaz cites this issue as his reason for marrying Ruth, although alone with her he promised marriage in order to "do the redeemer's part" for *her*. Thus in a private conversation with Ruth, Boaz made her welfare the sole object of his concern, but in a public discussion with men he makes Ruth the means for achieving a male purpose.[34]

The silence of the women on this question of the restoration of the name of the dead suggests that they do not share this male perspective. Conversely, the voice of the women on the question of marriage confirms that they have a different outlook. Often Naomi underscores the need for young widows to remarry, but never does she link this need with the imperative to restore a male name. Indeed, her advice in scene one is precisely the opposite: that Orpah and Ruth should find husbands in Moab. Besides, Naomi describes herself as "too old to have a husband," another indication that she was not oriented to restoring a male name. Even her speculation about a future husband and sons for herself bespeaks concern for her daughters-in-law rather than for the name of her dead husband and sons. Again, the scheme that Naomi proposes (scene three) has as its purpose finding a home for Ruth that it might be well with her. Ruth repeats this theme when she asks Boaz to marry her (3:9c). Nowhere, then, does either woman mention or imply the restoration of a male name. Their emphasis is life for the living.

Altogether the patriarchal cast of scene four is alien to the letter and spirit of the first three scenes, even if it is not alien to the culture of Israel. It alters emphases, and it views Ruth exclusively as a vessel for male progeny. Nevertheless, small ironies abound. If Orpah is a model to be emulated, the unnamed kinsman is a model to be avoided. If Boaz is now the patriarch in charge, it is two women who have summoned him to duty.

B. V. 13. Events move quickly. The privacy of intercourse follows immediately the public transaction. From being an object of discussion, Ruth returns to consummate a marriage.[35] Yet third-person narration distances the intimacy of this occasion.[36] Ruth and Boaz do not speak. The report of the occasion begins with the man acting and the female re-acting: "Boaz took Ruth and she became his wife" (RSV). The pattern continues—"he went in to her" (RSV)—only to be broken when deity intervenes: "but Yahweh gave her conception" (RSV*).[37] The gift of life resides neither in male nor in female, but in God. Only after this perspective is introduced do we read, "she bore a son." Intercourse between Ruth and Boaz is itself divine activity. That equation comes in both the structure and content of the report, and thereby the narrator announces that all is well. Ten years of a childless marriage in Moab (1:4-5) have been quickly redeemed in the union of Ruth and Boaz. Yahweh has given conception; blessing has transformed curse. This announcement of a private union for blessing mediates between public gatherings which, on the one side, legitimate the union and, on the other, celebrate it.

C. *Vv. 14-17.* At the celebration, women alone are present. Hence, this episode contrasts with the first in scene four (vv. 1-12), even as it corresponds to scene one (1:6-22). Women of Bethlehem, once excited by Naomi's return from the land of Maob, return themselves both to introduce and to conclude the last event. They commence with a blessing of Yahweh, and they address their words to Naomi, the one who told them that Yahweh brought her back empty. Now they answer her: "Blessed be Yahweh, who has not left you this day without a redeemer" (RSV*). The advent of a grandchild transforms death into life, emptiness into fullness:

> May his name be celebrated in Israel.
> He shall be to you a restorer of life
> and a nourisher of your old age. . . .
> (v. 15*a* RSV*)

But the celebration is more than the joy of a male child. The meaning of that child centers in his mother, a foreign woman who has forsaken all to follow Naomi. Thus the blessing climaxes in the exaltation of Ruth, who herself is set above not just a natural child and not just a male child but even above the ideal number of natural sons:

> . . . for your daughter-in-law who loves you bore him,
> she who means more to you than seven sons.
> (v. 15*b*)

These words of the women converge upon Naomi, and the storyteller reports then that she takes the child, holds him close, and becomes his guardian. The woman of emptiness has become the woman of plenty. And Ruth, the daughter-in-law faithful beyond death, is the mediator of this transformation to life.

Next the women of Bethlehem complete the circle of their words around Naomi as they name the child: "And the women of the neighborhood gave him a name, saying, 'A son has been born to Naomi.' They called his name Obed" (v. 17 RSV*). Their language of naming returns to the theme that Boaz introduced and the elders reinforced: "to restore the name of the dead to his inheritance." By concentrating upon it, the men shifted emphasis from justice for living females to justice for dead males. This shift was jarring in a story of women, even if it was justified in a world of men. But now the women redeem this male theme. They identify the child as the son of Naomi rather than of Elimelech. They perceive this infant as restoring life to the living rather than restoring a name to the dead.[38] They speak of Ruth the bearer rather than of Boaz the begetter. And they themselves name the baby. Repeatedly, these women stand as opposites to the elders. Each group has interpreted according to its kind. Reconciling these opposites is the newborn male child, the symbol of a new beginning with men. Not only does this infant mediate between adult males and females, but he also mediates between the ages. Of that generational function the narrator teaches when, having begun this story in premonarchic Israel, she or he concludes it with the coming of the monarchy. At the beginning we read, "in the days when the judges ruled" (1:1), and, at the end, "a son has been born to Naomi . . . he was the father of Jesse, the father of David" (4:17*bc* RSV).

A story beginning in deepest despair has worked its way to wholeness and well-being. Thus, it is a comedy in which the brave and bold decisions of women embody and bring to pass the blessings of God.[39] In the introduction, the curses of famine, exile, and death oppose divine blessing. And yet the storyteller does not attribute these curses to God. Indeed, the very first reference to deity is the narrator's report of blessing: "Yahweh had visited his people and given them food" (1:6 RSV*). Later in scene one, however, Naomi speaks openly of divine affliction. Though she does not fault God for her exile, she does blame the deity for the abundance of death in her life. Shadday has dealt bitterly; Shadday has brought calamity upon her (1:20-21). In the ensuing scenes, this divine curse is gradually removed through hidden and fortuitous means. Ruth "happened to come to the part of the field belonging to Boaz" (2:3 RSV). Conveniently, Boaz lay down "at the end of the heap of grain" (3:7 RSV). Called to duty by a foreign woman, this Israelite patriarch swore by Yahweh to do right for Ruth (3:13). When the matter finally turned out well (cf. 3:18), Yahweh gave conception to Ruth, and the women of Bethelehem blessed this deity in words appropriately addressed to Naomi (4:13-14). From being the agent of death, God has become the giver of life, although at no place has the divine world intruded upon the narrative by speech or by miracles. Clearly, the human struggle itself is divine activity, redeeming curse through blessing.

In scene one, Naomi and Ruth stand alone. They are women without men. They make their own decision; they work out their own destinies. This posture continues in scene two, though the situation is more complex, since in Boaz a strong male appears. Hence, it is all the more important to discern that the power of the story is not transferred to him. The women continue to shape their tale, as both structure and content confirm. Scene two is their struggle to survive physically even as scene three is their struggle to survive culturally. In both scenes Boaz is reactor to their initiative. Scene four commences with the shock of reminder. After all, it is a man's world, and concerns of women may well be subsumed, perhaps even subverted, by this patriarchal climate. Yet the women of Bethlehem do not permit this transformation to prevail. They reinterpret the language of a man's world to preserve the integrity of a woman's story. Accordingly, scene four concludes with the two themes coming together: a story of women making a new beginning with men. Scene four is, then, the answer to scene one. Having suffered and struggled, the image of God male and female rejoices at last in the goodness of daily life.

As a whole, this human comedy suggests a theological interpretation of feminism: women working out their own salvation with fear and trembling, for it is God who works in them. Naomi works as a bridge between tradition and innovation. Ruth and the females of Bethlehem work as paradigms for radicality. All together they are women in culture, women against culture, and women transforming culture. What they reflect, they challenge. And that challenge is a legacy of faith to this day for all who have ears to hear the stories of women in a man's world.

12. I SAMUEL 3: HISTORICAL NARRATIVE AND NARRATIVE POETICS

Michael Fishbane

Introduction

As is well known, literary texts accumulate meanings through the intersection of diverse frames of analysis. This accumulation may be the product of repeated readings by one reader, or it may be the collective achievement of many readers who share a common tradition, literary or religious. The capacity of any text to bear an intricate simultaneity of meanings is surely one sign of its complex thematics and rich texture; and surely one mandate of literary criticism is the disclosure of this simultaneity to conscious reflection. Where critics often disagree, however, is with respect to the integration of the planes of signification thus disclosed. For some, the analytical task is restricted to the isolation of micro- or macro-structures; for others, central weight is placed on traditional topics of narrative stylistics, like point of view, representation of character, or analysis of plot. The present essay is an attempt to analyze both the formal structure *and* the narrative stylistics of I Samuel 3, and to disclose its interpenetrating planes of meaning.

At first view, the text presents no complications. It begins when the young Samuel ministered before the Lord and the elderly Eli in Shiloh—a time when divine oracles were relatively uncommon (vv. 1-2). Asleep in the shrine, Samuel is thrice awakened by a direct address and goes each time to Eli for clarification. Twice the old priest calms the novitiate and tells him to return to sleep; on the third occasion, however, Eli realizes that the Lord has spoken and advises the youth how to respond should the event recur (vv. 3-10). The subsequent revelation announces divine judgment against the Elide priestly dynasty for the sins of Eli's sons and his own failure to reprove them (vv. 11-14). In the morning, Samuel reluctantly tells Eli the content of the oracle (vv. 15-18). The text concludes with a notice that Samuel grew in stature and that the oracular divine presence returned to Shiloh (vv. 19-21).

Set within the books of Samuel, this text purports to describe a historical event in the life of Samuel and the history of the Elide priesthood. Nothing fully undermines this supposition. But it may be contended that the text is much more than a simple factual report. Two converging factors bring this out, requiring I Samuel 3 to be reread and reinterpreted from an alternate perspective. The first factor is of a comparative nature. The present scenario of a priest who sleeps in a shrine, and to whom the deity "comes and . . . stands" and announces a vision or oracle, is paralleled by a recurrent *topos* known from ancient Egyptian and Mesopotamian sources. There, too, a priest (or cultic designate) sleeps in a shrine in order to receive a dream illumination from a deity who "comes and . . . stands" and announces the future.[1] The suspicion that the factual content of I Samuel 3 is further affected by narrative conventions is reinforced by such internal factors as the highly stereotyped patterning of the divine call to Samuel in verses 4-9 (three times plus a climax). Recurrent biblical instances confirm that such formal patterning was a widespread compositional convention, used in a wide range of genres. Texts like Numbers 22–24, Exodus 7–11, Judges 13–16, I Kings 2, and Amos 1–2 come particularly to mind.[2] (Note Ira Clark's discussion of this same pattern in chapter 9—ed.)

These comparative observations suggest that whatever the historical kernel underlying I Samuel 3, the report of it has been decisively mediated by a series of narrative conventions. Accordingly, the analytic task is not to distill some historical essence from the received narrative, as if the events of I Samuel 3 were independently accessible or confirmable; it is rather to analyze the particular discourse whereby the events are presented and formulated. Since the historical and the literary intricately interpenetrate, there is no historical analysis of I Samuel 3 which is not also a literary interpretation—and vice versa.

I

Access to I Samuel 3 is facilitated by its many structural levels, the most comprehensive of which is its ring-composition (or chiastic arrangement). The initial *mise-en-scène,* describing Samuel's youth, Eli's diminishing powers, and the absence of divine oracles (vv. 1-3; A), is balanced by the dénouement and conclusion, describing Samuel's growing stature as a man of God and the return of divine oracles to Shiloh (vv. 19-21; A'). Within this framework are three divine calls to a bewildered Samuel (vv. 4-9; B), the climactic fourth and subsequent oracle against the Elides (vv. 10-15; C), and Eli's request of Samuel to reiterate the divine revelation (vv. 16-18; B). The result is the structure ABCB'A'. The formal framework of A and A' thus focuses attention on the opening and closing situation, and on the state of the characters (Samuel and Eli). The climax commences with the series of calls to Samuel (B) and peaks with the doom-oracle (C) and its communication to Eli (B'). The concentric structure of this text thus sponsors two complementary fields of force: centrifugal and centripetal. In oscillating degrees the reader's attention is drawn from the peripheries to the center and from the center outward: but all converges at the center-climax, for it is the divine oracle which coordinates and gives referential perspective to the opening and closing situations.

A reading of I Samuel 3 on the basis of this formal design is not exhaustive, however. The alternative is to view the text incrementally so that C is seen as part of the dramatic development from A to A', from a situation characterized by the absence of a divine revelatory presence—"and the oracle of YHWH was infrequent in those days"*—to a remanifestation of that presence—when "YHWH continued to be seen at Shiloh."* (Asterisked biblical quotations are my own translation.) The movement of I Samuel 3 thus traces a trajectory from negativity (the absence of the divine word), through misperceived and so unactualized manifestations of God in the historical moment (B), to the acknowledged receipt (C) and transmission of the divine word (B'). This sequence climaxes not with the oracle of C but with the transformed situation described in A'.

The preceding two readings are complementary interpretations of the chiastic structure of the text. The one perceives that center in the renewal of the divine presence (C), the other focuses on its permanence and newly recurrent availability (A'); the one emphasizes the renewal of the divine word to Samuel, an individual (C), whereas the other speaks with reference to the changed situation for all Israel (A'). There is no need to disentangle these latter two loops of significance: individual and national motifs are complexly sustained throughout the text, and particularly in A/A' where a micro-chiasm reinforcing this point may be observed. Verse 1 refers first to *Samuel* who served the Lord (a), then to the *national* situation of divine absence (b); correspondingly, the closing v. 21 refers to the renewal of the divine presence for *all Israel* (b'), "because YHWH was revealed to *Samuel* at Shiloh through the oracle of YHWH"* (a'). Just as the macro-chiasm ABCB'A' sponsors alternate climaxes of individual and national import, and hardly separates them, so the micro-chiasm binds the two elements together as well.

II

The framework of the macro-structure (A and A') can be set against a wider horizon—one which underscores the growth of Samuel's religious stature from verse 1, when "the youth *[na'ar[* Samuel served *[mešārēt 'et]* YHWH,"* to verse 19, when "Samuel grew *[vayigdal]* and YHWH was with him *['immô]*, and let none of his words go unfulfilled.'"* Close analysis shows that just these phrases are used to develop the character of Samuel in the preceding chapter (I Samuel 2). Thus, following Hannah's prayer upon the birth of Samuel (2:1-10), the text, referring to Samuel, states "and the youth *[na'ar]* served *[mešārēt 'et]* YHWH"* (v. 11). Again, after a description of the sons of Eli and their activities (in 2:12-17) the reader is again informed that "Samuel served *[mešārēt]* the face of YHWH"* (v. 18), and that "the youth *[na'ar]* Samuel grew *[vayigdal]* with *['im]* YHWH"* (v. 21). Thereupon follows another depiction of the sins of Eli's sons (2:22-25) and a final notice that "the youth *[na'ar]* Samuel continued to grow *[vegadel]* . . . both with YHWH and mankind"* (v. 25). The entire sequence of episodes concludes with an oracle against the House of Eli (2:27-36).

It is thus apparent that the positive notices about Samuel's priestly novitiate and growth in relationship to YHWH alternate with and dramatically counterpoint the historical notices regarding the Elide priests. The ascendance of the one is deliberately set over against the decline of the other—evaluatively and developmentally. An accumulation of positive attributes thus marks the several descriptions of Samuel in verses 11, 18, 21, and 26, even as an intensification of Elide sins marks the episodes of verses 12-17 and 22-25, which climax in the judgment oracle of verses 27-36. Less noticeable is the fact that this concluding oracle balances the opening prayer of Hannah structurally and thematically: structurally, insofar as the prayer sets the context for Samuel's positive novitiate at Shiloh over against the decadence of the existing priesthood there; and thematically, insofar as both the prayer and the oracle refer to the royal anointed one *(mašîaḥ)* of YHWH (vv. 10, 35). The overall structural form of these several units in I Samuel 2 is chiastic, and may be graphically recapitulated as follows:

A. Hannah's prayer and reference to a royal *mašîaḥ* (2:1-10)
   B. Samuel serves YHWH (2:11)
      C. Sins of Elides (2:12-17)
         D. Samuel serves YHWH and grows with God (2:18, 21)
      C' Sins of Elides (2:22-25)
   B' Samuel serves YHWH and grows with God (2:26)
A' Divine oracle and reference to a royal *mašîaḥ* (2:27-36)

As remarked, this chiasm is both evaluative and developmental. The sequence of textual units climaxes in terms of the accumulated virtues of Samuel, on the one hand, and the judgment upon the priestly family of Eli, on the other. At the same time, the virtues of Samuel in I Samuel 2:11, 18, 21, 26 achieve a more forceful climax in I Samuel 3—since 3:1 and 19 reiterate these earlier references to Samuel's service and stature before God. The noticeable difference between these testimonies is that in chapter 2 they interweave the account of Elide decadence, whereas in chapter 3 they *bracket* the narrative of Samuel's call and the oracle against the Elides.

The reader of I Samuel 3:1 thus continues the historical narrative with backward glances at I Samuel 2:11, 18, 21, and 26. The macro-structural element A is thus strikingly bivalent: it concludes the developments of chapter 2 and recharges them. Other verbal elements further accentuate the relationship between I Samuel 2 and 3 and the distance between them. For example, while the oracle against the Elides refers to the fact that YHWH had first "revealed" *(niglōh)* himself to this priestly clan in Egypt (2:27), this divine presence had become increasingly absent until new words were "revealed" *[niglāh]* to Samuel (3:21). Or again, while speaking of the future failure of the Elide line, the oracle in 2:33 states that YHWH "will not cut off everyone of you, to make his eyes fail *[lekhallôt 'et 'ēynâv].*"* This phrase assumes ironic punning force in 3:2, where it is said of the declining—but still unreplaced—Eli that "his eyes began to get dim *['ēynâv hēḥēllû khēhôt]*"* and in 3:12, where Samuel is told that YHWH is about to bring about the fulfillment of the oracles "from start to finish *[hāḥēl vekallēh].*"* And finally, we read that YHWH "will lightly esteem *[yēqāllû]* those who are contemptuous"* of him (2:30), and that the divine judgment later announced to Samuel refers to the fact that Eli's sons "cursed *[meqallelîm].*"[3]

III

The description of the "negative" religious situation in I Samuel 3:1-3 (A) is richly textured. Semantic and phonemic elements interpenetrate to underscore the situation of lack, passivity, and torpor. The narrative reports that the divine word was rare or "precious at that time,"* and that "there was no frequent vision" (v. 1). This lack of spiritual vision is metonymically captured by the emphasis on Eli's failing sight. Indeed, the phrase "his eyes *['ēynâv]* began to grow dim"* in verse 2 is linked to the earlier "there was no *['ēyn]* frequent vision" thematically and alliteratively.

Similarly, a hard truth is expressed through the alliterative puns that unexpectedly link the description of Eli—"his eyes began *[hēhēllû]* to grow dim; he was unable *[yûkhal]* to see"*—with the reference to the "temple *[hēykhal]* of YHWH" in which Samuel slept (v. 3). The semantic nexus established by these alliterations juxtaposes Eli's lack of (in)sight to the temple in which Samuel lay with the ark—a simulacrum of ancient divine presence and symbol of potential divine illumination. In his blindness, Eli lay in the spiritual darkness outside the temple; while Samuel, the novitiate, lay within.

The emphsis on spiritual and physical blindness in I Samuel 3:1-2 condenses in verse 3 around the remarkable bivalent image of the "lamp of Elohim before it was extinguished."* This phrase follows the reference to Eli "sleeping *[šōkhēb]* in his place,"* and his blindness, and precedes the references to "Samuel sleeping *[šōkhēb]* in the temple of YHWH,"* and the "ark of Elohim." Linked to these two images of sleep, it is thoroughly ambiguous whether "the lamp of Elohim before it was extinguished"* is a metaphor referring to Eli, and the fact that this religious leader was not yet dead or blind, or whether it is a metaphor for the spiritual illumination dimmed at this time but not entirely extinguished ("there was no *frequent* vision").

Both levels of meaning are possible; and both highlight features of the social-religious reality that centers on Samuel. If the metaphor refers to Eli, the dominant contrast of verse 3 is between old age and youth, between the senescent priest who "sleeps in his place" and the youthful *mešārēt* who "sleeps in the temple of YHWH." If, on the other hand, the metaphor refers to the state of divine illumination at that time, the contrast is rather between the diminishing spiritual realities, as represented by Eli, and the lingering flicker of divine light that will be reignited through Samuel. On this last possibility, Samuel's sleep in the temple becomes a figurative depiction of his spiritual incumbency. At the same time, the emphasis on sleep (Eli's and Samuel's) reinforces the imagery of passivity that dominates verses 1-3 (A).

IV

The relative lack of action in verses 1-3 (A) shifts abruptly with the call sequence of verses 4-9 (B). The third-person oblique narrative report is intersected with direct second-person encounters that dramatize the threefold divine address to Samuel. Moreover, with the divine calls beginning in verse 4, there is a reversal of the "infrequent" silence of divinity up to that point (cf. v. 1). But not being used to hearing divine speech, Samuel misinterprets the supernatural address and three times goes to Eli (vv. 5, 6, 7). On the first two occasions Eli, who has also been without the divine oracle, misunderstands the event and sends Samuel back to the shrine to sleep (stem: *šakhab;* vv. 5-6).

Eli's commands to sleep sponsor a variety of ironic meanings when structurally linked to the uses of *šakhab* in verses 2-3 (A). At one level, the repeated emphasis in verses 5-6, where Samuel is directed back to the shrine, call particular attention to the opening spatial polarity, where Eli is described as "sleeping in his place," while Samuel was "sleeping in the temple." To be sure, Samuel's location complements the initial depiction of his status as an acolyte or novitiate, and, as such, occasions no particular attention. But there is already an incipient sense that the spatial polarity of verses 2-3 anticipates the centrality of the young Samuel, in contrast to the increasing marginality of Eli. The situation is thus precisely the reverse from the viewpoint of the protagonists. Samuel, who is in the spiritual-physical center of the shrine, does not know that the Lord has called him and that he has become a spiritually central personality. It is for this reason that he runs *out of* the sanctuary to Eli, believing the latter to be the voice of his vision and the central spiritual officiant at Shiloh. Consequently, Eli's repeated commands to Samuel to *šekhab* in the shrine have ironic overtones: the old priest sends his novitiate back to the temple, where he will receive an oracle announcing Eli's fall.

There is also ironic truth in Samuel's dependence on the old priest which is called to mind (and so accentuated) by a verbal link between verse 3 and verse 7. The novitiate's confusion during his visions is explained by the narrative comment that "Samuel did not yet *[terem]* know YHWH, and the oracle of YHWH was not yet *[terem]* revealed *[yiggaleh]* to him"* (v. 7). This comment comes between the second and third divine calls, and repeats the adverb *terem* earlier used in verse 3 with espect to Eli, "the lamp of Elohim before *[terem]* it was extinguished."*⁴ This verbal repetition establishes an unexpected structural coordinate between units A and B and effectively juxtaposes Samuel's as yet unillumined state with Eli's flickering but as yet not totally undiminished spiritual vision. It was Samuel's own consciousness of that fact that directed him to Eli in the first place. He was right in running to this "lamp of Elohim before it was extinguished," but for whom the divine call would have gone unanswered. The *"ṭerem"* of Eli's latent (declining) divine consciousness thus served to help actualize the *"ṭerem"* of Samuel's latent (incubating) knowledge of God.

The final irony attendant upon the verbal stem *šakhab* in A and B comes in verse 9, with the report of Samuel's compliance with Eli's command. Earlier, after Eli told Samuel to *šekhab*, it is reported that he (Samuel) "went and slept"* (v. 5). The reuse of this merism in verse 9 is, by contrast, noticeably prolix—recording that "Samuel went and slept *in his place [bimqômô]*."* In the Hebrew, the semantic disturbance of this merism is all the more obvious: "[and] went *Samuel* and slept *in his place*."* Now the repeated accent on Samuel in verse 9 may easily be understood as a reemphasis on the novitiate who comes and goes so obediently. But what of the clause "in his place"? This phrase recurs only in the opening remark (v. 2) that "Eli slept in his place *[bimqômô]*."* Given the transfer of imagery and significance from Eli to Samuel throughout A and B, there is meaningful contrast in this repetition of a phrase used first with respect to Eli and then prior to Samuel's receipt of the revelation-oracle. But the meaningfulness of the repetition is not—it must be stressed—that Samuel *literally* replaced Eli, for *bimqômô* is a locative clause, and never used in biblical Hebrew to indicate replacement.[5] All the same, the verbal repetition elicits a structural contrast that complements other thematics of the text. And so one is drawn to the figurative force of the phrase *bimqômô in this context*. Shiloh has begun to become for Samuel "his place," just as it once was the "place" of Eli. That it was Eli who sent Samuel to sleep in "his place" is thus the final irony structurally sponsored by the repetition of the verb *šakhab* in verses 2-9.

All the while he was spiritually unaware of God's call, Samuel awoke to that call with physical unrest and disorientation. He repeatedly ran to Eli and blurted out: "here *I* am, for you called *me*" (vv. 5-6, 8), a response whose self-referential quality is dominant. When, however, Samuel was aroused by the fourth call, having become aware that he was addressed by God, he said: "Speak, for *your servant* is listening" (v. 10). The contrast is marked. The disoriented running is replaced by orientation and focus; and the self-centered "I" of the confused novitiate has been humbly transformed. Samuel is now "*your* servant."

V

The stereotyped repetition of Samuel's call has functional meaning in I Samuel 3. It controls the reader's perception of time; provides a fixed counterpoint to the developmental nature of the incidents; organizes the tensions of the action; and provides the neutral ground against which stylistic variations can be perceived. The issues connected with the various stylistic uses of *šakhab*, *terem*, and *bimqômô* in A and B all have been discussed; so has the shift within B of pronouns (from first to second person).

The structural deployment and effect of one final term, *vayyôsef*, "and He [God] continued," may be noted at this point. It is of special interest both because it is related to the temporal relation of the calls, and because it is linked to the opening and final scenarios (A and A'). The term is used initially with respect to the divine calls to Samuel. It is naturally missing from the first occasion, but does precede the second and third calls, emphasizes the successive nature of the divine presence, and counterpoints the opening absence of that presence (v. 1) and Samuel's inability to perceive it (v. 7).[6] There is, thus, through the repetition of *vayyôsef*, a dramatic emphasis on the recurrent—even insistent— divine attempt to return to the shrine and religious consciousness. The hesitant and initially inconclusive occasion of God's calls, which leads up to the conclusive divine breakthrough in C, contrasts with the concluding verse of I Samuel 3 that announces that "YHWH continued *[vayyôsef]* to be seen at Shiloh"* (v. 21). There is final irony in the fact that when Eli admonishes Samuel to repeat the oracle to him, he adds the adjuration: "May Elohim do thus to you and all the more so *[yôsîf]*"* if the content of the oracle is withheld in any way (v. 17; B').

Through verbal repetitions, B' thus sponsors ironic contrasts with earlier phases in the narrative and provides a transition to the new reality of divine revelations in A'. B' also provides a dramatic reversal of the initial trope of darkness and dim (in)sight. When Samuel awakes after receiving the anti-Elide oracle, the first thing he does is "open the doors of the temple of YHWH"* (v. 15). The situation of darkness is thereby transformed into one of light—a light both physical (the light of day) and spiritual (divine illumination). The nighttime scenario of the incubation and revelation in B-C is thus an extension of the larger trope of darkness illumined by a flickering "lamp of Elohim" (A). And finally, this mixture of physical and spiritual illumination is structurally underscored by means of another remarkable verbal allusion and contrast. When Samuel reported the oracle to Eli in B', Eli recognized it as a divine communication, saying "it is from YHWH, let Him do as is fitting in *his eyes [ēynâv]*."* This response strikingly recalls the earlier reference to Eli's increasing blindness, when "his eyes *[ēynâv]* began to grow dim." Verbally textured in this way, this response formally draws attention to the thematic shift from human blindness and divine absence to human insight and divine presence.

VI

One final level of textual meaning in I Samuel 3 remains to be explored. This is the phonemic level of musicality, whereby meaning is *presented* simply and directly by repeated relations of sound clusters. No nontextual reality is represented or implied.[7] The musicality exists and functions on its own terms. Nevertheless, the phonemic clusters *may* reinforce or highlight other semantic levels in the text. This possibility is, in fact, the case in Jeremiah 20:1-9,[8] and may be observed in I Samuel 3 as well.

On a purely phonemic-allophonic level, the reader is struck by the repetition of the related sounds *k/kh/ḥ/g/q/* with *l*, as in *hēHēLLû . . . Lō'yûKHaL* (v. 2); *hēyKHaL* (v. 3); *hāKHēL veKaLLēh* (v. 12); *meQaLLeLîm Lāhem . . . veLō' Khîhāh . . . veLāKhēn* (vv. 13-14); or as in *YiGGāLeh* (v. 7); *yiGdaL* (v. 19); *niGlāh* (v. 21). But these similarities of sound also highlight other patterns and coordinates of meaning in the text. Thus, to simply follow the preceding Hebrew transcription: the description of Eli's eyes, which "began" *(heḥellû)* to grow dim so that he "could not" *(lo' yukhal)* see (v. 2) occurs in syntactic and semantic juxtaposition to Samuel's residence in the "temple" *(hêyKhal,* v. 3)—a contrast remarked on above. Similarly, the description of the onset of Eli's blindness is musically—and semantically—aligned with the curse against the Elides which was to be effected from "beginning to end" *(hāKhēl veKallēh,* v. 22). Eli's physical condition thus anticipates, and is punningly resumed by, the reference to the divine oracle. Moreover the foregoing sounds are also linked to the sin of Eli's sons who "cursed" *(meqallelîm)* but were "not reproved" *(lo'Khîhāh,* v. 13). Altogether these several sounds associated with the blindness of Eli, and the imminent destruction of the lineage for its curses and forebearance, accumulate a negative cohesion that contrasts with—while simultaneously echoing—the repeated verbs *LēKH* or *vayyē-LēKH,* which describe Eli's command to Samuel to "go" back to the temple. The phonemic reversal of the dominant *KH-L* sequence/pattern in *LeKH* formally highlights the thematic/religious reversal underway in the contrasted personalities of Eli and Samuel. Such phonemic reversals with semantic meaning occur elsewhere in the Hebrew Bible.[9]

Other phonemic patterns exist in I Samuel 3. For example, it is reported in verse 2 that Eli's "eyes began to dim" *(Kēhôt),* and in verse 13 that when his sons cursed Eli did not "reprove *[Kîhāh]* them." Like the foregoing examples, this phonemic assonance has semantic meaning as well. It juxtaposes Eli's physical blindness to his spiritual unattentiveness, and retrospectively reinforces the presentiment that Eli's lack of vision was spiritual as well as physical.

The consonantal sequence *rṣ* may serve as a final instance of the interpenetration of phonemic and semantic levels of meaning. The first occurrence of this pattern is at the very outset of I Samuel 3, where it is reported that there were infrequent *(nifRāṢ)* visions (v. 1); the last occurrence comes in the concluding report that YHWH was "with" Samuel's oracles so that "none of his pronouncements fell unfulfilled to the ground" *('aRṢāh,* v. 19). Compactly, this phonemic repetition highlights the thematic development of the entire chapter, which moves between the poles of a relative absence of revelations and their renewal. This thematic movement is mediated and coordinated, as it were, by another recurrence of the *rṣ* phonemic pattern in the verb *vayāRāS*—which refers to Samuel's alacrity when "he ran" to Eli upon first being awakened by an unperceived divine call (v. 5). Samuel's activity thus provides the transition between the absence of oracles and their renewal.

What is particularly striking in the above is the way purely formal phonemic repetitions complement levels of meaning achieved by other means. Surely these phonemic/semantic meanings add to the historical "fact" of the composition and bring out more forcefully that in the Hebrew Bible historical narrative is always narrative history, and so is necessarily mediated by language and its effects. It is thus language in its artistic deployment that produces the received biblical history—a point that must serve to deflect all historicistic reductions of these texts to "pure" facts. And if all this requires a reconception of the truth-claims of the biblical historical narrative, then it is to this point that reflection has long been due.

13. KING DAVID OF ISRAEL

Kenneth R. R. Gros Louis

> When one rules justly over men,
>   ruling in the fear of God,
> he dawns on them like the morning light,
>   like the sun shining forth upon a cloudless morning,
>   like rain that makes grass to sprout from the earth.
> Yea, does not my house stand so with God? (II Sam. 23:3-5 RSV)

These words are spoken by King David near the end of II Samuel, shortly after he has delivered to the Gibeonites for execution two of Saul's sons and five of his grandsons, shortly before the narrative takes us in a flashback to the cave of Adullam, where, many years before, David had hidden himself from Saul and where "every one who was in distress, and every one who was in debt, and every one who was discontented, gathered to him" (I Sam. 22:2 RSV).

> Upon the King!
> Let us our lives, our souls,
> Our debts, our careful wives,
> Our children and our sins lay on the King!
> We must bear all. O hard condition,
> Twin-born with greatness, subject to the breath
> Of every fool . . .
> What infinite heart's-ease
> Must kings neglect, that private men enjoy!

These words are spoken by Shakespeare's Henry V, formerly Prince Hal, shortly after he has, unrecognized, moved among his men on the eve of their battle with the troops of France, shortly before he passes by an opportunity to inquire about his once-beloved Falstaff, who has, we know, died babbling of green fields, drawn even at his end to a psalm that assures him that his cup will runneth over.

Even though separated by centuries and world views, these passages contain a strikingly similar perception. David's statement on kingship acknowledges that the just king, ruling under divine law, brings men out of darkness, makes them warm and secure, nourishes them; the king is like another force of nature, of natural order, like the dawn or the sun or the rain. Henry V would not dispute these attitudes toward kingship nor would many in Shakespeare's audience, but Henry, unlike David, also feels the burden of the office; he recognizes, as David only rarely does, the relationship between moral individual order and political community order; he knows that one called upon to execute justice and shape policies for the common good must not show in himself signs of selfishness or frailty or weakness; he knows that there is more than a ceremony and a banner separating Prince Hal from King Henry V.

While this may seem a circuitous way to begin a discussion of King David, it suggests, I believe, a means for analyzing the narrative of his accomplishments in the OT. An amazing number of incidents, few of them narrative fillers, are contained in the account, from the time David is called from the sheep to be anointed by Samuel to the day of his death. We see him in a variety of roles—as giant-slayer, shepherd, musician, manipulator of men, outlaw, disguised madman, loyal friend and subject, lover, warrior, dancer and merrymaker, father, brother, son, master, servant, religious enthusiast, and king. We see him pursued and pursuing, in God's favor and out, in the hearts of his people and out, triumphant and downcast. What are we to make of this enormous portrait? Where do we begin? How do we reconcile the David who slays Goliath with the David who has Uriah the Hittite murdered? The man who lies to the priest Ahimelech with the man who feeds the lame Mephibosheth at his own table? The man who seems to ignore his apparent heir Solomon with the man who weeps for the rebellious Absalom? The man who listens quietly to Joab's implicit and explicit criticisms with the man who scorns his wife's bitterness over his display of exuberance in public? The man who schemes to eliminate his enemies with the man who twice refuses to kill Saul, who is seeking his life? The answers to these questions are hinted at by the analogy with Prince Hal; for it is Hal, we remember, who, having become king, greets his former tutor, drinking companion, and friend, the expectant Falstaff, with the words: "I know thee not old man, . . . I banish thee on pain of death not to come near me."

The opening and closing of the David narrative may provide a frame for our understanding of David's years as king of Israel, for presumably differences between the beginning and ending of a narrative are a direct result of what has happened in between. In I Samuel 16, the Lord gives specific instructions to Samuel to go to Jesse the Bethlehemite, for as the Lord says, "I have provided for myself a king among his sons." Samuel is afraid to go; the elders of the city who come to meet him tremble and fear for their lives. "Do you come peaceably?" they ask. "I have come to sacrifice to the Lord. . . ." When all have come for the sacrifice, including Jesse and his sons, Samuel, through whose eyes we are seeing this, looks on Jesse's first son and thinks surely the Lord's anointed is before him. But we learn, as Samuel learns, that he is not the one to be anointed. The Lord says, "Do not look on his appearance or on the height of his stature, because I have rejected him; for the Lord sees not as man sees; man looks on the outward appearance, but the Lord looks on the heart." Other sons come and the tension mounts for Samuel and therefore for us until all of Jesse's sons have passed before him and none is to be anointed king. "Are all your sons here?" Samuel asks Jesse. "There remains yet the youngest, but behold, he is keeping the sheep." Samuel asks him to come, and soon in comes David, running, with beautiful eyes, handsome, and the Lord says, "Arise, anoint him; for this is he," and the narrative tells us that the spirit of the Lord came mightily upon David as, in contrast, the opening of chapter 14 tells us that the Spirit of the Lord departed from Saul.

Obviously, there is an element of wonder in David's selection—it is a surprise to Samuel; it is surprising to Jesse, who left David with the sheep during the visit of the prophet; and it is surprising, therefore, to us as readers. At the same time, it is done very simply—Samuel is sent to Bethlehem with specific instructions; the Lord clearly knows who is to be the next king, and the anointing is done quickly, without fanfare, without "outward appearance." The implication, because the hand of the Lord is involved, is that David will alter the atmosphere in Israel, a tense atmosphere as suggested by Samuel's concern about going to Bethlehem and by the elders' trembling upon his arrival.

Consider the end of David's life in I Kings 1. David, we have been told, is old and advanced in years, cold, and a maiden has been brought to keep him warm. We hear that Adonijah, one of his sons, has exalted himself saying, "I will be king." (Adonijah, that son not very well raised, whose father had not at any time displeased him by asking, "Why have you done thus and so?"). Adonijah is, like David, a very handsome man. Some in David's court follow him; others do not. He gives a sumptuous banquet, selectively inviting those who support his claim. Nathan and Bathsheba, plotting and scheming for their own interests, inform David (twice) of Adonijah's self-exaltation and remind him of his promise to make Solomon his heir. David recalls his promise so well that Bathsheba, by verse 31, can say: "May my lord King David live for ever!"—a blessing that rings somewhat hollow in this context of preparing for David's death. The performance is then carefully planned. Solomon is to ride on David's mule, the priest and Nathan the prophet are to anoint him, a trumpet is to be blown, and all are to shout, "Long live King Solomon." The "spontaneous" demonstration takes place, is repeated a second time, and a third time. After the third time Jonathan rushes to Adonijah to tell him that Solomon rides on the king's mule, that he has been anointed, that a trumpet has been blown: Adonijah flees, and Solomon's succession is assured.

The difference between this episode and the opening episode tells us a great deal about David's reign. For one thing, we hear nothing of the presence of the Lord in the second episode. Many people recall oaths made in the Lord's name and the Lord is called upon for safety, but the stage is filled with human characters who, as the Lord had pointed out to Samuel earlier, and as is only reasonable, see as men see. They are dazzled, as the Lord said to

Samuel, by the outward appearance. Adonijah is beautiful, he has
horsemen and chariots, fifty men to run before him; he sacrifices
sheep, oxen, and fatlings, and gives a sumptuous banquet. Those
who favor Solomon put on a good show of their own, banking
heavily on outward appearance—Solomon rides on David's mule,
he is anointed before crowds of people, the trumpet blows, the
people shout, "Long live King Solomon." As Jonathan reports to
Adonijah, "the city is in an uproar." What a difference between
this noisy display—a scene repeated three times in the narrative—and the simple words to Samuel: "Anoint him; for this is
he." David's court is heavily politicized, people are looking out for
themselves. As David moves toward death, those around him
scheme to secure their own futures. What has gone wrong? Why is
David leaving as his legacy a divided, insecure kingdom?

Consider again our introduction to David. After he is anointed
by Samuel, we are given two accounts of his arrival at Saul's court
and of his coming into contact with Saul. Scholars who write about
these episodes point out that they are inconsistent, that Saul
should not have to ask who David is after the slaying of Goliath.
But surely whoever put the narrative into this final form was aware
of the inconsistency too. The appearance of such inconsistent
accounts in close proximity in a narrative is more than an author's
nodding; it is the equivalent of deep sleep. Assume, then, that the
author of Samuel has a reason for including two seemingly
inconsistent accounts of David's coming into Saul's life. What,
then, *is* the reason? At the end of chapter 16 in I Samuel, we are
told that after the spirit of the Lord departed from Saul, he
suffered from moments of depression, of melancholy. One of his
servants, seeking someone skilled in playing the lyre who might
calm him during these moments of torment, recalls: "Behold, I
have seen a son of Jesse the Bethlehemite, who is skilful in
playing. . . ." Here, the most distinguishing characteristic of
David is his power of music; but David is also a man of valor, of
war, prudent, of good speech, a man of good presence, *and the
Lord is with him.* David is a great success as Saul's comforter, so
much so that "Saul loved him greatly, and he became his
armor-bearer." David comes into an enclosure, then into court,
into a private and personal relationship with Saul; when Saul is in

his melancholy mood David is sent for, plays the lyre (while the two of them are presumably alone), and Saul is calmed.

At the opening of chapter 17 we are told that the Philistines have gathered their armies for battle. Suddenly we shift from an inside private court scene to a very large public outside stage. The Philistines stand on the mountain on one side and Israel stands on the mountain on the other side with a valley between them. We are then given an account of Goliath and of his challenge to the Israelites, a challenge to which no one responds. In verse 12 the narrative shifts—"Now David was the son of an Ephrathite of Bethlehem in Judah, named Jesse, who had eight sons." Three of his sons are fighting for Saul, but not David: "David was the youngest; the three eldest followed Saul, but David went back and forth from Saul to feed his father's sheep at Bethlehem." There follows this sentence: "For forty days the Philistine came forward and took his stand, morning and evening." The juxtaposition is striking. David is going back and forth from his private enclosure with the sheep, bringing food to his brothers; Goliath is going back and forth, too, but on a public stage, coming forward to challenge the Israelites. David is instructed by Jesse to bring food to his brothers, and then to return. There follows a series of private things left behind. "David rose early in the morning, and left the sheep with a keeper. . . ." He gets to the battlefield and sees the Israelites and the Philistines drawn up for battle again on the two mountains. (Think how stunning it is for David coming from the sheepfold to see these armies on the two mountains with the valley between them.) He leaves his "things" in charge of the keeper of the baggage and runs to the ranks. When he gets to the ranks, Goliath speaks, "and David heard him." He has many times gone back and forth, but this time he comes, *leaves* the sheep with the keeper, *leaves* his things with the keeper of the baggage, and hears Goliath for the first time.

Following this gradual movement of David from a personal to a public world, he soon becomes a very public figure indeed. His motives are ambiguous, as his own brother (17:28) seems to recognize—on one hand, the reward for killing Goliath is great; on the other hand, Goliath is an uncircumcised Philistine who had defied the armies of the living God. David youthfully and brashly presents himself to Saul, who, after agreeing to let him fight

Goliath, clothes him with his own armor. And we are surely meant to recall that earlier David the musician had been Saul's *armor-bearer*. David kills Goliath with no sword—the Lord, David points out, "saves not with sword and spear." (How David's statement will haunt us when, after the affair with Bathsheba, the Lord instructs Nathan to tell David, "the sword shall never depart from your house . . .") (II Sam. 12:10). It is at this point, with David victorious over Goliath, that Saul asks what would seem to be, given the earlier narrative of David and Saul, his unnecessary question: "Whose son are you, young man?" (17:58).

The two accounts, however inconsistent they may seem, present us with two views of David at Saul's court and two views of Saul's relationship to David. In the first, he comes as Saul's personal musician, he calms him privately at court with his music and Saul loves him greatly; in the second, he becomes Saul's public champion, gradually, as depicted in the narrative, moving away from the private enclosure of his father's home, his sheep, his deliveries to his brothers, and into the public world of war and armor, visibility, wealth and influence. David has a private relationship with Saul the man; he also develops a public relationship with Saul the king. Saul the man can love his comforter and recall the refreshment brought to him by his music; Saul the king cannot bear to hear the Israelite women singing, "Saul has slain his thousands, and David his ten thousands" (I Sam. 18:7).

Henry V had said of kingship, "O hard condition, / Twin-born with greatness, subject to the breath / Of every fool . . . / What infinite heart's ease / Must kings neglect, that private men enjoy." David never quite understands the necessity of Henry's implicit advice. He is, in his running battle with Saul, continually puzzled: "What have I done?" he asks repeatedly. His friend Jonathan cannot understand either—"What has he done?" Jonathan asks his father when Saul gives orders that David be killed. A public figure has many responsibilities and obligations, as David knows. This first king of Israel also comes to recognize, however, and only through harsh experience, that a public figure has many personal desires as well, and that to satisfy them may not be in the best interests of the people who depend on him. The two books of Samuel give us a portrait, a very rich one, of the first real king;

these books also give us an insight into the enormous difficulty of ruling well. We are offered, by the two accounts of David's introduction to Saul, a way into the narrative, and that is, to note the differences between David's private encounters and his public activities. For, unlike Henry V, he is not able to merge them, to suppress private needs for public ones. At times in the narrative he is solely a public figure, at times solely a private figure; but when his personal desires and his public obligations come into conflict, or when prviate and public needs have equal validity for him, he is lost.

The narrative caan be analyzed in these terms. Davd, when he is conscious of his position, when he recognizes most clearly his own responsibilities and the needs of those who depend on him, seems aware of himself as a public figure. His major public relationships are with the prophet Samuel, with the priest Ahimelech, with the wealthy Nabal, with Achish, the king of Gath, with the army commanders Abner and Joab, with the prophets Nathan and Gad, with two of his own sons, Solomon and Adonijah, and with the cursing Shimei. What is David like with these people? How would we characterize him? The traits that emerge most clearly are these: he is shrewd and calculating, cautious, patient, vigorous in the defense of himself and his followers. Most important, he acts in the public welfare, even if it means at times suppressing his own desires, humbling himself, letting himself be criticized. He never, for example, challenges the instructions given to him by the prophets Samuel, Nathan, and Gad. He is willing to be led by them, to acknowledge the divine source of their advice. His responses are wise, we realize, but they are also politic. It is not good, David must know, to go against the prophets; for he must have heard what happened to Saul when he disobeyed Samuel's explicit instructions concerning the Amalekites. David's shrewdness is seen further in his three lies to Ahimelech, lies that lead to Ahimelech's death and the destruction of his city. With Achish, David feigns madness, letting his spittle run down his beard to avoid what he believes is the king of Gath's mistrust of him; later, he prudently asks Achish to give him a town so that he will not come to rival the king in his own city. He clearly is concerned about his public image when he responds to Nabal's rude rejection of his request for food by telling his men to gird on their swords. At the same time, he can be patient and humble when the public need or political considerations demand it. Early in the narrative he taunts and criticizes Abner for not properly protecting King Saul (I Sam. 26:15-16). And yet, despite his sharp rebuke of Abner, David later gives him a sumptuous banquet and becomes his co-conspirator, perhaps knowing all the time of the enmity between Abner and Joab, knowing that Joab will be, as he usually is, an efficient assassin, that David can then blamelessly say, as he does, "I and my kingdom are for ever guiltless before the Lord for the blood of Abner" (II Sam. 3:28). David's whole relationship with Joab is the most illuminating of his public activities. Joab is commander of the army, the military leader of Israel; and David, as king, seems to recognize the need to be cautious with him, even though there is no personal affection between them. That is why David remains quiet when Joab accuses him of being deceived by Abner, why he leaves Joab alone even while he mourns the murdered Amasa and Abner, why he tolerates Joab's abusive rebuke as he mourns his son Absalom, who was killed *by* Joab. The public needs of Israel are presumably best served if the king and the commander of his army are not in open conflict. This does not mean, as we know, that David forgets what Joab has done and said to him. Similarly, David prevents his followers from killing Shimei even though Shimei curses him and hurls dust and stones at him—it is no time, David may think, as he flees from Jerusalem, to begin a blood feud with the Benjamites. But he does not forget Shimei either.

Shrewd and cautious when he needs to be, patient with those who rebuke him, David calculates rightly that it is good politics to kill the self-proclaimed murderer of Saul and Jonathan and the actual murderers of Saul's son Ishbosheth, but bad politics to kill Joab and Shimei—even though his attitude to them, as we know from his final words to Solomon, is basically the same as it is to those he does execute. In his public moments, as leader of his troops, dispenser of justice, in dealing with members of his government and with potential enemies, David excels.

But as Prince Hal recognized, and painfully accepted when he banished Falstaff from his sight, a leader also has personal and private desires that, if unchecked, if not banished, can damage the public welfare he has been asked to maintain. The king has his emotions and feelings, he can respond on a personal level to the desires of others; but while these emotions can and should be followed if they call forth magnanimity, they must also be suppressed if they arouse pettiness, if they activate man's frailties and weaknesses.

King David can be magnanimous. In his darkest hour as king, as he and his followers leave Jerusalem, he can feel concern for Ittai; he can be moved by the loyalty of Ziba; he can be touched by Barzillai's desire to die in his own city. The insights we get into David the man leave us with good feelings about him. He can acknowledge the loyalty of Rizpah and give proper burial to the executed sons and grandsons of Saul; however thirsty, he can recognize a display of loyal affection by his three mighty men and pour on the ground the water they bring to him from the well of Bethlehem. In these moments David's personal compassion and concern for others enhances his public image as king. What he does with Ittai, Ziba, Barzillai, Rizpah, and the three mighty men results from a personal link he feels toward them; and his actions seal that link without interfering with the public welfare.

At times, however, David's compassion weakens the public security, as a personal decision spills over into the public realm. In what seems not unpraiseworthy, for example, he asks in II Samuel 9, "Is there still any one left of the house of Saul, that I may show him kindness for Jonathan's sake?" After hearing about Mephibosheth, Jonathan's son who, the narrative tells us several times, is lame in both his feet, David takes him in as one of his own sons. And yet, shortly before when he conquered Jerusalem, David had said, "Whoever would smite the Jebusites, let him get up the water shaft to attack the lame and the blind, who are hated by David's soul." Yet here is the lame Mephibosheth—and the nrrative emphasizes his lameness—in David's own house, the same Mephibosheth who will later remain with the rebel Absalom, hoping, the narrative tells us, to get back the kingdom of his father.

Although David may have thought he was being shrewd in keeping Mephibosheth under his surveillance, there is also an element of pride and careless self-confidence in his desire to help him, in wanting to do something that would look generous at the moment of his greatest triumph. A hint of that pride appears in several earlier episodes—when David is pleased by the flattery of Saul's servants and decides it might not be such a bad thing to be the king's son-in-law, when he is swayed by the clever speech of Abigail, when he wants desperately to have the ark of the Lord come to *him*.

These less attractive sides of David's character dominate his affair with Bathsheba, an affair that represents the most obvious example of his personal desires overwhelming his public duties. His errors are monumental. He stays home, open to temptation, "in the spring of the year, the time when kings go forth to battle" (II Sam. 11:1). He abuses his power as king in sending for and sleeping with Bathsheba, in satisfying his own private desires. He calls for Uriah, deceives him by asking about the war; bribes him with a gift; gets him drunk so he will lay with Bathsheba. When David asks him why he is not sleeping with his wife, Uriah says, "The ark and Israel and Judah dwell in booths; and my lord Joab and the servants of my lord are camping in the open field; shall I then go to my house, to eat and to drink, and to lie with my wife? As you live, as as your soul lives, I will not do this thing" (II Sam. 11:11). Here is David on his couch, staying home from the battle and sleeping with another man's wife, and Uriah reminds him what his men are doing out in the open fields, his men, and the ark and Israel and Judah, dwelling in booths. At this point there is nothing for David to do but kill Uriah. It is the act of a desperate man. As he displays his remarkable disloyalty, he also, we notice, takes advantage of the loyalties of others. He sends the instructions that Uriah be killed to Joab, knowing that Joab will carry them out because he is loyal. He gives the letter to Uriah knowing, because Uriah is loyal, that he will not look at it. He *uses* the very loyalties that he is undermining. When he hears that Uriah is dead, he simply says, "Do not let this matter trouble you, for the sword devours now one and now another" (II Sam. 11:25) (the *sword* again, from the man who killed Goliath with no sword, the man who once proclaimed that "the Lord saves not with sword and spear"). How appropriate David's punishment is. "Thus says the Lord . . . 'I will take your wives before your eyes, and give them to your neighbor, and he shall lie with your wives in the sight of this sun. For you did it secretly; but I will do this thing before all

Israel, and before the sun'" (II Sam. 12:11-12). It is almost as if the narrative is emphasizing to us the private nature of David's sin, having the Lord make it public because David is a public figure. David's personal desire for Bathsheba and his personal desire for secrecy lead him to adultery, betrayals, lies, deceptions, murder. As a result of his enjoyment of his "heart's ease," the heart's ease that Henry V points out can be enjoyed only by private men, he undermines the security of the state—"the sword shall never depart from [his] house." And in a short time, his son Absalom will kill another of his sons, Amnon.

David and Absalom, David and Saul—the two relationships dominate the narrative and obviously invite comparison. In many ways, they epitomize the conflict explored in the narrative of the leader or king who is also a man. David is impressive as a public figure; he is attractive as a man in those private, personal encounters with his followers. With Bathsheba, however, David's personal life overcomes his public obligations with disastrous consequences. The relationships with Saul and Absalom are even more complex because with both David is involved in personal *and* public ways. His personal feelings toward them have equal validity with his public obligations toward them. Under the circumstances, the narrative suggests, a king is most severely tested.

We have noted how carefully the narrative makes us aware of David and Saul's relationship as a private as well as public one, even to the point of seeming narrative inconsistencies. The incredible tension and ambivalence that both experience is explained by the dual nature of their relationship. Saul is afraid of David, but in awe of him; he hurls spears at him and schemes against him with the Philistines, his daughter, his son, and servants, but he repeatedly calls David back to court; he believes that David plots against him, pitifully saying to his servants, "No one discloses to me when my son makes a league with the son of Jesse, none of you is sorry for me or discloses to me that my son has stirred up my servant against me, to lie in wait, as at this day" (I Sam. 22:8); his view of David is epitomized in his conversation with the Ziphites when he tells them to look for David's haunts, "the lurking places where he hides" (I Sam. 23:23). But he also calls David more righteous than he is, he weeps to hear David's voice, he swears peace to him and calls himself a fool. As David's king, he fears the popular acclaim David receives from the people; and yet he knows the truth of Ahimelech's words: "And who among all your servants is so faithful as David, who is the king's son-in-law, and captain over your bodyguard, and honored in your house?" (I Sam. 22:14). As David's friend, he loves him like a son; and yet he still believes David is lying in wait to ambush him.

David, on his part, is the slayer of Goliath, the man anointed by Samuel to be king of Israel; and yet, as he is schemed against and pursued by Saul, instead of defending himself he moves into the wilderness and hides in caves. Twice he rejects the advice of his followers and spares Saul's life, the life of the man seeking to kill him (and this is the David who threatens Nabal with total destruction because he will not feed him). From his encounter with Goliath we know, of course, David's sense of awe at the concept of the Lord's anointed; we also assume that he must feel some personal gratitude toward Saul; but it is more than politics that prevents David from killing Saul. Saul is his king: "the king of Israel," says David, "has come out to seek my life, like one who hunts a partridge in the mountains" (I Sam. 26:20). Saul is his friend: "Why does my Lord pursue after his servant? For what have I done? What guilt is on my hands?" (I Sam. 26:18).

Because of his relation with Saul, David surely understands the complexity of his ambivalence toward Absalom. What could be more poignant than a conflict between a king/father and his apparent successor/son? But hasn't David experienced something like this once before, albeit in another of the roles? The similarities are many. Absalom kills Amnon; David is angry but he does nothing about it. Is it because he recognizes that what Absalom did to Amnon had some justice, because what Amnon did to Tamar was comparable to what he had done to Bathsheba and Uriah the Hittite? Absalom flees, the narrative emphasizes, "and so he fled," "and so he fled," "and so he fled." Is David reminded of his own fleeing from Saul, and is it because of what Saul did to him that he will not pursue Absalom? Joab shrewdly instructs a woman to obtain a judgment from David in which David convicts himself. Does David remember that in his decision with Nathan the prophet he also convicted himself? Does he realize that he *must* maintain justice with Absalom, and yet also realize that he has already abandoned justice with Uriah? He seeks a compromise by permitting Absalom to return but live apart. Absalom then works through Joab to discover David's thinking. Is David reminded of how he worked through Jonathan to discover Saul's thinking and does he want to avoid doing to Absalom what Saul did to him? Absalom is beautiful, and he steals the hearts of the men of Israel—and notice what men they are: those who come to the king with a suit seeking judgment. Is David reminded of those who gathered to him, to his beautiful person in the cave of Adullam, those in debt, those in distress, those who were discontented, those, in other words, with suits seeking judgment? And does he now feel what Saul felt when he heard the women of Israel sing of David?

All the public need points to David's obligation to destroy Absalom or punish him or prevent him from increasing his authority. But David's own relation to him as father, and his own past, paralyze him. His uncharacteristic outburst at Absalom's death—"O my son Absalom, my son, my son Absalom! Would I had died instead of you, O Absalom, my son, my son!"—marks the culminating realization that his public duty as king has been neglected because of the private emotions he feels for his son, emotions augmented because he too was like such a son to another king of Israel. It takes Joab to underline the conflict for him:

"You have today covered with shame the faces of all your servants, who have this day saved your life, and the lives of your sons and your daughters, and the lives of your wives and your concubines, because you love those who hate you and you hate those who love you. For you have made it clear today that commanders and servants are nothing to you; for today I perceive that if Absalom were alive and all of us were dead today, then you would be pleased." (II Sam. 19:5-6)

Joab is right. As king, David must welcome his conquering army; but as father to a dead son killed by that army, and a son who arouses memories of his own past, David finds that very difficult to do. When David had wanted to make his Lord a house, the Lord had declared to him, "The Lord will make *you* a house. . . . I will raise up your offspring after you . . . I will establish his kingdom . . . I will be his father, and he shall be my son." But the Lord had also added, "When he commits iniquity, I will chasten him with the rod of men, with the stripes of the sons of men"; at the same time, the Lord promises, "I will not take my steadfast love from him" (II Sam. 7:11-15). It is a hard standard that God sets for man.

As the united kingdom David once ruled begins to crumble, David sings his song to the Lord, "My rock, and my fortress, and my deliverer" (II Sam. 22). It is an extraordinary song. In it, David almost phases himself out as a personality. With Saul, Bathsheba, Absalom behind him, he speaks in a voice so public that it has no personal tone or emotion at all. He has become, in a terribly painful way, the perfect king, alienated from his personal desires as a man, alienated from his personal identity, instructing his people. The biography he gives himself in the song is obviously invented, but for the public welfare. "I have kept the ways of the Lord," he says, "and have not wickedly departed from my God. For all his ordinances were before me, and from his statutes I did not turn aside. I was blameless before him." This clearly is not personally true. The song is didactic, purely public, a series of meditations on kingship, on the power of God, on the importance of following God's guidance. There is no moment in the song when we hear that personal voice which earlier sang, "I am distressed for you, my brother Jonathan; very pleasant have you been to me; your love to me was wonderful, passing the love of women" (II Sam. 1:26). As his death draws near, David gives his son Solomon kingly and public advice, warning him to walk in the ways of God. But for this first king, private desires impinge even at the end. Of Joab he tells Solomon, "Do not let his gray head go down to Sheol in peace"; of Shimei he tells Solomon, in his last words, "bring his gray head down with blood to Sheol" (I Kings 2:6, 9).

The narrative explores what it means to be a king, what it means for a man with his own personal desires and needs to be entrusted with the public welfare. The promise held out for Israel by Samuel's public anointing of David has been disappointed at the end of David's life, as we see members of his court struggling to achieve their personal desires, even at the expense of the state. The narrative in between has alternated between showing us David in his private moments and David in his public moments—a pattern established by his dual introduction into Saul's court, a pattern highlighted by his relations with Saul and Absalom, in which personal and public desires have equal validity. David can overcome and learn from the machinations of Saul, as Prince Hal moves beyond the guilt and paranoia of his father; he can put up with Joab, his blunt Hotspur; but he cannot, in the end, abandon entirely his heart's ease—he is unable to suppress his personal desire for Bathsheba, he is unable to carry out his public duty toward Absalom; he cannot, as does Prince Hal, banish Falstaff.

14. I SAMUEL 25 AS LITERATURE AND HISTORY

Jon D. Levenson

I. The Literary Craft of the Narrator

The Hebrew Bible is as much a work of literary artistry as it is a writing of history. Unfortunately, the literary dimension has received far less attention over the years than the historical. The reason for this is that the Bible has been seen as first and foremost a record of events that disclose and transform the very nature of human existence. The form in which that record is clothed, at least until the present century, has been regarded as rather extraneous to the fundamental character of the book, an entertaining digression perhaps, but a digression nonetheless. The fact is, however, that the categories of literary artistry and historiography are not so independent as many a scholar of the Bible may think. Some elements of artistry are apparent in any work of historiography, and this aesthetic dimesion is of the utmost importance in works executed before critical canons of objectivity and chronological consistency held sway. Until modern times, the distinction between story and history was rarely made, and history told in a flat, unappealing style (like that to which many academic historians today aspire) was not likely to be remembered. In a society like that of ancient Israel, history was something recited. It survived and was ultimately transcribed because of its rhetorical force.

The historian in the modern mode, however, must make an

effort to disengage the event from its recitation. He cannot rest content, as do many Orthodox Jews and fundamentalist Christians, with the assumption that the narrative in our hands reflects in an uncomplicated way what really happened. Instead, the historian must continually second-guess the text, striving to look beyond the literary piece in front of him in an effort to recover the historical facts, however elusive or speculative these latter may be. For the student of literature, the text may be the beginning and the end of his labors. His goal is to advance our appreciation of it. For the historian, the text is but a means to the end of ascertaining historical fact. The irony is that the historian cannot reach his goal without a lucid perception of the other dimension, the literary, lest he take elements of artistic convention for simple indications of fact. And so, in discussing the tale of David and Abigail in I Samuel 25, we must first explore the literary dimension, how the story is told, and only then can we begin to penetrate beyond the artistry of the storyteller in order to reconstruct the original political significance of his story.[1]

1. Nabal and the Heartlessness of a Churl

The characterization of Abigail's repulsive husband, Nabal, begins with his very name, which is a form of character assassination. The Hebrew word *nābāl,* often translated as "fool," designates not a harmless simpleton, but rather a vicious, materialistic, and egocentric misfit. Other biblical passages present the *nābāl* as an embarrassment to his father, a glutton, a hoarder, and even an atheist.[2] Most significant for our purposes is Isaiah 32:6, in which the refusal to feed the hungry and give drink to the thirsty, precisely the sin of Nabal in I Samuel 25, is listed among the characteristics of a *nābāl:*

> No longer will the fool *(nābāl)* be called noble,
> Nor the villain be termed honorable.
> For the fool utters foolishness *(nĕbālâ),*
> And his mind plots evil,
> To do foul things,
> To preach disloyalty against the Lord,
> To keep empty the gullet of the hungry,
> To deprive the thirsty of drink,
> As for the villain, his actions are vile;

He devises plots
To deprive the lowly of their rights through lies,
Even when the claim of the poor is just.
But the noble man counsels only noble things,
And stands his ground in his nobility.* (Isa. 32:5-8)

It is interesting that, although the *nābāl* appears elsewhere as a glutton, as we have seen, only in Isaiah 32:6 and in I Samuel 25 is this particular sin attributed to him, and only in these two passages is the pun on *nābāl* and *nĕbālâ* ("fool" and "foolishness" or "scandal") made. As Abigail says to David: "Let not my lord pay attention to this worthless fellow, to Nabal, for like his name is he: "Fool" is his name, and foolishness is about him"* (v. 25). The most likely explanation for these curious circumstances is that Abigail here applies to her husband an old proverb of which we find a parallel or variant in Isaiah 32:5-8. If so, the suspicion naturally arises that the historical figure's real name has been suppressed in order to give him an appellation indicative of his character, one that will show that he is called what he is. To be sure, the Semitic linguist can, if he searches hard enough, find an etymology for the name Nabal more flattering than the word for a vile misfit. One scholar, James Barr, discusses four uses of essentially the same word in languages related to Hebrew, one use with the meaning "flame," another with the meaning "sent," a third meaning "to be noble," and a fourth meaning "skilled, clever." Barr seems to favor the etymology "sent"; Nabal's name would then mean something like "messenger." To be sure, there is no way to disallow Barr's approach. If he is right, then Abigail's pun on "fool"/"foolishness" *(nābāl/nĕbālâ)* is a product of her wit and not that of the narrator. She puns on Nabal's name; the narrator does not. The problem is that if there are so many perfectly ordinary etymologies for this name, why is it that Abigail's husband alone in the entire Hebrew Bible bears it? The fact is that there are many biblical names that are tendentious in character. For example, the instigator of revolution in Judges 9 is named Gaal ben Ebed, which means something like "Loathing son of a Slave." The loyal Yahwist of I Kings 17 is named Obadiah, which means something on the order of "Servant of YHWH."

And the royal servant of Jeremiah 38 bears the name Ebed-me-lech, "Servant of a King," hardly a coincidence. In short, many names in the Hebrew Bible have been changed in accordance with the character or role of their bearers. "Nabal" is most likely no exception. The storyteller wants us to know what this fellow is like from the start.

This process of deliberate, overt characterization continues in verse 3, in which it is remarked almost parenthetically: "he was a Calebite." Ancient Hebrew was always written in consonants, with essentially no indication of vowels. Since different words can have the same consonants, there is a greater ambiguity than in most other languages. For example, in English the consonants *ctlg* probably suggest to the reader "catalogue," but, in fact, they could just as well represent "cytology." In Hebrew, furthermore, it is possible to write with the consonants of one word and the vowel indicators of another. The word in verse 3 that I have translated as "Calebite" *(kālibbî)* indicating a member of the tribe of Caleb, might also be read, according to its vowels, as "doglike," hardly a compliment in light of the biblical view of dogs. But according to its consonants, the phrase in question means "and he was like his heart" *(kĕlibbô),* amost certainly an allusion to Psalm 14:1 (53:1):

> The fool *[nābāl]* has said in his heart *[bĕlibbô]*,
> "There is no God."

If this is correct, then we have here an instance of scribal sarcasm. The consonantal text alludes to the prideful and ultimately stupid and arrogantly unperceptive character of this man, who seems to have recognized no authority other than his own. As we shall see, Nabal's heart and his miserly nature again appear in association later in the chapter.

As if all this unsubtle characterization were not enough to convince us of Nabal's viciousness, both his servants (v. 17) and his wife (v. 25) unashamedly describe him (although not to his face) as "a worthless man," "a good for nothing." All of this name-calling amounts to a kind of descriptive overkill, which, as we shall see, constitutes part of the narrator's peculiar artistry. His purposes do not allow ambivalence about the moral worth of his characters.

More subtle is the narrator's introduction of Nabal: "There was a man in Maon, whose business was in Carmel, and the man was very important, owning three thousand sheep and one thousand goats"* (v. 2). It is significant that Nabal's property is described before he is; he is introduced in terms of his possessions. The difference between the person and his holdings is further underscored by David's initial message: "Thus shall you say to my brother: 'Prosperity to you, prosperity to your household, and prosperity to all that you own'"* (v. 6). Thematically, this touch is quite revealing, for I Samuel 25 is the story of how this fool and his property came to be parted. It is precisely Nabal's attitude toward his holdings which destroys the potential for the *šālôm* with David that the latter seeks. Nabal's refusal to give causes his loss, even the loss of his life. The introduction of Nabal the great rancher and the characterization of him immediately as "harsh and evil in deeds" prepare us artfully for his rash reply to David's tidings of peace, a reply that triggers the action of the tale.

Nabal's response lacks the polish and restraint that characterize David's message:

Nabal answered the servants of David: "Who is this 'David,' and who is this 'Ben-Jesse'? Nowadays, many are the slaves who break away from their masters! And am I to take my bread and my wine and the meat I have prepared for my shearers and give it to men from I know not where?"* (vv. 10-11)

These verses are more an outburst than a speech, as we expect from the type of person of whom it is said:

> Fine talk does not become a fool *(nābāl),*
> Nor a lying tongue, the noble person.* (Prov. 17:7)

The reply of Nabal is intended to insult David, whose men, after all, did include "any man in distress, any who had a creditor, and any who was of a bitter disposition"* (I Sam. 22:2). In speaking with David's men, Nabal is hardly a diplomat! More painful to their leader is the probable reference to David's flight from the court of Saul, described elsewhere as his "lord" (II Sam. 12:8). In short, Nabal declares from the start his refusal to see in David anything other than a brigand. David offers a courtly greeting, but

Nabal answers not with courtesy, but with an insult fit for delivery to a terrorist. Nabal, unlike his wife, does not sense in David a future king, but only a brigand, perhaps because he is blind to the traces of native nobility that Abigail sees so clearly. Nabal's rejection of David, however, is immensely ironic, for he is about to find *himself* in the role of a master whose slaves break away, telling their mistress of her husband's stupidity and ethical vacuity. This defection is doubly ironic, since it is precisely concern for his staff which Nabal cites as his reason for his refusal to honor David's demand. We sense here a man who is either dangerously out of touch with his own workers or a deliberate liar, who seeks only to cover his callousness and greed with a mantle of humanitarian motivation. Probably the narrator intends us to believe that Nabal is both—out of touch and a liar.

One fine point of diction brings out this element of autocratic arrogance in Nabal. When David's men are mentioned in connection with their leader, they are termed "boys, servants"* (vv. 5, 9, 12), or "men"* (v. 13); but when the focus is on Nabal, they are termed "slaves"* (v. 10, twice). The point is clear: David is a leader, whereas Nabal is a slave-owner, a man with no personal feelings toward social inferiors, who are, to him, chattels. In this connection, it is surely no coincidence that of the three major figures in the drama, the two others, Abigail and David, pointedly refer to themselves as "slaves" to someone, Abigail to David (vv. 23-31; see esp. v. 41), and David to God (v. 39). Nabal, like the fool who says in his heart, "There is no God"* (Ps. 14:1; 53:1), is no one's slave.

When we next see Nabal, he is indulging himself in a lavish banquet, in which he becomes so drunk[3] that he is unapproachable till the next morning. The irony is again pointed. First, Nabal apparently never misses his wife; he goes into shock or has a heart attack (v. 37) when he later finds out why she was gone. It is not simply that he is incapable of fine sentiment, such as that which dominates the moving exchange between Abigail and David during Nabal's debauched celebration. Rather, he is incapable of even the basic concerns of a man possessed of the requisite maturity for matrimony. When we learn what Nabal has been doing during his wife's touching rendezvous with David, we recognize what we have sensed subliminally all along, that he and

Abigail are irremediably mismatched, and, more ominously, we begin to feel that Nabal lacks the self-possession necessary to retain his clever spouse. He is neither a crafty villain nor even a pathetic misfit, neither a Iago nor an Othello. He has no tragic depth; he is only a despicable fool.

Alongside this negative revelation of Nabal's character through the banquet, of the absence in him of concern for and appreciation of his wife, lies a revelation of his positive crassness. The banquet after the shearing was traditional in Israel.[4] What was not traditional was to feast like a king while knowing that hungry and thirsty men (one of them a true king to be!) encamp nearby, men who believe that their protection of Nabal's flocks has earned them a claim in his provisions. Nabal will have to pay for this callous disregard of David in the same currency with which he pays for his failure to appreciate Abigail. That currency is the marriage, after Nabal's punishment through death, of the two people he has neglected. His character drives them into each other's arms. He cements their union.

Nabal does not survive his revealing celebration:

> Abigail returned to Nabal while he was having a feast fit for a king. His spirits were high, for he was very drunk. So she told him nothing, important or trivial, until dawn. And at dawn, when the wine was going out of Nabal, when his wife told him these things, his heart died within him and it turned to stone. About ten days later, God struck Nabal and he died.* (vv. 36-38)

It is as though the moral balance of the universe would become misaligned if Nabal were able to sink into such depths of gluttony and ego-gratification with impunity:

> At three things the earth shudders,
> Four it cannot tolerate:
> A slave who becomes king,
> A fool *(nābāl)* who gorges himself,
> A spurned woman who finally marries,
> And a slave-girl who displaces her mistress.* (Prov. 30:21-23)

Nabal's indulgence, like his lording over David and his marriage to Abigail, indicates a malfunction of the moral order which cannot be allowed to endure. Indeed, his behavior at the "feast fit for a king," during which his wife is secretly proclaiming herself a servant to the true king, David, is but the last indulgence before his fall. "Before calamity, pride," goes the proverbial wisdom, "and before ruin, high spirits"* (Prov. 16:18). The description of Nabal's actual death is an exquisite portrait of a villain's inability to stand the light of justice. The phrase, "when the wine was going out of Nabal," just three words in Hebrew, captures graphically the full measure of the man's materialism, his unsanctified corporeality. It is a pun as well, since the word *nebel* (or *nēbel*), which sounds like "Nabal," to which it is identical in written form, means "wineskin" or "jar." In short, the man is equated with his bladder. The account of his demise in two stages, first the death of his heart and then of himself, augments this effect by portraying a huge body, alive but subhuman, breathing but not feeling, not responding, a living being turned to stone for ten days. As the consonantal form of verse 2 indicates, "he is like his heart"—dead, spiritually dead even when physically alive. And what is the catastrophe that finally does him in? The loss of various perishables and exactly five sheep out of his three thousand. Nabal suffers a fatal stroke over a negligible loss. How the death fits the life!

The theme of a "heart of stone" was a familiar one in the culture of ancient Israel, and we modern readers must not allow ourselves to miss its connotations. In a vision of coming redemption, the prophet Ezekiel announces this promise in the name of God:

> I will give you a new heart,
> And a new spirit I will place within you.
> I will remove the heart of stone from your body,
> And I will give you a heart of flesh.* (Ezek. 36:26)

In the case of Nabal, of course, the direction of movement is the reverse. His heart turns to stone, and he lingers between death and life for ten days until the fatal blow from God. His manner of "living" (the author would dispute the term) is the antipode of redeemed existence, just as his destiny—one of loss and death—is the antipode of David's destiny of increasing wealth, power, and glory. This antithesis between niggardliness and death, on the one hand, and redemption and enhanced life, on the other, is reminiscent of the confrontation between Pharaoh and Moses. God hardens Pharoah's heart, too, so that he does not yield to Moses' pleas (Exod. 7:3). And Nabal's retort to David's plea—"who is this 'David,' and who is this 'Ben-Jesse'?"*—recalls strikingly Pharaoh's retort to Moses in Exodus 5:2: "Who is "YHWH" [God] that I should obey him and let Israel go? I don't know YHWH, and I won't let Israel go!"* In fact, Nabal sees in David only what Pharaoh saw in Israel—an uppity slave. The imagery is significant: in ancient Israel, the heart was considered to be the source of thinking. It is Pharaoh's refusal to think of God that ensures the hardening of his heart and ultimately his humiliation. For Pharaoh, like the churl in the tale of David and Abigail, is, in the last analysis, a fool:

> The fool *[nābāl]* has said in his heart,
> There is no God."* (Ps. 14:1; 53:1)

2. Abigail and the Ideal of Femininity

The characterization of Abigail, like that of her husband, begins in overtly evaluative language: "the woman was very intelligent and beautiful in appearance, but the man was harsh and evil in deeds."* The full significance of this contrast will not emerge until the eñnouement of the tale. To the listener acquainted with Israel's traditions, however, the contrast is most pregnant, for Abigail's qualities, intelligence and beauty, are precisely those of the man who the audience may already suspect will become her new husband:

Samuel said to Jesse, "Are these all the boys?" He answered, "The little one is left. He is tending the sheep." Samuel said to Jesse, "Send for him and bring him here. We won't sit down till he comes here." So he sent for him and brought him, and he was a red-head, with pretty eyes, and of good appearance . . .* (I Sam. 16:11-12)

Here, the physical appearance of the characters, in a fashion worthy of Hawthorne, bodies forth their underlying spiritual status. Abigail is as well matched with David as she is mismatched with Nabal. And if she is at all like everyone else with whom David has come in contact—Saul, Jonathan, Michal, and, indeed, all

Israel and Judah—the outcome of their chance meeting can only be passionate: "David came before Saul and stood in front of him, and Saul loved him greatly, and he became Saul's armor-bearer."[5]

The theme of the episode can already be intuited merely from the brief description of Abigail, which is as unambiguously laudatory as that of her husband is derogatory. The narrator has declared his sympathies at the outset and so painted his figures that we can only share them. Nonetheless, he does not rest content with an introduction that lacks subtlety; rather, he develops the action in such a way as to convince us that his initial evaluations of the protagonists were indeed apt.

The contrast in action with Nabal begins when Nabal's slaves, having heard their master's rash rejoinder to David's message, approach Abigail to remedy the abuse. We have already seen that their frank characterization of Nabal as "such a good-for-nothing that there is no use talking to him" discloses much about Nabal's rapport with his subordinates. Now we see them looking to Abigail with exactly the confidence which they despair of placing in her husband. Her relationship to the servants is much more like that of David to his men, one characterized by mutuality and solidarity. This comparison probably accounts for the arrangement of scenes in such a way that the servants' approach to Abigail follows without interruption David's reception of his spurned envoys: "David's servants turned and made their way back and came and told him all these things. David said to his men, 'Let each man buckle on his sword,' and each man did so. David also buckled on his sword"* (vv. 12-13). No armchair general he! And note the contrast with Nabal: When David hears "all these things," he manfully prepares for battle, but when Nabal hears from Abigail "these things," his heart turns to stone and he dies. He loses his courage, his wife, and his life.

The intelligence of Abigail, of which verse 3 notifies us, appears clearly in verse 19, when she, like Jacob about to confront the brother he wronged, sends gifts ahead. The difference is that the narrator here utilizes this notion in order to dismiss from the scene all whose presence might intrude upon the romantic dimension of her encounter with David. Note that nowhere in verses 23-35 are David's men mentioned. Instead, we witness a moving personal encounter behind the courtly language. Abigail's dismissal of her servants must be intended to heighten exactly this quality, for, as we see at the very end of her address, her goal is more than the safety of Nabal's household: she offers victuals to David's men; to David, she offers herself.

Her argument is a rhetorical masterpiece. She first disarms David by taking full blame for Nabal's irresponsibility ("upon me be the guilt," v. 24).[6] David has just sworn to annihilate all males (*maštîn běqîr*, "those who piss on a wall," v. 22)[7] in Nabal's household. But what is he to do to a woman, a beautiful one at that? Abigail, for her part, has to be careful neither to exculpate Nabal nor to appear disloyal to him. To deny her husband's guilt is to sink to his level, earning the undying enmity of David. To "call a spade a spade" is to break faith with her husband and thus to prove her unfitness for the wifely role. Of the ideal wife (*'ēšet-ḥayil*) of Israel's proverbs, one characteristic is that:

> She opens her mouth to speak with wisdom,
> Instruction in fidelity is on her tongue.* (Prov. 31:26)

In short, she must win David without betraying Nabal. Abigail devises the perfect solution to the dilemma: she intercedes on behalf of Nabal (v. 24), although conceding that he has no case and no hope of survival (vv. 25-26). In other words, while overtly defending him, she covertly dissociates herself from him, so that by the end of her address, only she appears as the potential beneficiary of David's change of heart: "When YHWH has made good his promises to my lord, may you remember your maid-servant"* (v. 31). It is also essential that Abigail neither appear to be bribing David, lest she injure the warrior's pride, nor come empty-handed, lest she seem to underestimate the man's resolve and the seriousness with which he takes the matter. She chooses her words carefully in order to navigate between the Scylla of insult and the Charybdis of levity. Whereas Jacob offers Esau *minḥâ,* "tribute," Abigail euphemistically offers David a *běrākâ,*[8] "a blessing," which she asks "be given to the boys who march under my lord's command"* (v. 27). Far be it from David to take protection money for himself!

Her eloquent plea to David is structured in two tiers. First, Abigail assures David that the vengeance of YHWH will visit

Nabal if only David restrains himself from usurping the divine prerogative, and she offers the present as a token of her confidence in the rightness of David's cause. Next she speaks of God's commitment to his chosen servant, one that vouchsafes to him a security that should enable him to overlook this temporary irritation, which must in no case impede David's ascent to the throne. The overall direction of her speech is thus one that moves from a bribe of sorts to a gracious gift, from vengeance to promise, from Nabal to David's secure dynasty, from the momentary to the eternal. She thus lifts simultaneously David's sights and the reader's awareness of the providential destiny imperiled in this brief episode. In each of the two tiers, the less and the more sublime, she smuggles in a personal note too brief for her to be accused of self-service, but unmistakable in intent: "I myself did not see my lord's men whom you sent,"* (v. 25); "when YHWH has made good his promises to my lord, may you remember your maidservant"* (v. 31). These two sentences lend the effect of an *inclusio:* Abigail begins and ends with a statement about herself, especially in relation to David. But whereas the David of verse 25 is the leader of a band of guerrillas, the David of verse 31 is God's anointed king.

In marked contrast to Nabal, Abigail recognizes David's coming kingship. She is the first person in the Bible to say that David will be chosen *nāgîd 'al yiśrā'ēl,* "ruler over Israel"* (v. 30).[9] Her assertion that YHWH will build David a *bayit ne'ĕmān,* "a secure dynasty" (v. 28), is an undeniable adumbration of Nathan's prophecy in I Samuel 7:16, which utilizes the identical language. It is this element which led the rabbis of talmudic times, according to the medieval commentator Rabbi David Qimchi, to count Abigail among the seven women who they believed had been graced by the holy spirit, the source of prophecy. There is no question that this theme of the "secure dynasty" of David became central in the books of Kings, where it serves to ground the hope of an afflicted kingdom.[10] The author, however, does not mean to present Abigail as literally a prophetess. He does mean her to be a woman of providence, a person who in this case from intelligence (*śekel,* v. 3), rather than from special revelation, sense the drift of history. Endowed with the highly valued initiative and efficiency of the ideal woman of proverbial wisdom, Abigail rides the crest of the providential wave into personal success. This is her lasting merit:

> Charm is a delusion and beauty fleeting;
> It is the woman who fears God that is to be praised.
> Give her of the fruit of her labors,
> And let her deeds praise her in the city-gate.* (Prov. 31:30-31)

The sphere of action of a woman in biblical times was severely restricted. The offices of king and priest were male prerogatives, and only a handful of women are recorded as having functioned as prophets. None has left us an anthology of her oracles. Nonetheless, in narrative, women seem often to play a central, even the central role, a circumstance that one would not expect on the basis of their legal status. We need think only of Eve, Sarah, Hagar, Rebecca, Rachel, Deborah, Ruth, Naomi, Hannah, Bathsheba, Jezebel, and Esther to realize that the subordination of woman in Israel did not mean her insignificance. What it did mean is that she had to affect things not through the realm of public life, but from behind the scenes, through manipulation of those enfranchised to act, the men. In some cases, her means of manipulation were nonverbal, as in the cases of the daughters of Lot, who got their father drunk, or of Esther, who employed her physical beauty, together with cunning speech, to benefit the Jews. For the most part, however, a woman's weapon was her tongue. She manipulated the man in her life, usually her husband, through skillful speech. Now in some cases, the influence of woman over man leads to death, as in the case of Eve and the forbidden fruit; or of Bathsheba, whose clever persuasion of her senile husband ultimately brought about the deaths of Joab, Shimei, and Adonijah, and the exile of the high priest Abiathar; or of Jezebel, who employed her sharp tongue against her submissive husband, Ahab, to have the innocent farmer Naboth executed (Gen. 2:25–3:24; I Kings 1–2:21). In other instances, however, a woman utilizes her verbal and, in some cases, physical gifts for the sake not of death, but of life. One thinks, for example, of Ruth, whose charm and persuasion, much of it suggested by Naomi, change a situation of famine and death into one of plenty and birth, or of the wise woman of Tekoa, whose rhetorical skill saves the life of

Absalom in II Samuel 14. It is in this latter category that Abigail falls. Only her speech saves David from bloodguilt and, therefore, forfeiture of the throne. She disarms the warrior whom her powerful husband could not handle. Again, of the ideal woman, the book of Proverbs (31:11-12) remarks:

> Her husband's whole trust is in her,
> Rich fare is not wanting.
> She repays him with good, not evil,
> All the days of her life,*

3. I Samuel 25 and the Craft of the Hebrew Narrator

Before we leave analysis of the literary artistry within I Samuel 25 to speak of its place in the larger framework of the books of Samuel, we must offer correction to some of the regnant generalizations about the nature of Israelite prose narrative, as our investigation shows many of them to be flawed. The most influential discussion has been the brilliant first chapter of Erich Auerbach's *Mimesis,* in which the narrative methods of Homer and the Hebrew Bible are presented as antithetical types:

It would be difficult, then, to imagine styles more contrasted than those of these two equally ancient and equally epic texts. On the one hand, externalized, uniformly illuminated phenomena, at a definite time and in a definite place, connected together without lacunae in a perpetual foreground; thoughts and feelings completely expressed; events taking place in a leisurely fashion and with very little of suspense. On the other hand, the externalization of only so much of the phenomena as is necessary for the purpose of the narrative, all else left in obscurity; the decisive points of the narrative alone are emphasized; what lies between is non-existent; time and place are undefined and call for interpretation; thoughts and feelings remain unexpressed, are only suggested by the silence and the fragmentary speeches; the whole, permeated with the most unrelieved suspense and directed toward a single goal (and to that extent far more of a unity), remains mysterious and "fraught with background."[11]

The generality of Auerbach's observations comes in for censure in an article by Robert Alter:

An arresting starkness of foreground, an enormous height of background, are beautifully illustrated in the story of the Binding of Isaac which

Auerbach analyzes, but those terms would have to be seriously modified for the psychologically complex cycle of stories about David . . . where, in fact, there is a high degree of specification in the foreground of artifacts, costume, court customs, and the like.[12]

Alter is quite right to observe that Auerbach's conclusion is colored by the restriction of the scope of his investigation to the Binding of Isaac. In fact, that story is remarkable among biblical narratives precisely because of its disproportionate degree of internalization, its timeless, colorless backdrop, its suppression of feeling in a speechless drama. These characteristics are inextricably associated with the austerity of its theological theme, the unconditioned, unquestioning, and undivided obedience of the man of faith to his God. One could retort that Genesis 22 is a distillation of the quintessential Hebraic spirit. But even if this claim is valid, that chapter does not therefore become representative of Israelite storytelling. In stories with a different theme, we expect a different narrative technique.

It is a far cry from the Binding of Isaac in Genesis 22 to the episode of I Samuel 25. As we have seen, two of the three major figures in the latter tale can be viewed, in part, as personifications of certain character types common in Israelite Wisdom literature, especially the book of Proverbs. One of them even bears as his personal name the designation of such a type. In this little tale, we are close to the world of moral allegory, of which perhaps the best example is Bunyan's *Pilgrim's Progress,* with its figures with names like "Obstinate," "Pliable," and "Christian." It is essential to this genre that the author declare his purposes early. Allegory fails if who represents what is less than transparent. Ambiguity destroys the intended moral function of the genre. Because the events refer to a realm of ideas outside themselves, the action alone, without comment, cannot tell the story, as they can and do in the test of Abraham. The author (or redactor) of the moral allegory must editorialize, whether in his own voice or through the voice of his cast. If he only editorializes, however, he ends up with a sermon, not a narrative. The *desideratum,* then, is a story in which the author both defines his characters and lets the action and speeches prove his definition correct, in which the narrative bodies forth and bears out the author's moral vision. He must declare his sympathies openly and then win us subtly for his point of view. It is this goal which the characterization we discussed in sections 2 and 3 serves. In the case of Nabal, the author defines him in his own voice through his name, his gentilic *(kālibbî),* and through the remark that he was "harsh and evil in deeds." But the narrator does not rest content with attacking foolishness in his own voice. Instead, he characterizes Nabal in the voice of both his slaves and his wife, who term him a *ben/îš (hab) bĕlîya'al,* a "good-for-nothing." Most important, the action of the tale itself proves the correctness of this insult when Nabal dismisses David's messengers, mistakes the future king for a fugitive slave, indulges in a drunken banquet, suffers a stroke upon the loss of five sheep, and dies unmourned. In the case of Abigail, the author first defines her himself as "very intelligent and beautiful in appearance." Then he speaks to the same effect through the voice of David, who offers "a blessing on your good sense and a blessing on you" (v. 33).[13] Last, the author proves his characterization correct, as we have seen, in virtually everything Abigail says and does throughout the tale. She makes amends for her husband's crassness, senses David's coming kingship, dissuades the proud warrior from vengeance, and ends up as his wife. First Samuel 25 is thus different from the stark, silent world of Genesis 22 and from the sensuous, powerfully visual world of the Homeric epics. Like the former, it has no concern with external detail, nothing like a "wine-dark sea" or a "rosy-fingered dawn." But like the Homeric poems and unlike Genesis 22, it is dominated by revealing discourse and polished speeches, almost grandiloquent in style. Clearly, Auerbach's dichotomy cannot yield any profound insight into the narrative artistry of I Samuel 25; it only spotlights the need for greater literary sophistication and sensitivity on the part of students of the Hebrew Bible.

4. *The Episode of Nabal and Abigail as Narrative Analogy*

In his study of the Hebrew Bible as literature, Robert Alter draws attention to "the repeated use of narrative analogy, through which one part of the text provides oblique commentary on another."[14] In consideration of any narrative unit, the critic must broaden his horizon beyond the passage in front of him to ask why the unit is placed where it is and whether other units in the text as we have it comment upon it, implicitly or otherwise. It is not hard to see why I Samuel 25 is spliced between the two variants of the tradition of David's sparing of Saul's life. In each case, David perceives a powerful advantage in killing, but is restrained by a theological consideration. In chapters 24 and 26, that consideration is the foulness of slaying "God's anointed"; in chapter 25, it is, in Abigail's words, that "when God has appointed you ruler over Israel, it should not be a cause for you to stumble or to lose your courage that you shed blood without cause." To be sure, in David's mind and Abigail's too, the death of Nabal would hardly be an example of his shedding innocent blood; similarly, Saul's death in I Samuel 27:1 could be justified by a plea of self-defense. Rather, the point is that, regardless of the ethical situation, a king is neither to slay nor to be slain.[15] The difference between I Samuel 25 and its neighbors is that in the latter, David seeks out Saul solely in order to demonstrate his good will, whereas in our tale, only the rhetorical genius of Abigail saves him from bloodying his hands. In short, the David of chapters 24 and 26 is the character we have been seeing since his introduction in chapter 16 and whom we shall continue to see until II Samuel 11. He is the appealing young man of immaculate motivation and heroic courage. But the David of chapter 25 is a man who kills for a grudge. The episode of Nabal is the very first revelation of evil in David's character. He can kill in cold blood. This time he stops short. But the cloud that chapter 25 raises will continue to darken our perception of David's character.

Just as Abigail feared, David's shedding of innocent blood was to be his downfall. The David whom we glimpsed ominously but momentarily in I Samuel 25 dominates the pivotal episode of Bathsheba and Uriah, in which David contrives the death of a faithful warrior to seize his gorgeous bride (II Samuel 11–12). As a consequence, in the prophet Nathan's words: "Now your family will have no rest from the sword ever because you spurned me by taking Uriah the Hittite's wife as your own wife"* (II Sam. 12:10). The crime that David (without knowing that he was speaking of himself) said must be expiated fourfold will result in the deaths of four of his sons, the nameless offspring of the adulterous union, then Amnon, Absalom, and Adonijah, successively. The episode of Uriah and Bathsheba is David's peripeteia. His reign after it becomes one of incessant rebellion. He dies with execution orders on his lips.

For our purposes, the relevance of this pivotal episode lies in the fact that there is just enough similarity between it and the Nabal narrative that one cannot read one without recalling the other. In both cases and in them alone, David moves to kill a man and to marry his wife. In the instance of Nabal, as the storyteller would have it, Abigail's persuasiveness and an act of God frustrate the murder and legitimize the marriage. With Uriah, such luck is not to be David's. First Samuel 25 is a proleptic glimpse, within the context of David's ascent, of his fall from grace. In the story of Abigail, a beautiful woman's wisdom preserves David's fitness for royalty; in the case of Bathsheba, a woman's beauty brings about the decline and fall of a king secure in his throne to the point of arrogance. There is in the symmetry of these two situations, one of the future king ascending and one of the established king in decline, an implied critique of kingship. So long as David may yet be denied the throne God has designated for him, he values a woman's wisdom above her beauty and retains his innocence. Once his throne is not in doubt and his "secure dynasty" has been affirmed by the mouth of a prophet as an eternal grant of God (II Sam. 7:16), then he yields to a woman's beauty in spite of wisdom, and, although his dynasty will endure, his family life becomes a shambles. "At the turn of the year, the season when kings go out to battle," David becomes an armchair general: he sends others to fight while he stays in Jerusalem and devises his fatal tryst.

The history of rebellion which is the bitter fruit of David's fall also finds an anticipation in I Samuel 25. Recall Nabal's response to David's envoys: "Who is this 'David' and who is this 'Ben-Jesse'? Nowadays many are the slaves who break away from their masters!"* (v. 10). This particular contemptuous dismissal of David sounds very much like the battlecry of the rebel, Sheba Ben-Bichri: "There happened to be a good-for-nothing *[îš bĕlîyaʿal]* there whose name was Sheba Ben Bichri, a Benjaminite. He blew on the shofar and cried out, 'We have no share in David, We have no lot in Ben-Jesse. Away to your tents, O Israel!'"* (II Sam. 20:1). It is hard to imagine an Israelite's hearing the rejection of David on the lips of the one *'îš bĕlîyaʿal* (Nabal, v. 25) without thinking of the latter, more consequential cry of the other (Sheba).

Here, again, the tale of David and Abigail plants an ominous seed, which sprouts in the doomed rebellion of Sheba but matures in the days of David's grandson Rehoboam, when the northern tribes raise the identical cry, with a momentous effect on David's "secure dynasty" (I Kings 12:16-17). Only within this broad historical perspective can we appreciate the tragic poignance of Abigail's prayer that "all the enemies who seek to harm my lord may be like Nabal." The old folktale of the handsome prince who rescues the beautiful lady from the ogre to whom she is married has been redone so as to constitute a critical link in the story of David and in the tragic history of the Israelite monarchy.

II. The Historical Events Behind the Tale

We have seen that the tale of David, Nabal, and Abigail is related with a subtle, consummate artistry. For some purposes, a literary analysis such as that we have provided in section 1 is all that a proper study of the episode requires. For the student of literature, this may be the case. But, for the historian, this kind of analysis is only the first step in the mastery of the text. For after the aesthetics of the passage are disclosed and analyzed and their effect on our reading of it is savored, it remains to be determined what the historical raw materials were upon which the artist's genius worked. The Hebrew Bible, after all, makes a claim to historicity, a claim that the pure literarian devoted to a close reading of his texts is inclined to put aside. The fact is, however, that for the biblical scholar, a point arrives at which the artistry ceases to be the goal of our endeavor and becomes an obstacle in the way of our recovery of the historical meaning of the passage. To be sure, the concept of historical fact, "what really happened," is problematic in any historical inquiry, and all the more so when, as in biblical history, the evidence is so scanty and the literature so tendentious that we are reduced to hypothesis. In the passage under consideration, the obstacles posed by the received form of the text are formidable, for, as William McKane remarks, the narrative is told through a kind of "theological filter,"[16] which can obscure the sociopolitical significance of the events. We need not subscribe to simplistic positivism, however, to believe that it is possible to provide an educated speculation that enables us to recover the facts in spite of the filter.

One event that seems to be historical fact rather than aesthetic or theological invention is David's marriage to Abigail, since a wife of David's by that name is referred to elsewhere.[17] The only historically momentous reference is this one:

> After this, David inquired of God, "Should I go up to one of the cities of Judah?" God answered, "Go up!" David asked, "To which one should I go up?" And he answered, "To Hebron." David went up there, together with his two wives, Ahinoam the Jezreelite and Abigail, the wife of Nabal the Carmelite. The men who had joined him David also brought up, with their households, and they settled in the towns around Hebron. The men of Judah came and anointed David there as king over the House of Judah."*[18] (II Sam. 2:1-4a)

There are several very curious aspects to this brief notice of David's assumption of kingship at Hebron. For one thing, the text is tantalizingly cryptic. We are told nothing about how David the brigand came to be seen as a royal figure, the successor, it would seem, to King Saul. Nor do we hear any explanation of how a non-Calebite like David managed to assume kingship at the capital of the Calebite patrimony, Hebron. One would have expected some resistance to David's falling heir to the Calebite grant, which figures so prominently in the history of that region.[19] Finally, it is strange that the passage takes explicit but apparently superfluous note of David's wives. Why is their presence important? This last oddity includes the curious point that Abigail is described as "the wife of Nabal the Carmelite," as if her past marital history, far from being something the Davidic historian would want to forget, were actually somehow pertinent to the present situation. But how?

All three aspects can be explained under one assumption, that David's marriage to Nabal's wife was the pivotal move in his ascent to kingship at Hebron. If this assumption is correct, then David's anointing is no longer so discontinuous with the material before it. On the contrary, it follows quite unremarkably upon I Samuel 25, especially once Saul has perished. Furthermore, if David is the successor to Nabal the Calebite and the husband of a prominent

Calebite lady, then his acceptance in Hebron and the reference to Abigail as the wife of Nabal are no longer extraordinary.

The notion that marriage could play a critical role in a man's ascent to kingship in Israel is well known. As Matitiahu Tsevat observes, "the early history of the Israelite kingdom affords several examples of the fact that the marriage of a former king's wife bestows legitimacy on an aspirant who otherwise has no sufficient claim on the throne.[20] The two clearest examples occur within David's immediate family. Absalom, on Ahitophel's advice, has intercourse with David's concubines as part of his effort to wrest the throne for himself; and Adonijah asks for the hand of Abishag, David's last mistress, to which Solomon, with characteristic discernment, replies, "You might as well ask for the whole kingdom!"* (II Sam. 16:20-23; I Kings 2:13-25). Less explicit, but still probably relevant, is Abner's acquisition of Rizpah, one of Saul's concubines, in II Samuel 3:6-10, a move that causes Saul's son and heir Ishbaal to suspect Abner's loyalty to the House of Saul. Nor is the underlying notion unique to Israel. Tsevat finds a reflex of it at Ugarit, a Bronze Age site on the Syrian coast, and Roland de Vaux finds it still alive in Persia in the sixth century B.C.E.[21]

If this practice is pertinent to David's marriage to Abigail, then the man whose name has been altered to "Nabal" must have been a very powerful figure in the Calebite clan of his day. If his three thousand sheep and one thousand goats are not a gross exaggeration, then it was perfectly true that his feast was "fit for a king," for he must have been at the pinnacle of economic status. Nehemiah is said to have fed one hundred fifty Jews and an unspecified number of Gentiles on one ox, six sheep, and some fowl every day. Solomon is reported to have provisioned his immense court daily with twenty oxen and one hundred sheep as well as other animals of unspecified number (Neh. 5:17-18; I Kings 5:3). James Montgomery considered the "shrewdest estimate" for the number of people Solomon fed to be from four thousand to five thousand.[22] If these figures are even remotely accurate, Nabal alone could have supplied Solomon's daily ration of sheep for a month! Note, too, that Abigail has, while in his court, no fewer than five ladies-in-waiting (v. 42). Obviously, Nabal was no commoner. I suspect that he was the chief *(rōʼš bêt ʼāb* or *nāśîʼ)* of the Calebite clan, a status to which David laid claim through his marriage to Nabal's lady. It may well be that David picked a quarrel with Nabal with precisely such a matrimony in mind. In this connection, it is interesting that alongside the familiar genealogy of David, which makes the Calebites distant cousins of David and his clan, there exists another genealogy, also in Chronicles, which makes the Davidic family (in fact, all of Bethlehem) *descendants* of Caleb.[23] In short, David came to be seen as the heir of Caleb and the latter's patrimony of Hebron. The most likely hypothesis is that David's marriage to Abigail served as a kind of legal fiction by which he became grafted into the Calebite bloodline. The new political reality came to be expressed, as is often the case, by a new genealogy,[24] that of the House of David, heirs of the Calebites, and thus of Hebron.

A test case of our hypothesis about the historical significance of the marriage of David and Abigail is the identity of Ahinoam the Jezreelite, who is mentioned together with Abigail in the account of David's procession into Hebron. We should be able to find an equally distinguished identity for her. Of course, it is quite conceivable that we have lost the account of her past. Or have we? Only one other person in the Hebrew Bible bears her name, and she *mirabile dictu,* is a contemporary of David's. In fact, her husband is King Saul! (In I Sam. 14:50.) Could it be that David swaggered into Hebron with the wife of a Calebite chieftain on one arm and that of the Israelite king on the other? A remark of Nathan's to David suggests that there was but one Ahinoam, wife of Saul, then of David: "I gave you the household of your lord and the wives of your lord in your bosom, and I gave you the House of Israel and Judah. A little more, and I would have given you more like these"* (II Sam. 12:8). Nathan alludes to David's marriage to Saul's wives[25] as if it were well known. When could the marriage to Ahinoam have taken place? Note that Ahinoam is always mentioned before Abigail and that she bears David a son before Abigail does.[26] The likelihood is, therefore, that she was already wed to David when the conflict with Nabal erupted.[27] If so, David had already laid claim to Saul's throne while the latter was still alive. In fact, the chronology of II Samuel 2:10-11 corroborates this nicely, since it attributes a reign of two years to Saul's own son and successor Ishbaal and one of seven and one-half years to

David at Hebron. This suggests that David may have been King of Judah for five and a half years while Saul ruled the remainder of the tribes.[28] In that case, the end of I Samuel 25 should be translated: "David had married Ahinoam of Jezreel, so that the two became his wives. But Saul gave his daughter Michal, who had belonged to David, to Palti, son of Laish, from Gallim"* (vv. 43-44). The suspicion grows that verse 43 and verse 44 are connected by more than a similarity in subject matter. Saul's action in verse 44 is a *quid pro quo* to David's in verse 43. He deprived David of Michal when David asserted his right to the throne through marriage to Queen Ahinoam. Thus, if Saul was paranoid, as I Samuel asserts, the likelihood remains that David was out to get him, to claim his women and thus his throne and to become the King of Israel and Judah, as indeed he did. Saul's pursuit of David, if this speculation holds, was an instance of realism and not psychosis. Temporarily stymied in the north, David had moved into his home country of Judah, and, upon the opportune demise of Nabal, the Calebite chief, he successfully appropriated the latter's wife and office and parlayed the advantage into kingship in Judah and eventually in all Israel. The charming tale of the handsome warrior and the beautiful, clever lady masks a political struggle with the greatest consequences.

15. THE SONG OF SONGS

Kenneth R. R. Gros Louis

The history of criticism on the Song of Songs presents two major obstacles to an understanding of the poems as literature. The first of these is found in the numerous allegorical interpretations that explain that the Song uses the imagery and language of secular, profane love to depict the sacred and divine love between God and Israel, or between Christ and his church, or between Christ and the individual soul. The various extensions, by-products, and offshoots of these interpretations complicate matters, and it is overwhelming to discover that by the end of the seventeenth century over five hundred allegorical interpretations of the Song have been written, one of them over fifteen hundred pages in length devoted to explicating verses one and two. These interpretations, largely theological in nature, present problems for the student of literature because they depend on complex cross references and allusions to other Old Testament passages.

The second obstacle is presented by those commentators and critics from the late eighteenth century to the present who vigorously reject these allegorical presentations and take us instead into ancient fertility rites, into marriage rituals, and into passionate, honest, sexual love between a man and a woman. Although the interpretations of these latter-day secularists initially seem to provide a more familiar footing, the many disagreements among them soon remove any sense of comfort and leave us with a new uneasiness. Not only do they debate whether the Song is a series of unrelated lyrics or a structured mini-drama—and there are of course extensions, by-products, and offshoots of these theories as well—but they also cannot seem to agree on who is speaking, or when, or to whom. Some editors, for example, assign the comparison of a lover to a mare of Pharaoh's chariot in 1:9 to the woman, some assign it to the king, and some to a shepherd youth. Similar disagreements exist concerning the identity of the speaker who describes Solomon's procession, of the one who praises the woman's beauty in chapters 4 and 7, of those who have a little sister with no breasts, and of the speakers of numerous other verses and passages.

Each edition or anthology supplies a somewhat different Song of Songs. And always, somewhere in our minds, are those hundreds of allegorizations of the poems. Unfortunately, the complexities offered by the variety of interpretations and by their number will not serve to attract students to the literary value of the Song of Songs or supply them with an appreciation of the lyrics. As with other narratives of the Bible and other poems, our primary interest is in the Song as as literature, and we should ask of it the same questions we ask of any poetry. One question to the reader is the basic one of the purpose of the work. If the Song is a series of lyrics sketching a dramatic situation, the answer will come from an understanding of the author's process of selection. A poet has hundreds of options in selecting a particular image or a particular metaphor; yet the process of selection in a work of art will determine what that work of art will say about its subject. Through the careful selection and structuring of images, metaphors, and motifs, the author of the Song has created a unique expression on the subject of love. The movement and weaving of the central images creates a world with dynamics of its own, a world in which a particular dramatic situation unfolds.

The strong images suggest to the reader the world in which the characters live and reveal this world as it is experienced through the eyes and minds of these characters. The reader sees a young woman at court being stared at by the courtly ladies as an object and as an unusual presence, defending her own values in life and her vision of love. The reader pictures, through the voice (or thoughts) of the young maiden, a man bounding over hills and mountains, gazing in through the lattice, whispering to her that it is spring, urging her to come back to the country with him. The reader experiences the longing of the young woman as she twice wanders through the streets and squares of the city in search of her beloved. The reader witnesses the brilliant procession of Solomon, at first only a column of smoke seen in the dust-filled distance, and, gradually, as it gets nearer, becoming the spectacle of sixty mighty warriors and a dazzlingly wrought litter made from the cedars of Lebanon. The reader, by listening to earnest exchanges of love, enters the world of the young man who describes his beloved in natural and living images from his world, comparing her hair to a flock of goats moving down the slopes. The reader's imagination is present in the central scene when in the woman's dream there is a knocking at the door, a hesitation, an empty door frame. And the reader hears that pledge given in love's name and that invitation to go forth into the fields and into the villages.

The world presented in the lyrics comes to life in a way that arouses all our senses. It is a world flowing with liquids: wine and oils, nectar, honey, milk, dew, and water. It is a world that is heavily scented, with trees and spices, flowers and perfumes, cedars and pines, with myrrh and frankincense, henna blossoms, roses and lilies, and aromatic roots. It is a world offering raisins, apples, grapes, figs, and pomegranates for the tastes. It is filled with the sounds of animals, of flocks, of kids and goats, of ewes and fawns, lions and leopards, gazelles and stags, of doves and foxes. It is bright with the colors of fruits, trees, and flowers, with a green couch, a purple seat, a scarlet thread, a man with raven black hair. It is a world filled with jewels; gold, silver, glistening sapphires.

These carefully selected images, which suggest worlds of experience and visions of life, are elements of the dynamic that produces the dramatic movement of the lyrics. The movement is also propelled by tensions within and between the characters. Given the short length of the Song and its subject, love, it is surprising that so much tension is developed. It is expressed through the questions that are asked, more than a dozen, through requests that are made, through expressions of hope, frustration, and longing—"draw me after you," "do not gaze at me," "tell me . . . where you pasture your flock," "sustain me . . . refresh me," "arise, my love . . . come away," "I sought him . . . I called him," "come with me from Lebanon . . . depart from the peak of Amana," "open to me, my sister, my love," "return, O Shulammite . . . that we may look upon you," "come, let us go forth into the field," "O that his left hand were under my head, and that his right hand embraced me!" "My companions are listening for your voice; let me hear it. Make haste, my beloved." These requests, most of them imperatives, and the hopes they express, indicate that important decisions are being made, decisions that will affect the course of human lives. They involve choice, commitment, even some danger and pain. There are moments of joyous revelation in the lyrics—"behold, you are beautiful," "behold, he comes," "behold, there he stands," "I found him . . . I held him, and would not let him go," "behold, it is the litter of Solomon." But such moments of joy are balanced by somber and puzzling tensions and warnings—"let us make haste," "I am sick with love," "I adjure you . . . that you stir not up nor awaken love until it please," "the little foxes . . . spoil the vineyards," "the watchmen found me . . . they beat me, they wounded me," "if a man offered for love all the wealth of his house it would be utterly scorned," "My vineyard, my very own, is for myself."

The opening chapter of the Song reveals the tensions and the characters involved in this dramatic situation. "O that you would kiss me with the kisses of your mouth!" the series of lyrics begins. "Draw me after you, let us make haste. The king has brought me into his chambers. We will exult and rejoice in you." Through the pronouns a constellation of characters begins to emerge. The speaker, a woman, has been brought into the king's chambers where a group of people, the "we," prepare a welcome. It is unlikely that the woman is speaking to the king, since it would be unusual to refer to the same person as "you" and "the king" in consecutive lines.

The tension begins in the opening verses, within the mind of the woman. The reader, beginning to discover her past life and her present predicament, wonders why it is necessary for her to make haste if she is already in the king's chamber, whether it is haste to get away from someone and someplace. In fact, the expression of distress centers on her presence in the king's chambers: "Draw me after you, let us make haste. The king has brought me into his chambers." Next she turns to the courtly women, who welcome

her with exultant rejoicing and extol her love more than wine; but
for the maiden they are a source of distress. She says to the court,
"I am very dark, but comely, O daughters of Jerusalem. . . . Do
not gaze at me because I am swarthy, because the sun has scorched
me." The courtly women find her unusual, strange, foreign,
tanned deeper than any woman who is from the court, and they
stare at her. She explains why she is scorched: "My mother's sons
were angry with me, they made me keeper of the vineyards." The
young woman, referring to her past life before she was brought to
the court by the king, seems indeed to be from the country. The
tensions within the mind of this country maiden and the tensions
between her and the courtly environment now become manifest in
the unfolding of her visions and in the murmurs of voices that
emanate from her mind and that echo in her memory.

The tension that arises from her thoughts of the country is
sustained throughout the lyrics. The other great tension within the
woman is the tension of her love. "But, my own vineyard I have
not kept!" she begins, in a metaphorical expression of the fact that
she had fallen in love and opened her life to another. In her heart
she immediately speaks to this beloved, "Tell me, you whom my
soul loves, where you pasture your flock, where you make it lie
down at noon; for why should I be like one who wanders beside the
flocks of your companions?" And to her heart the voice of her
beloved answers. "If you," the voice tells her, "do not know, O
fairest among women, follow in the tracks of the flock, and pasture
your kids beside the shepherds' tents." The voice inside her
reminds her that she should know the answers to her questions, for
she too is from the country.

The lover whom she seeks pastures his flocks and lives in a
shepherd's tent, a world away from the court and the king. The
young woman is recalled to her presence at court, however, by the
voice of the king, who speaks in a manner much different from that
of her beloved's voice. "I," the king begins, "compare you, my
love, to a mare of Pharaoh's chariots. Your cheeks are comely with
ornaments, your neck with strings of jewels. We will make you
ornaments of gold, studded with silver." The speaker here comes
from a world where mares, trained and harnassed, proudly
precede the great man's chariot. This world, a world of ornaments,
jewels, gold, and silver, is not the world of the shepherd youth or

the country maiden. From these poles, the court and the country, the king and the country lover, arise the tensions in the lyrical expressions of the young woman, and these tensions mount as the two worlds are developed in the Song.

While the king reclines on his regal couch in his chambers, speaking to her of jewels and precious metals crafted into sublime ornaments by courtly artisans, the mind of the maiden wanders beside the flocks where she has told herself she belongs, wanders to him whom her soul loves. And she thinks now of a different kind of ornamentation and of a different couch and of something very different than royal chambers: "While the king was on his couch, my nard gave forth its fragrance. My beloved is to me a bag of myrrh, that lies between my breasts. My beloved is to me a cluster of henna blossoms in the vineyards of En-gedi." Her lover's voice now continues, "Behold, you are beautiful, my love; behold, you are beautiful; your eyes are doves. . . . Our couch is green, the beams of our house are cedar, our rafters are pine." This opposition of the natural world outside—the couch of green, the house of cedar—and the courtly world within the king's chambers—the regal couch, the rafted ceiling—establishes the dramatic impulse that will move through the remainder of the lyrics.

Within the mind of the young woman a counterpoint is created from her visions of the worlds and the characters she sees and out of the voices that speak to her, beckon her, and praise her. She is in a situation where she is bound to her king but is also bound to her love, and the manner in which the two men are portrayed reveals her vision of their worlds and the nature of their characters. She envisions, for example, the approach both of her beloved and her king. "Behold, he comes" she says of her beloved in 2:8, "leaping upon the mountains, bounding over the hills. My beloved is like a gazelle, or a young stag." This hyperbolic expression of great longing displays her sense of him as a force of nature, and the description stands in striking contrast to the king lying on his couch in his chambers. A gazelle and a stag represent swift and free animals of the countryside, not harnessed and trained creatures such as the courtly mares of Pharaoh's chariots.

The approach of the king to the city in chapter 3 offers a markedly different portrait from the coming of the country lover to the woman; each detail of the king's approach seems to oppose the image she has of her lover. She recalls a column of smoke in the distance, the dust caused by the mass of people coming with Solomon. The fragrance of perfumes distilled from myrrh and frankincense and all the fragrant powders of the merchant contrast with the natural scents of the henna blossoms and of the bag of myrrh, which she associates with her beloved. "Behold, it is the litter of Solomon! About it are sixty mighty men of the mighty men of Israel, all girt with swords and expert in war, each with his sword at his thigh, against alarms by night." This public figure, protected within the palanquin midst the security offered by the great column of warriors, is in his heavy awesomeness very unlike her lover, solitary, leaping upon ragged mountains and bounding over hills like a gazelle or stag. Solomon's palanquin is made from the wood of Lebanon, its posts of silver, its back of gold, its seat of purple, its interior "lovingly wrought . . . by the daughters of Jerusalem." The artificial, civilized, sophisticated quality of this structure, a creation of artisans and courtly hands, draws to the mind of the reader that very different description earlier of the natural green couch and the house of the living cedars of Lebanon with rafters of living pine. Here the cedars of Lebanon, the wood that is associated with the lovers throughout the lyrics, has been cut down to make a litter for Solomon. Dazzling though the palanquin may be, it lacks the natural and living quality that marks the world of the lovers. Finally, the king's splendid crown, "with which his mother crowned him on the day of his wedding," is another reminder that above all else he is king and ruler, head of court and country. When speaking of her country lover, who to her is a cluster of henna blossoms, not the wearer of a crown, the description is very different from that of a king: "As an apple tree among the trees of the wood, so is my beloved among young men. With great delight I sat in his shadow, and his fruit was sweet to my taste. He brought me to the banqueting house, and his banner over me was love." The pair of lovers is a couple unto itself, even a world unto itself, not a part of a court or a column. The banner is not part of an awesome royal procession but a metaphorical one of love, existing in the hearts of two individuals.

The voices of both the country lover and the king entreat her to come away with them, but the appeals represent opposing viewpoints. The voice of her lover comes to her when she is presumably at court, and she sees him, who has just come bounding as a gazelle or stag, gaze at her through the windows from outside. As he looks in through the lattice he says to her, "Arise, my love, my fair one, and come away; for lo, the winter is past. . . ." He paints a picture of nature coming to new life in the spring, the time of singing. He speaks of flowers making their appearance on the earth, of the fruition of the fig trees, of the blossoms and fragrance of the vines. "Arise, my love, my fair one, and come away," he repeats. "O my dove, in the clefts of the rock, in the covert of the cliff, let me see your face, let me hear your voice, for your voice is sweet, and your face is comely. Catch us the foxes, the little foxes, that spoil the vineyards, for our vineyards are in blossom." He asks her to come out from inside back into the world of nature and living things and back to the *safety* of the mountains. There their love can live and grow; there no one will gaze at her, for to him she is comely, not "very dark, but comely– as she believes she is for the women at court.

It is the invitation for the lovers to meet "in the clefts of the rock, in the covert of the cliff" that illustrates the differences in perspective between the lover and Solomon. The king also asks her, in 4:8, to come away with him, but he is asking her to come away from the world that the country lover cherishes, her world: "Come with me *from* Lebanon, my bride; come with me *from* Lebanon. Depart *from* the peak of Amana, *from* the peak of Senir and Hermon, *from* the dens of lions, *from* the mountains of leopards." For Solomon, a man from the city, the clefts of the rock and the covert in the cliff represent, in opposition to what they represent for the lovers, places that are *not* safe. When the king thinks of the beasts of the countryside he thinks of lions and leopards, revealing a hint of disquiet and a sense of the danger and wildness of nature. The young man, on the other hand, had spoken of flocks of sheep, of goats, ewes, doves, and, at worst, "the foxes, the little foxes," animals that are all accepted as parts of a living and ultimately harmonious nature. Solomon beckons her to come away with him to civilization, to court, and to the city, which, as the reader knows, are all protected by watchmen and by mighty men, "each with his sword at his thigh, against alarms by night."

Both the descriptions of the approaches of the two men and the tenor and content of their invitations to the woman to come away give a sense of the worlds to which the two men belong. It is in their descriptions of her, however, in their words of love to her, that the reader can understand the impact of this woman on each of them and discover the nature of the image each holds of her. The difference in perspectives is a sign not only of their different backgrounds, but also of very basic differences in attitude toward the woman they love.

Some of the similes and metaphors the country lover uses to describe the young woman initially seem more bizarre and difficult than those used by the king. In chapter 6, the country lover tells her, "Your hair is like a flock of goats, moving down the slopes of Gilead. Your teeth are like a flock of ewes, that have come up from the washing. . . . Your cheeks are like halves of a pomegranate. . . ." These similes, spoken by him in chapter 4 as well, would seem as unusual and out of place to the king as they might to any of us who are also not of the countryside. But in the voice of the country lover, from whose perspective poetry can in fact be created from a flock of goats, the similes have a correctness and an exact naturalness that are authentic and sincere expressions of beauty. We note as well the perfection and bountifulness of the lovers' world, in which all the ewes "bear twins," and "not one among them is bereaved."

There is a simplicity to the lover's view of her as he tells her, "You have ravished my heart, my sister, my bride, you have ravished my heart with a glance of your eyes, with one jewel of your necklace." It is a single glance, a single jewel of which he speaks to her, not of "strings of jewels" and "ornaments of gold, studded with silver" which the king lavishes on her when he fits her out as a courtly woman. For the country lover the woman is a garden and a fountain, "a well of living water, and flowing streams from Lebanon"; she is a source of nourishment and growth for all that is in his world. A self-sufficiency seems to emanate from their love. With each other they have wealth beyond physical wealth. "I come to my garden, my sister, my bride," he says. "I gather my myrrh with my spice, I eat my honeycomb with my honey, I drink my wine with my milk." Through his thoughts of her and through his love for her, a simple country meal of spice, honey, and milk is transformed into myrrh, honeycomb, and wine; his world is metamorphosed through love into a world as rich as that of Solomon. The same occurs for her when she speaks of him in response to the courtly ladies' question, "What is your beloved more than another beloved . . . ?" "My beloved is all radiant and ruddy," she says, recalling for the reader her own darkness. "His head is the finest gold. . . . His lips are lilies, distilling liquid myrrh. His arms are rounded gold, set with jewels. His body is ivory work, encrusted with sapphires. His legs are alabaster columns, set upon bases of gold." This hyperbole is composed of metaphors, not similes, for she does not use these riches as standards of comparison; rather, he *is* these things to her, he supplants them in her mind. The gold that interests her is not the gold of kings but the gold that is her beloved's head. The standards she uses for comparison, rather, are evident in the similes of natural things that tell the reader what is of value in their world: "His eyes are like doves beside springs of water. . . . His cheeks are like beds of spices yielding fragrance." And climactically, "His appearance is like Lebanon, choice as the cedars. . . . This is my beloved and this is my friend, O daughters of Jerusalem."

Lebanon is a code word for the common vision of life and love that unites the two lovers even when they are apart. In 4, as he calls her a garden fountain, "flowing streams from Lebanon," he says to her that even "the scent of your garments is like the scent of Lebanon." And she soon answers, "Awake, O north wind, and come, O south wind! Blow upon my garden, let its fragrance be wafted abroad. Let my beloved come to his garden and eat its choicest fruits." Though separated, they live through common poetry; the sounds, colors, and fragrances of this world fill their minds and trigger their longing for each other.

Solomon, who asked her to come away from Lebanon with him, who had made a palanquin from the wood of Lebanon, and his court, quite understandably see, speak to, and describe the young woman in a different way and from a different perspective. The natural world is less their environment than the sophisticated and civilized world that prevails at court and in the city. As in Solomon's hint of disquiet when speaking of the mountains and hills of Lebanon, there may even be a negative image of the natural world outside civilization. Early in chapter 2, Solomon speaks to her, describing his feelings for her; "As a lily among brambles, so is my love among maidens." The simile suggests something positive about the lily and something negative about the brambles. For the young woman and her lover all nature is good, even the sun that scorches, even the foxes that spoil the blossoming vineyards, even the clefts of the rock and the coverts in the cliff.

For Solomon and his court, the mare of Pharaoh's chariot takes precedence as an image of strength and beauty over gazelles and stags or goats and ewes. Gold and silver, not pomegranates and lilies, dominate the thoughts and perceptions of the court. Throughout the lyrics, the country woman is an object to be gazed at by the courtly maidens, a curiosity from elsewhere. As her heart is drawn to her beloved and she goes to the nut orchard to look at the blossoms, "to see whether the vines had budded, whether the pomegranates were in bloom," the courtly maidens call her back as they see her thinking of her lover. "Return, return, O Shulammite, return, return, that we may look upon you." She says rightly, "Why should you look upon the Shulammite, as upon a dance before two armies?" She resents the fact that she is somehow viewed as entertainment for them.

When the courtly maidens try to compliment her, they also reveal their perspective and their world. It is difficult for someone from a city to try to draw images from nature and make poetry. "How graceful are your feet in sandals, O queenly maiden!" they exclaim, giving an incidental reminder that she has not always worn sandals. "Your rounded thighs are like jewels, the work of a master hand. Your navel is a rounded bowl that never lacks mixed wine." This is not the kind of imagery the young lover would use; these objects of comparison are things of duty, things made, things crafted by the trained hands of artisans, things artificial. Even when the women attempt to relate her to nature, their city consciousness draws geographical locations from the city into the imagery. "Your neck is like an ivory tower. Your eyes are pools in Heshbon, by the gate of Bath-rabbim. Your nose is like a tower of Lebanon, overlooking Damascus. Your head crowns you like Carmel, and your flowing locks are like purple; a king is held captive in the tresses." It is difficult for them to speak in terms of natural objects; it is far easier to think of places of which the young woman reminds them most. The flowing locks in which they admit the king is held captive are to them like purple, not like a flock of goats. Purple is a color the lovers never use. It is a color of royalty, the color of the regal seat in the palanquin.

When the king speaks to her, he speaks with an admiration that reveals a very different attitude toward the woman than that found in the expressions of love proffered by the country lover. The king speaks to her, and of her, as an object, a sexual object, something to be enjoyed. "How fair and pleasant you are, O loved one, delectable maiden! You are stately as a palm tree, and your breasts are like its clusters. I say I will climb the palm tree and lay hold of its branches. Oh, may your breasts be like clusters of the vine, and the scent of your breath like apples, and your kisses like the best wine that goes down smoothly, gliding over lips and teeth." The images are all of things that need to be enjoyed through the senses, things that are "delectable." It is an expression of desire that seems shallow when compared to that intense desire uttered and felt by the country lover, who is, she has said, "a friend" and who calls her, five times, "my sister, my bride."

It is the congruence of their desire, this more gentle affection, their common background, and the unity of their poetic vision that leads her to her decision. "I am my beloved's, and his desire is for me," she says to him, deciding in favor of the fields and villages rather than the court and royal chambers. "Come, my beloved, let us go forth into the fields, and lodge in the villages; let us go out early to the vineyards, and see whether the vines have budded, whether the grape blossoms have opened and the pomegranates are in bloom. There I will give you my love."

This decision is not only an answer to the king but also at last a reply to her beloved. She uses the same imagery to answer him as he had used in that earlier invitation to come away: "Arise, my love, my fair one, and come away: for lo, the winter is past, the rain is over and gone. The flowers appear on the earth . . . the vines are in blossom; they give forth fragrance." Her answer and acquiescence are an echo of his expression of desire, his request that she, too, come out into the movement of nature, blossom, and bear fruit. She also tells him, "The mandrakes give forth fragrance, and over our doors are all choice fruits, new as well as old, which I have laid up for you, O my beloved." The phrase, "new as well as old," marks a continuity in that movement of nature which they now join.

She turns, for the last time, in chapter 8, to Solomon, who now learns what he is not and what his life is not. "O that you were like a brother to me, that nursed at my mother's breast! If I met you outside, I would kiss you, and none would despise me. I would lead you and bring you into the house of my mother, and into the chamber of her that conceived me. I would give you spiced wine to drink, the juice of my pomegranates." If she met the king outside, in her world, and if he were part of that world on its terms, then they could be friends. But her "brother," of course, is her beloved. Solomon has lost, for her love was hers to give and could not be demanded, owned, or bought. Solomon may own much property and have great wealth, and we know that he has "sixty queens and eighty concubines, and maidens without number," but this wealth and the expectations that might come with it can claim no fulfillment. The young woman says to Solomon, summarizing her freedom and the fact of her decision, "My vineyard, my very own, is for myself."

The tensions that are resolved with her decision involve not only the tension of opposition between the country and the court or between the country lover and the king, but also tensions within the woman that have to do only with herself and with the nature of love. Love is not a neutral object but a powerful force that she has had to come to terms with, control, and accept. She has suffered some pain from love throughout the lyrics, repeating that she is "sick with love" and warning the courtly women three times about its power: "I adjure you, O daughters of Jerusalem, that you stir not up nor awaken love until it please." She has experienced frustrated love, longing, the temptations of love, and love's overwhelming force, which she respects and expresses near the end of the Song: "for love is strong as death, jealousy as cruel as the grave. Its flashes are flashes of fire, a most vehement flame. Many waters cannot quench love, neither can floods drown it. If a man offered for love all the wealth of his house, it would be utterly scorned."

The sensual and sexual elements of the love between the man and the woman, though tempered by a gentle and sincere affection, are also a source of tension. She dreams of him twice. In chapter 3, "upon [her] bed by night," she seeks him in the city, searching through the streets and squares, not finding him until she passes the watchmen, presumably beyond the city's walls, in the country. The sexual dimension of this dream is more pronounced in her second dream in chapter 5, when she imagines him knocking on her bolted door, urging her to "open to me, my sister, my love, my dove, my perfect one." He has again bounded over the hills, for his head is "wet with dew." She is tempted, but she pauses, making up excuses: "I had put off my garment, how could I put it on? I had bathed my feet, how could I soil them?" But then his hand touches the latch, and she is aroused. Her palms sweat, dripping "with liquid myrrh." She opens the door; it is too late; he is gone. She again searches through the streets and squares of the city. But this time her sense of guilt over her hesitation and refusal ("My soul failed me when he spoke") is transformed into the dream vision of her being beaten and wounded by the watchmen. Psychologically, the progress of her decision to join him is remarkably correct. Only when she herself has decided that the time is right, when she herself has seen and felt that it is spring, does she call her beloved and invite him to go forth with her into the fields and lodge in the villages. Her decision to wait until the time when she believes it is right to give him her love is a source of quiet and proud reflection at the end of the lyrics. "I was a wall," she tells the courtly women, "and my breasts were like towers; then I was in his eyes as one who brings peace." On her example the courtly women have already learned this and summarize their feelings. "We have a little sister, and she has no breasts. What shall we do for our sister, on the day when she is spoken for? If she is a wall, we will build upon her a battlement of silver; but if she is a door, we will enclose her with boards of cedar." This fierce condemnation of promiscuity underscores the poet's vision of love as a singular and unique bond between a man and a woman.

The Song of Songs presents us with totally different ways of viewing reality, different perspectives on love, and different perceptions of human experience. The tensions are characterized in terms of various oppositions: the private vs. the public, the country vs. the court, the natural vs. the artificial, the simple vs. the sophisticated. The young woman whose story this is cannot get away from her own roots, nor does she want to. The young lovers are one with nature; they live in it, they describe each other according to its terms, they participate in its cycles. By contrast, Solomon and his court are inside, and inside in many different ways. They are literally inside, as seen when the women in the king's chambers gaze at the young woman's sunburned complexion. They are inside the city, enclosed by walls, guarded by watchmen supported by sixty mighty men protecting it against alarms by night. They are inside figuratively, within their limited perception of nature and its cycles, in their inability to create images and metaphors without using for comparison the artificial works of master hands or the well-known buildings and sites of other cities. Because they are inside they are limited, enclosed unto themselves and their world.

The dominant image pattern of the Song is, in fact, that of enclosure. The enclosures are many, each of them preventing full access to human experience: the king's chamber, the tents of Kedar, the curtains of Solomon, the wall behind which the young man stands, the lattice though which he gazes, the walls of the city, the woman's veil; she is a locked garden, a sealed fountain; Solomon comes through the wilderness enclosed within a palanquin; the woman dreams in her bedroom of her lover knocking on a bolted door. The images carry the suggestion of the danger of being walled about, metaphorically and literally, and the lyrics advocate the need to open ourselves to the sights and sounds, the smells and tastes, of the natural world. Enclosures provide security, as the woman herself recognizes as she dreams of taking her lover to her mother's house and into the room where she was conceived, but enclosures also exclude what is outside. And what is outside, the lyrics suggest, is life. The lyrics are about getting out from inside, about the opening up of nature in the spring, about the opening up of ourselves and the experiencing without bias of all that nature and life have to offer, and they are about the awakening of love and the opening of oneself to another.

The living things and natural elements that are chosen to fill this natural world reveal a pattern in the poet's vision of the world in which the lovers live. The lovers speak and dream of henna blossoms, roses and lilies; goats and hinds, ewes and fawns; doves; milk, water and dew; wine, myrrh, and frankincense; apples and pomegranates. Through the choice of these fruits and flowers, animals, birds, and liquids, the poet has worked into our imaginations, almost without exception, things red and things white. He suggests through this pattern the underlying strength of the lovers' vision of the world. It is passionate but innocent, fiery but pure. Red and white, with all their ancient and modern connotations, epitomize the lovers.

The poet of the Song has created a world where beauty is sensual and where sensuality is beautiful. The personal is balanced and leavened by the aesthetic. He includes those moments of frustration and tension in the lyrics to avoid the sentimentality of tenderness between two individuals; he transfers the love of the humans to the objects of nature. The two lovers exist for the reader only in the love they have for each other, and this is as it should be. The lyrics depict their world as they see it, a world metamorphosed by love. The master touch of the Song is that the world presented in the poem comes from inside the lovers, and it is something like the world as it appears at the most intense moment of love. The lyrics are not, after all, about love; rather, they are about what love thinks it sees.

16. NARRATIVE ART IN THE BOOK OF JUDITH

Dolores Gros Louis

Among the wide variety of genres represented in the Old and New Testament are several self-contained narratives especially suitable for close reading and careful study. Outstanding in this group is the book of Judith, a work whose narrative technique seems particularly appealing to a modern audience.

Written—or at least preserved—in Greek, Judith is included in the Roman Catholic canon but considered apocryphal in the Hebrew and Protestant traditions. There are many ways to categorize the book. First, it is a pseudo history. Its main event is fictional, as are all its major characters, and its alleged history is grossly inaccurate. Second, it may also be viewed as a war story. The author spends a great deal of time, particularly in the first half of the book, imaginatively describing the declaration of war, the mustering of troops, the movement of armies, the sacking of cities, the burning of fields, the surrender of the defeated and the terrified, and the victors' triumphant processions; as the story moves toward its climax, he focuses on the arguing of military advisors, the suffering and fear of a besieged town, and the people's ultimate rout of the enemy. Third, Judith is a religious story, an account of one woman's triumph through her complete faith in an omnipotent and omniscient God. In this connection it is also a strongly didactic story, emphasizing the need for prayer, fasting, tithing, purification, and strict adherence to the dietary laws. Finally, Judith shows intriguing qualities as a tightly structured suspense story.

Most critics and commentators consider Judith a masterpiece of Jewish narrative art. Biblical scholars agree that it was probably written about 150 B.C., after the victories of Judas Maccabeus but while the Jews were still struggling for independence and freedom against the successors of the hated Syrian king Antiochus IV Epiphanes. The author's depiction of Nebuchadnezzar closely reflects the character of Antiochus, who reigned in the years 175 to 164 B.C. Some commentators feel that Nebuchadnezzar might even be an accepted pseudonym for Antiochus, who was a cruel persecutor, vengeful and ambitious, and who, like Nebuchadnezzar in the story, is reported to have decreed "to destroy all the gods of the land, so that all nations should worship [him] only, and all their tongues and tribes should call upon him as god" (3:8)! The biographical details about Nebuchadnezzar included in Judith are thoroughly anachronistic. He is said to be the king of the Assyrians, although he really was king of the Babylonians. Nineveh is named as his capital, when, in fact, it was Babylon—indeed Nineveh had been destroyed some years before Nebuchadnezzar became king. Furthermore, the story is set after the Jews' return from Exile, which was, of course, several generations after Nebuchadnezzar's death. These and other historical and geographical inaccuracies would have been so obvious to readers in the second century B.C. that they are generally believed to be deliberate errors by the author, signaling that the work is to be read as a fiction.

While it *is* fiction, it is realistic in many ways. Despite its factual errors and some conventional exaggerations in numbers, Judith is filled with carefully rendered details, such as those of chapter 10, in which the step-by-step process by which Judith transforms herself from a plain widow into an elegant beauty is described. The particular items of kosher food that she assembles for her visit to the enemy camp are elaborately listed. Beyond these details, the incidents of the plot form a careful and logical sequence. Indeed, even a seemingly unnecessary incident, that dealing with Achior, will turn out later to be crucial. Nothing supernatural occurs in the book of Judith; there are no miracles. The story's psychology is believable. Holofernes' banishing of Achior, for example, is consistent with his tyrant's egoism, as is his foolish trust of Judith.

The setting, an element of special importance in this fiction, also is realistic, though it may not have been, in a geographic sense, real. Most scholars identify Bethulia as the city of Shechem, north of Jerusalem; but whether Bethulia is Shechem, or whether settlements such as Shechem merely served the author as a model, the setting of the story's fictional Bethulia is carefully conceived and important to the plot in several ways. Bethulia is described as a city built upon a mountain or hill. At the foot of it are the springs that provide the city's water supply. These essential "springs below Bethulia" (6:11) are mentioned early in the story, when Achior is delivered to the bottom of the hill, although at that point they do not appear to have any importance. Also at the foot of the hill is the narrow valley leading to the plain. This difficult passage to the mountainside city causes Holofernes to decide to lay seige to Bethulia instead of attacking it, a lucky decision for the Jews since it gives Judith the time to devise and carry out her plan. By holding Bethulia's springs for over a month, Holofernes is certain that he can make the people surrender and thus win the city without risking a single life in an assault up the mountain.

But the setting of Bethulia is important for more than its own defense. Twice strategic location is emphasized. In chapter 4, we are told of its key role:

Also Joiakim, the high priest, who was in Jerusalem at that time, wrote to the people of Bethulia and Betomesthaim, which faces Esdraelon opposite the plain near Dothan, ordering them to seize the passes up into the hills, since by them Judea could be invaded, and it was easy to stop any who tried to enter, for the approach was narrow, only wide enough for two men at the most. (4:6-7)

Later, chapter 8, the consequences of the fall of Bethulia are made even clearer:

For if we are captured all Judea will be captured and our sanctuary will be plundered; and he will exact of us the penalty for its desecration. And the slaughter of our brethren and the captivity of the land and the desolation of our inheritance—all this he will bring upon our heads among the Gentiles. . . . Now therefore, brethren, let us set an example to our brethren, for their lives depend upon us, and the sanctuary and the temple and the altar rest upon us. (8:21-24)

Thus, not only its own fate but that of all Judea and of the temple in Jerusalem depend upon the defense of Bethulia. This fact greatly increases the importance of Judith's opposition to Ozias, when he is willing to capitulate in five days. For if Bethulia surrenders, "all Judea shall lie waste, and our sanctuary shall be spoiled."

Finally, after the success of Judith's secret plan in the Assyrian camp, the dénouement also depends on the topography. Judith instructs the Jews: "let every valiant man take his weapons and go out of the city, and set a captain over them, as if you were going down to the plain against the Assyrian outpost; only do not go down" (14:2). Obviously, Judith depends on the mountain site and the narrow approach to prevent the Assyrians from attacking the Jews immediately. The Jews on the straits of the mountain can seem to threaten attack without exposing themselves or actually starting a battle.

It is clear that Judith divides into two parts. The first part consists of chapters 1–7, in which Judith herself does not appear. Here we learn the elaborate history of Nebuchadnezzar's campaigns and of the dispatch of his chief captain, Holofernes, to conquer all the western peoples (including the Jews) who had refused to aid him in his war against Arphaxad. Holofernes' great threat to Judah is described in some detail, and we witness the siege of Bethulia, the suffering, the thirst and hunger of the people there, and hear of their ultimate despair. The second part begins with the introduction of Judith and comprises the remainder of the book. Here we read about Judith's background, her plan (which is not at first revealed to us), the plan's success, the ultimate rout of the Assyrians, and the thanksgiving of the Jews. Finally, the rest of Judith's life history is summarized.

The two parts, which are almost even in length, are not of the same quality. Some critics, in fact, barely conceal their impatience with what they consider the tediousness of the first part and only grudgingly concede that it is, in fact, part of the book of Judith. From a literary perspective, though, part 1 is integrally related to part 2 and is significant in a number of ways. The opening chapters build up the ferocity of Holofernes and the great strength of his army, and describe his devastating progress through the many western countries and the fearful surrender of the coastal cities (chaps. 2–3). Thus the reader's own fear is aroused for the fate of the Israelites in chapters 4 and 7, where the siege is depicted. It is in chapter 4 that the Israelites are first made part of the war fiction, and in chapter 7 that the siege of Bethulia and the people's despair set up the need for the desperate action that Judith plans. The fear that the reader is made to feel, then, enhances appreciation of Judith's courage when she goes to Holofernes' camp in chapter 10.

Thus, the first part of the book, from the end of chapter 2, also introduces a major theme—that of *fear*—which runs throughout the story. All the coastal people felt "fear and terror" of Holofernes; they "feared him exceedingly" (2:28). Then, hearing that he had decreed to "destroy all the gods of the land, so that all nations should worship Nebuchadnezzar only" (3:8), the Israelites fear for their religion as well as for their country. Their first fear, in fact, is for their religion. Chapter 4 opens:

By this time the people of Israel living in Judea heard of everything that Holofernes, the general of Nebuchadnezzar the king of the Assyrians, had done to the nations, and how he had plundered and destroyed all their temples; they were therefore very greatly terrified at his approach, and were alarmed both for Jerusalem and for the temple of the Lord their God. For they had only recently returned from the captivity, and all the people of Judea were newly gathered together and the sacred vessels and the altar and the temple had been consecrated after their profanation.

This is why the Israelites are the only western people to resist Holofernes, who asks, "Why have they alone of all who live in the west, refused to come out and meet me?" (5:4).

The fear of the Jews for their religion in the face of the pagan threat of Holofernes leads us to the second important theme introduced in the first part of the book, the contrast between military power and the power of God. Holofernes' question about the Jews—"How large is their army, and in what does their power or strength consist? Who rules over them as King, leading their army?" (5:3)—is answered in part two when the mighty Holofernes is destroyed by the Jews' king and captain, God, working through the hand of a woman. This theme is illustrated in Achior's testimony to the invincibility of the Jewish people as long as they do not sin. He says to Holofernes, "But if there is no transgression in their nation, then let my lord pass them by; for their Lord will defend them, and their God will protect them, and we shall be put to shame before the whole world" (5:21). Again, there is a clear correspondence between the two parts of the story. Achior's warning here influences Holofernes' credulity when, in part two, Judith repeats what he had said and adds that the Jews *are* about to sin.

Achior's testimony in chapter 5, which includes a brief history of the Jewish people, serves a didactic purpose also, giving the first- and second-century B.C. readers—*and* later readers—a capsule summary of the help and defense God gave the Jews when they were faithful to him. Their history also adds credibility to Judith's total faith in her God, the faith that moves her to appeal to her people not to abandon *their* trust in God.

In addition to their sharing common themes, the artistic integration of the two parts of Judith is exemplified by the device used to frame the story of the Jews' resistance—the accounts of two dances, which form an ironic parallel between part one and part two. The first dance is that of the submissive coastal people for Holofernes: "And these people in the country round about welcomed him with garland and dances and tambourines" (3:7). After this, Holofernes nevertheless destroys their shrines and sacred groves and moves on to camp threateningly near Judah. The second dance, near the end of the story, is performed by the Israelites after they have chased away the leaderless Assyrians:

Then all the women of Israel gathered to see her, and blessed her, and some of them performed a dance for her; and she took branches in her hands and gave them to the women who were with her; and they crowned themselves with olive wreaths, she and those who were with her; and she went before all the people in the dance, leading all the women while all the men of Israel followed, bearing their arms and wearing garlands and with songs on their lips. (15:12-13)

In addition to the garlands and dancing, timbrels also appear in the next chapter, so there are many similarities between these two dances. And yet beyond the similarities lies the immense difference in context that allows the two dances to represent in vivid terms the contrast between the Jews' triumph and the abject capitulation of Holofernes' earlier opponents.

The triumph of Judith and her people is the material of part 2, and it begins in chapter 8 with Judith's opposition to the despair of the people and her opposition to the weakness of their governor, Ozias, the unbelieving believer (juxtaposed, perhaps, to Achior, the believing *un*believer!). At the end of part 1, Bethulia has very little hope. Ozias says, "If these [five] days pass by, and no help comes for us, I will do what you say"—that is, deliver the whole city to Holofernes—"and they were greatly depressed in the city" (7:31-32). Judith is introduced abruptly in chapter 8, but a long parenthesis tells a lot about her. This parenthesis, which gives her history, starts with "At that time Judith heard about these things," and goes to "When she heard" in verse 9. This repetition signals the end of the parenthesis describing her and the continuation of the story. She is beautiful, rich, and very pious. Since her husband's death she has humbled herself in sackcloth. She has lived mainly in a rooftop tent and has fasted every day that is allowed, that is, every day except the Sabbath and the festival days, when fasting is forbidden. If Judith is not too good to be true, she is certainly beyond reproach. Her character as a model is indicated by her name, which means, simply, Jewess. Judith, of course, dominates the book that has her name. She is the one who devises and carries out the plan that saves not only Bethulia but all Judea. Her action in the story of part 2 is related to the events of part 1. It is also related to the two major themes of part 1: Judith brings an end to the great fear repeatedly described there; she also answers, in both words and actions, the thematic question of military strength as opposed to God's power.

As a heroine without any flaws, Judith is a static character; she does not change or develop during the story. Yet, as the story proceeds, she does become more interesting as her intriguing qualities are gradually dramatized. These qualities, not mentioned in the parenthetical introduction, are her courage, both moral and physical, her initiative, her wisdom, and her cleverness.

These four qualities are sometimes overlooked by scholars, some of whom attribute Judith's amazing victory to her beauty alone. Charles Torrey, in his *Apocryphal Literature,* says the author of Judith "is very aware of the one thing that gives the story its measure of plausibility, Judith's extraordinary beauty, with her consciousness of its power; it was this weapon that saved the city."[1] Another scholar, Robert Denton, remarks that Judith "relates the daring exploit of a heroic woman who used her remarkable endowments of beauty and personal charm to rescue her people from disaster in time of war."[2] Judith's beauty certainly *is* important to her plan. It helps render plausible Holofernes' gracious acceptance of her and his inviting her to his tent. The author repeatedly describes her extraordinary beauty and its great effect on men, both Israelites and Assyrians. In chapter 10, after she changes herself from a plain widow, we read: "When they saw her, and noted how her face was altered and her clothing changed, they greatly admired her beauty" (10:7), and as she goes out of the city, "the men of the city watched her until she had gone down the mountain and passed through the valley and they could no longer see her" (10:10). The Assyrians are equally impressed: "When the men heard her words, and observed her face—she was in their eyes marvelously beautiful" (10:14). This is repeated in what seems to be a sort of inside Jewish joke: "And they marveled at her beauty, and admired the Israelites, judging them by her, and every one said to his neighbor, 'who can despise these people, who have women like this among them? Surely not a man of them had better be left alive, for it we let them go they will be able to ensnare the whole world!'" (10:19).

But it is not only Judith's beauty that saves Bethulia and the land of the Hebrews. She also has courage. First, she has the moral courage to speak up to and rebuke the city's governor and elders: "What you have said to the people today is not right; . . . Who are you that have put God to the test this day, and are setting yourselves up in the place of God among the sons of men?" (8:11-12). Second, she has physical courage, of course, in going alone with her maid to the very camp of Holofernes.

Judith displays initiative, also. Instead of following Ozias' request that she passively pray for rain to relieve the besieged city, Judith announces her secret plan of action through which "the Lord will deliver Israel by my hand" (8:33). After she kills Holofernes, Judith again takes the initiative in directing the men of Bethulia in their overthrow of the Assyrian army. And in the last chapter, again it is Judith who composes a psalm of praise to

God and who leads the people in singing and dancing. Judith's initiative and courage are both founded on her complete faith in God and her awareness of her own perfect obedience to God and his laws. She trusts God, and she trust herself as his loyal servant.

Judith's wisdom also is related to her faith. In challenging Ozias' proposal she presents the theological argument that man cannot possibly know what God is thinking and that the omnipotent God may do whatever he wishes, whenever he wishes. It is not for man to put God to the test, she says; it is God who puts man to the test. Therefore, it is wrong, she argues, to threaten God by promising to surrender the city unless God helps it within five days. Acknowledging Judith's wisdom, Ozias, the governor, points out that she speaks with "a true heart," and that she has wisdom because "your heart's disposition is right" (8:28-29). Judith's prayer, which constitutes chapter 9, shows both her wisdom and her faith. She believes in God's omnipotence and in his complete foreknowledge: "For thou hast done these things and those that went before and those that followed; thou hast designed the things that are now, and those that are to come. Yea, the things thou didst intend came to pass, and the things thou didst presented themselves and said, 'Lo, we are here'; for all thy ways are prepared in advance, and thy judgment is with foreknowledge" (9:5-6). Judith's main concern, both in her prayer and in chapter 8, is for the temple. She asks God's help mainly because the Assyrians "intend to defile thy sanctuary, and to pollute the tabernacle where thy glorious name rests, and to cast down the horn of thy altar with the sword" (9:8).

In addition to her virtues of beauty, courage, initiative, faith, and wisdom, Judith also exhibits great cleverness. In chapter 11 she captures Holofernes' interest with her words as much as with her beauty. It is true that many of her words are lies, but almost as many are cunning double entendres. For example, she says to Holofernes, "And if you wilt follow out the words of your maidservant, God will accomplish something through you, and my lord will not fail to achieve his purposes" (11:6). The thing to be brought to pass, of course, is her secret plan to kill Holofernes, not the plan for victory which she presents to him. "My lord will not fail to achieve his purposes" seems to refer to Holofernes, though in fact it refers to God. Another irony appears when she flatters

Holofernes: "For we have heard of your wisdom and skill, and it is reported throughout the whole world that you are the one good man in the whole kingdom, thoroughly informed and marvelous in military strategy" (11:8). But, as we know, Judith certainly believes that God is far more knowledgeable and far more powerful; she is aware of the differences between human power and divine power. In the same chapter (vv. 9-10), Judith shrewdly reminds Holofernes of Achior's belief that the Israelites can be defeated only if they sin, and this in turn makes him receptive to Judith's lie that the Bethulians, on the edge of starvation, are about to break the dietary laws. Incidentally, this point shows the necessity of an incident that seems at the time unnecessary, the delivery of Achior to Bethulia. It is Achior's report of Bethulia to Holofernes that allows Judith to echo him later, and so make her story convincing. In 11:16 there is another double meaning, when Judith tells Holofernes, "and God has sent me to accomplish with you things that will astonish the whole world, as many as shall hear about them." These words flatter and encourage Holofernes, but to Judith—and to the reader—they mean, of course, not Holofernes' victory, but his defeat. The crowning irony of this chapter is Holofernes' great admiration for Judith's words. At the end of the chapter, we are told: "Her words pleased Holofernes and all his servants, and they marveled at her wisdom and said, 'There is not such a woman from one end of the earth to the other, either for beauty of face or wisdom of speech!'" (11:20-21). And Holofernes says to her, "You are not only beautiful in appearance, but wise in speech" (11:23). The words he praises are words the reader knows are lies, ironies, and double entendres, with which he himself has been beguiled.

As the story proceeds, Judith continues to speak in double entendres. In chapter 12, referring to the supply of kosher food she has brought with her, she says to him, "As your soul lives, my lord, your servant will not use up the things I have with me before the Lord carries out by my hand what he has determined to do" (12:4), and again, "and Judith said, 'Who am I, to refuse my lord? Surely whatever pleases him I will do at once, and it will be a joy to me until the day of my death!'" (12:14). And this is the day of the murder of Holofernes! When he asks her to come and feast with him, she says, "I will drink now, my lord, because my life means

more to me today more than in all the days since I was born"
(12:18). He, of course, thinks that she is excited because he is
about to sleep with her; in fact, her excitement stems from her
knowledge that she is soon to behead him.

Judith's cleverness is best illustrated by the entire intricate
plan—only gradually revealed to the reader—which she has
devised for killing Holofernes and returning home safely. First,
she gains his confidence and interest by her wit, beauty, flattery,
and by the hope she holds out to him of a sure and easy victory. She
also gains time by telling him that the Jews of Bethulia will not sin
until they receive permission from Jerusalem to consume
forbidden foods, the firstfruits, and the tithes (11:12-15). To
assure her eventual escape, Judith gains permission to go out to
the valley of Bethulia to pray at night. She follows this pattern for
three nights before her actual escape after the beheading. When
she does escape, we discover that even the food bag was part of her
scheme, for on her return trip she carries in it the head of
Holofernes and the jeweled canopy from his bed. All these details
have been thought out by Judith ahead of time, but not explained
to us. We have to go back in our minds to see how the plan was
conceived.

At this point, we can see that the book of Judith is a strikingly
well constructed story, and one that should appeal to a modern
audience. It is not a mystery story, but rather a story of intrigue
that shares a number of qualities with modern spy stories and
thrillers. It depends first of all on the depiction of a well-organized,
well-entrenched enemy. The job of defeating such formidable
opposition requires courage and resourcefulness, and the focus is
on *how* that defeat is accomplished. To increase suspense, there is
a time limit of four days. The plan, as it develops, entails
penetration of the enemy's base by means of disguise. Judith
disguises both her purposes—it is the opposite of the one she
announces—and her character—the chaste and pious widow
becomes an adorned and alluring woman. In fact, the plan is what
we know today as an undercover operation; Judith is a double
agent posing as a defector. Exploiting the psychology of the
enemy, the operative engineers a careful deception, strikes the
enemy down at the very moment that he thinks himself victorious,
and then escapes undetected.

Of course, Judith is much more than a good popular story. As we have seen, the character of Judith is closely interwoven with the plot, and the didactic elements of her exemplary pious behavior are skillfully handled. In the end, plot, character, and major themes all contribute to the development of the theological lesson on the nature of God and of man's proper relationship to him. Characterization and plot have already been discussed; I would like now to look more closely at Judith's major themes—fear and power. These themes, appropriate to a war story, are also presented from a religious perspective. The atmosphere in the first part of the book is dominated by fear of Holofernes: "So fear and terror of him fell upon all the people who lived along the seacoast. . . . Those who lived in Azotus and Ascalon feared him exceedingly" (2:28). The children of Israel "were very greatly terrified at his approach" (4:2). After Judith's appearance, the reader may well fear for her in the enemy camp, but she herself expresses no fear. After the climax of part two, the beheading, fear grips the Assyrians: "Fear and trembling came over them" (15:2). The book concludes with the end of fear; the last verse in Judith states: "And no one ever again spread terror among the people of Israel in the days of Judith, or for a long time after her death" (16:25). Opposed to this early fear of men is the fear of God. The heroine's faith kept her from fearing Holofernes; but "she feared God with great devotion" (8:8). The fear of God is also expressed in her song: "But to those who fear thee thou wilt continue to show mercy . . . but he who fears the Lord shall be great for ever" (16:15-16).

The related theme of power also presents a dichotomy between the human and the divine. With many detailed accounts of countries, captains, archers, foot soldiers, chariots, and horses, part 1 builds up the enormous power of Nebuchadnezzar and of Holofernes. The men of their armies are "men confident in their strength" (2:5). Neuchadnezzar announced, "For as I live, and by the power of my kingdom, what I have spoken my hand will execute" (2:12). Holofernes "set out with his whole army, to go ahead of King Nebuchadnezzar and to cover the whole face of the earth to the west with their chariots and horsemen and picked troops of infantry" (2:19). When the Israelites refuse to submit to Holofernes, he asks his advisors about the extent of their power.

All but one of his advisors answer that Israel is powerless: "For we will not be afraid of the Israelites; they are a people with no strength or power for making war" (5:23). Only once in this first section of fear and hopelessness is there an affirmation of the power of the God of Israel. Again this is a kind of Jewish joke since it is the enemy of Israel, the Ammonite Achior, who affirms the great power of the Israelites. This alleged power of the Israelites' God is discounted by Holofernes. He reasserts his faith in the power of Nebuchadnezzar: "Who is God except Nebuchadnezzar? He will send his forces and will destroy them from the face of the earth, and their God will not deliver them—we the king's servants will destroy them as one man. They cannot resist the might of our cavalry. . . . They cannot withstand us, but will utterly perish. So says King Nebuchadnezzar, the lord of the whole earth for he has spoken: none of his words shall be in vain" (6:2-4). Holofernes' report underlines Nebuchadnezzar's hubris in ascribing power to himself which the narrative demonstrates is beyond human attainment.

In the second part of the book, in fact, Judith reminds the rulers of Bethulia of the omnipotence of the Lord Almighty: "he has power to protect us within any time he pleases, or even to destroy us in the presence of our enemies" (8:15). Judith's long prayer (chapter 9) makes explicit the superiority of God's power over any human power, and her victory illustrates that superiority. Part of her prayer reads:

Behold now, the Assyrians are increased in their might; they are exalted, with their horses and riders; they glory in the strength of their foot soldiers; they trust in shield and spear, in bow and sling, and know not that thou art the Lord who crushest wars; the Lord is thy name. Break their strength by thy might, and bring down their power in thy anger. . . . Give to me, a widow, the strength to do what I plan." (9:7-9)

Just before she beheads Holofernes, Judith, the widow who has conceived not rain or fertility, but a wise plan, prays to the "Lord God of all might" (13:4); and as she returned to the gates of Bethulia, she calls out, "God, our God, is still with us, to show his power in Israel, and his strength against our enemies, even as he has done this day!" (13:11, 14). Just as the theme of fear is restated in Judith's psalms of praise, so also the theme of God's supreme power is recapitulated there: "But the Lord Almighty has foiled them by the hand of a woman. . . . The sons of maid servants have pierced them through; they were wounded like the children of fugitives, they perished before the army of my Lord. I will sing to my God a new song; O Lord, thou art great and glorious, wonderful in strength, invincible" (16:6, 12, 13).

These two major themes—power and fear—are important to a persecuted people, as the Israelites of this book were. In this pseudo history of war these themes are introduced at the beginning, even in the first verse with the name of Nebuchadnezzar. The military and political significance of power and fear are immense, but the Book of Judith teaches that God's power is omnipotent and, therefore, that one should fear and obey only God. Those who have faith in God's omnipotence, as Judith does, will not fear a Holofernes, for "God breaketh the battles." And those who fear the omniscient Lord, as Judith does, will serve him and obey his laws only, for "thou art merciful to them that fear thee." This message was dramatized in the story of Judith in order to encourage the Jews' faith in God and obedience to his laws. But the book not only teaches; it also delights. Its irony, its suspense, its intricately constructed plot, all make it an accessible and entertaining story.

17. THE JESUS BIRTH STORIES

Kenneth R. R. Gros Louis

T. S. Eliot's poem "Journey of the Magi" and the complete lyrics of the Christmas carol that begins, "We Three Kings of Orient Are," describe essentially the same dramatic action. But obviously, the narrators of the poems bring different perspectives to that action. The kings are not alike. Concrete descriptions of them differ. It is unclear why they are taking a journey or what it is they hope to find. The journey is not described in either poem. Are the kings equally satisfied in both poems? How do they express their approval or disapproval? What sense do we get of the world the kings live in? How are these worlds depicted? Are there other characters in the poems? What are they like? How do they interact with the kings?

Obviously, what we recognize as we consider the poems is that the same basic event can be described by writers in vastly different ways, that a writer, even when depicting an event that is well known—such as the circumstances surrounding the birth of Jesus, selects and augments his material, that he offers, through and because of what he has selected, altered, and expanded, a point of view. We must be alert, in other words, to the voice of a narrative, the voice that, whether we like it or not, leads us to whatever meaning or significance we derive from the narrative.

Matthew and Luke open their Gospels by describing the same event, the birth of Jesus, a birth that from their perspective was miraculous. A way into the narratives might well be to compare them to other miraculous birth stories from classical and modern literature. Suppose we do this: we will find it interesting, but, as it turns out, not very revealing in illustrating Matthew and Luke as literature. If we compile a list of the standard devices of miraculous birth stories and note the standard variations on the themes, we soon recognize that this is somehow not about the Gospels—it is information comparable to the knowledge that a sonnet has fourteen lines, usually one of two structures, and is often about frustrated love. That knowledge, like our knowledge about miraculous birth stories in regard to Luke and Matthew, is minimally helpful to us in understanding a particular sonnet. The danger with literary comparisons of this type—that is, not of subject matter, but of genres, subgenres, topoi, conventions, archetypes, modes, forms—is that our interest soon turns to the object of comparison itself and away from the individual objects being compared. We end up studying miraculous birth stories and not the particular birth described in Matthew and Luke.

Another possible approach is to combine the two stories and discuss the Nativity as one narrative, the birth of Jesus. But the more we consider this, the less comfortable we become with it. We don't, after all, combine the third chapter of Genesis and Book IX of *Paradise Lost* as one narrative about the fall of man; nor, in perhaps a better example because they are closer together in time, do we discuss Shakespeare's history plays and Holinshed's chronicles as one narrative about the kings of England. In the latter instance, in fact, just the reverse is true—we note what Shakespeare adds that is not in Holinshed and vice versa, and ask, as critics, why? Still, Milton and the narrator of Genesis 3 describe the same basic events, as do Shakespeare and Holinshed, and as, we know, do Matthew and Luke. If we are talking about these Nativity stories in religious or theological terms, then perhaps it is proper to combine them and to point out, for example, that the magi and the shepherds *both* came to the birth of Jesus. But in discussing these passages as literature, we need to keep them separate—if Matthew knew about the shepherds, he *chose* to leave them out; if Luke knew about the magi, he *chose* to leave them out—why? If, on the other hand, the shepherds and magi are purely literary inventions, then why does Matthew select magi as Jesus' visitors and Luke shepherds?

Our two writers, Matthew and Luke, describe the same event, a miraculous birth and a birth, we know from their narratives as a whole, of someone whom they believe is very important—the King of the Jews, the Savior, the son of God. Our question is really their question—how are they going to do it? Many stories must have circulated about this man Jesus, conflicting versions of his birth and life and death, of his family and disciples of his sayings and influence. How do Matthew and Luke decide what to select? What questions go through a writer's mind—Shakespeare's, say, as he read Holinshed, or Milton's, as he read Genesis 3—as he considers his sources and subjects? For Matthew and Luke, perhaps questions like these: How will the birth be described? What is the audience like? How much does it know? Does it need to be persuaded of the importance of the birth? How can this best be done? Does the birth of a child to a virgin need to be made believable? How can *that* best be done? What narrative context should the birth be set into? What events, of many known, should be emphasized? What characters should be included and which ones then emphasized? Who should speak? What should they say? Should the sources be made known? In what ways should the birth set the pattern and tone of the rest of the narrative, for this is, after all, only the introduction to a longer account of Jesus? Our problem is to see how Matthew and Luke answered their questions—those of any writer—by looking at the narratives and then asking why certain choices, why certain decisions, were made.

Before discussing the narratives as literature, it might be useful to summarize them in order to demonstrate how surprisingly different they are. Matthew's Gospel opens by tracing Jesus' genealogy from Abraham (Luke postpones a similar genealogy until the end of chapter 3 in his gospel, at a time when Jesus is thirty years old). In 1:18, Matthew tells us, "Now the birth of Jesus Christ took place in this way"; but instead of hearing about the birth, we are told why Joseph does not divorce Mary after she becomes pregnant and how the birth of Jesus fulfills a prophecy in Isaiah. Chapter 2 opens with the coming of the wise men from the East, a visit that troubles King Herod, who becomes more troubled when he learns from his chief priests and scribes that indeed a ruler to be born in Bethlehem had been prophesied in

Micah. Herod summons the wise men and instructs them to complete their journey and then let him know where the child is so that he too might worship him. The wise men, however, after finding the house where Jesus has been born and giving him their gifts of gold, frankincense, and myrrh, are warned in a dream not to report to Herod and to return home by a different route. Joseph also is warned in a dream that Herod plans to destroy the child and is told to flee to Egypt—this, too, Matthew tells us, was prophesied in Hosea. Herod, in a rage, orders that all male children two years old or under be killed. This decree parallels the circumstances of Moses' birth, and transforms the description of deported Jews in Jeremiah into a terrible prophecy. But when Herod himself dies (2:19), Joseph, following the instructions given in two dreams, returns to Israel and settles in Nazareth. Thus, Matthew concludes his second chapter, Isaiah's description of the branch (Hebrew *nēṣer*—11:1) is fulfilled as the family settles in Nazareth.

Luke's Gospel opens with a formal preface to "most excellent Theophilus," announcing the intention to write an "orderly account" of those things of which Theophilus has only been "informed." The narrative begins with the story of Zachariah, a righteous but childless priest. During a religious service in the temple, Gabriel appears and stuns Zachariah by telling him that his wife Elizabeth, though old and barren, will bear a son, whose name shall be John and who will "make ready for the Lord a people prepared." Because Zachariah questions Gabriel's words, he is struck mute, much to the amazement of the people who meet him as he leaves the temple. In the sixth month of Elizabeth's pregnancy, Gabriel appears before Mary in Nazareth and announces that she, though a virgin, will bear a son, whose name shall be Jesus and who "will be great, and will be called the Son of the Most High." The angel explains that nothing is impossible for God, as evidenced by Elizabeth, who was called barren and is now pregnant. Mary visits Elizabeth, and both rejoice in their mutual good fortune; Mary especially realizes that she has been favored and that "henceforth all generations will call [her] blessed." John is born, and many neighbors and relatives gather at Zachariah's house, urging that he be named for his father. Elizabeth, however indicates that the boy will be named John, and Zachariah further amazes the crowd by writing on a tablet, "His name is John."

Those in the hill country are much puzzled—"What then will this child be?" Zachariah, his power of speech renewed, prophesies that he "will be called the prophet of the Most High," and John, we are told, grown strong in age and spirit, goes into the wilderness. Meanwhile, Joseph and Mary leave their home and journey to Bethlehem to obey the decree from Caesar Augustus that all the world should be "enrolled." The time comes for Mary to give birth, but because the inn is filled, she wraps the child in swaddling clothes and lays him in a manger. An angel of the Lord appears to shepherds in the region to tell them the "good news" of the birth of a "Savior, who is Christ the Lord." The shepherds decide to visit the manger and there inform everyone what they had been told by the angel. Jesus is circumcised after eight days, and his parents, following the law, bring him to Jerusalem to present him to the Lord.

What is striking about the narratives is that even though they describe the same basic event they are totally different. And the differences are not only in details, but in essentials, in structure, in emphases, in point of view toward the birth and those concerned with it. Joseph and Herod play central roles in Matthew's narrative, but they are only names in Luke's; Mary, only a name in Matthew, is central to Luke's narrative; Zachariah, Elizabeth, and John do not appear in Matthew; Bethlehem is the site of Jesus' birth in both accounts, but the circumstances and location differ greatly; wise men visit Jesus in Matthew, shepherds visit him in Luke. The list could be extended by noting the details that are unique to only one narrative or the other. The only things they have in common, in fact, are several names and places, and two important details—the mother is a virgin and the child's name is given as Jesus by an angel of the Lord. Clearly, the same momentous historical event is being reported, but in two markedly different narratives. Finally, it is important to note that one account is not an elaboration of the other—there is nothing in Matthew's version that might suggest what is in Luke's, or vice versa. What are we, as readers of literature, to make of these two stories? What does each reveal about the point of view of the narratives toward the implications of the birth of a man whom both present as the son of God? (And surely these questions are provocative, if only because of our surprise at discovering that the

Nativity story with which we are so familiar is actually a composite of two stories in the Gospels.)

To begin with, we notice the importance of dreams and prophecies in Matthew. In two short chapters, there are five dreams, and five prophecies are recalled (neither dream nor prophecy occurs in Luke). This is either clumsy narration or some end is intended. If we read the narrative with dreams and prophecies in mind, in fact, we discover that nothing happens—no action is begun or ended—that does not result from a dream or that is not the fulfillment of a prophecy. Joseph thinks of divorcing Mary, but does not do so because of the angel's advice in his dream; the wise men might have returned to Herod, but a dream warns them away; Joseph takes his family on a difficult journey to Egypt because of instructions received in a dream; and their return from Egypt is occasioned by another dream, as is the decision not to return to Judea. Mary's conception of Jesus fulfills a prophecy; Jesus is born in the city prophesied to be "by no means least among the rulers of Judah"; that Joseph and his family are in Egypt and move to Galilee instead of returning to Judea fulfills two prophecies; even Herod's mass murder of male children represents a fulfillment of the words of Jeremiah. The *only* action in the narrative not directly related to dreams and prophecies is the journey of the wise men; but even they, having calculated astrological changes, follow a star, even their decision concerning the time to seek Jesus is in a real sense predetermined for them.

What does this apparently not accidental emphasis on dreams and prophecies suggest to us about the narrative's view of history and of the role of individuals in history? This is, after all, a narrative describing a major historical event. Presumably, a narrative that describes actions as the outcomes of dreams or as the fulfillment of prophecies invites us to view history as the result of predetermined patterns and not of individual choice. Such a narrative is not going to be very interested in individual personalities; the pattern, the fulfillment of the plan, is what is important. If we return to the Matthew narrative, we find many confirmations for this suggestion. For one thing, the dreams always *alter* human decisions—Joseph had resolved to divorce Mary quietly until his dream; the wise men had presumably planned to return to Herod until their dream; Joseph presumably had decided to remain in Bethlehem until his dream and he does not leave Egypt until he is told to do so in another dream. Also, the prophecies are always given to us *after* facts and events are described—we know Mary the virgin is pregnant before the narrative recalls the prophecy; that Jesus is born in Bethlehem before Herod's chief priests and scribes tell him that; we know of the family's flight to Egypt, of Herod's mass murder, of Joseph's going into Nazareth, before the prophecies that these events fulfill are recalled. The narrative obviously could have reversed the pattern, but the effect of concluding actions by recalling prophecies fulfilled is to make the prophecies seem like afterthoughts, recalled to confirm information the narrative has already given us.

We get additional evidence of the narrative's view of history when we consider the reasons for the long genealogy at the beginning, and for the allusions to the three sets of fourteen generations that intervened between Abraham and David, David and the deportation, the deportation and Jesus. The history of man has been planned, as the narrative demonstrates by Abraham's line and the triple-fourteen pattern, and it is still being directed from elsewhere, as demonstrated through the devices of dreams and prophecies. As the genealogy further suggests, history is dominated by men, presumably a logical conclusion if central historical importance is attached to Abraham, David, and Jesus. This may explain why Matthew's narrative is so heavily male-dominated. The angel instructs *Joseph* to name the baby Jesus, Herod plays a central role, the wise *men* take the journey to Bethlehem, an angel appears to *Joseph* four times in dreams. Mary is barely mentioned. We conclude the narrative remembering *men*—Joseph, the wise men, Herod, Jesus, Jesus' ancestry. Such a view of history explains, perhaps, why the account of Herod's mass murder is emphasized—the killing of all the *male* children in the region of Bethlehem would be in this narrative an event of major historical importance; the view may also explain why so few women are mentioned in the genealogy and why the narrative does not even allude by name to the woman who caused David's downfall—she is "the wife of Uriah." All the more striking it is then, after several dozen repetitions of the pattern "x the father of y," to read in 1:16: "Joseph *the husband of* Mary, of whom Jesus was born, who is called Christ." Alert readers of literature should know who is to be the subject of this narrative.

A conception of history as divinely planned and of men in history as instruments of the plan is going to create a very special kind of literature, one that describes major occurrences and largely ignores details, human emotions and responses, and dramatic action. Matthew's narrative offers us few descriptions of individual responses and movements—those few which are mentioned are almost narrative fillers between a dream and the next prophecy.

If we turn from Matthew to Luke, we begin to recognize how complex the differences are between the two narratives. Instead of a structure dominated by dreams, prophecies, and events, the structure of Luke is controlled by the carefully and fully worked out parallels between the births of John and Jesus, and the varied responses of those connected with the births. Instead of a male-dominated narrative, Luke, if not female-dominated, is at least more balanced in presenting us with the responses and emotions of Zachariah, Elizabeth, and Mary. Further, instead of having characters suddenly appear somewhere or being directed to go elsewhere, as in Matthew, Luke moves his characters from place to place with narrative logic. Zachariah has a reason for being in the temple and for coming out of it, Mary's trip to Elizabeth is described, there is movement among Zachariah's neighbors and kinfolk, Joseph has a specific reason for going to Bethlehem, the shepherds discuss their decision to visit the manager after the angel's announcement to them. Events in Luke are connected, in other words—history, or the reporting of history, or the creation of literature involves not only recording events or their causes, but also describing what happens to people in time and space as events unravel. By contrast, Matthew tells us "the birth of Jesus Christ took place in this way" and then proceeds to describe Joseph's decision, his dream, and the prophecy concerning Mary; the birth is not described at all. The next we hear—another event—is that Jesus has been born in Bethlehem. Matthew reports that the angel directs Joseph to go to Egypt, but he then shifts to an account of Herod's rage—his interest, in other words, is in the *instruction* to Joseph and not in the human problems and difficulties involved in carrying it out.

Luke, on the other hand, is much more interested in human emotions and responses—in Zachariah's fear and disbelief, the multitude's puzzlement over his delay in the temple, Elizabeth's responses to the baby in her womb, Mary's wonderment at Gabriel's announcement, Elizabeth's ecstasy during Mary's visit, and so on. History may be worked out in advance, as the songs in Luke suggest to us that it is, but Luke is as interested in the people involved in history as he is in the history that results from what they do. The tight parallel structure indicates his belief, similar to Matthew's, in the ordering and patterning of human events; but Matthew would not have included the details Luke does about human responses and movement nor the asides typical of Luke that fill out the narrative for us. Luke does not have to tell us, for example, that Zachariah is of the division of Abijah or that the angel is on the right side of the altar or that the friends and neighbors of Zachariah gossip about John, or that the enrollment to which Joseph goes is the "first enrollment." Matthew would not have told us these things nor included such details and responses, which to him do not seem relevant to the larger patterns of history.

A different sensibility is at work in Luke, creating a different kind of literature. The very preface to Theophilus suggests that the narrator has a strong sense of self; he conceives of his function in time and space—*he* will be the reliable narrator, writing an "orderly account" of what has recently transpired. He seems aware of his audience—an official, someone in power, skeptical perhaps, but knowledgeable about contemporary events, interested in the human details of a remarkable birth. The personal voice speaking to a specifically identifiable auditor differs remarkably from Matthew's impersonal, somewhat majestic, voice giving us the long genealogy from Abraham to Jesus. That Luke's account is not dominated by dreams and prophecies that determine or alter human decisions and actions does not mean that his characters are not fulfilling prophecies or following divinely inspired instructions; it means rather that the narrative centers on human consciousness as it participates in history *instead* of on the prophecies being fulfilled and the instructions being given. Mary's song to the Lord, for example, may *be* a hymn inserted for the benefit of the reader, but it nevertheless accurately reflects Mary's wonder at having been selected to be the mother of the son of God.

Similarly, the song praising John (1:14-17) may *be* inserted for instructional purposes; but the narrative recalls that John "will be filled with the Holy Spirit, even from his mother's womb," when we are told in 1:41 that John, hearing the voice of Mary, leaped in his mother's womb.

Different sensibilities are indeed at work in Luke and Matthew, with different concepts of history, of the individual in history, of the function of self in the creation of art. For Matthew, the birth is another major event, like the birth of Abraham, the selection of David as king, the deportation to Babylon. History, the total of these significant moments, is made up of announcements and instructions from angels and the fulfillment of prophecies. The time and space the characters move in is not time and space as we know them. For Luke, however, the birth of Christ has suggested a different kind of emphasis. The point of view in Matthew's version of the Nativity is closer to that expressed in the Christmas carol of the three kings. But Luke, like T. S. Eliot in "Journey of the Magi," wants to know how people respond to events, how they get from place to place, what they're doing when they are not present in the narrative. Notice the narrative neatness of Luke—the scene at the temple has its beginning, middle, and end, Mary's going *to* and *from* Elizabeth's house is mentioned, the amazement at Zachiariah's writing the name John is discussed in the countryside, John is in the wilderness when he is not in the narrative, Joseph is *required* to go to Bethlehem.

There are several obvious reasons for the parallel structure in Luke involving the John and Jesus births. What happens to the virgin Mary is more believable because something comparable has happened to the old and barren Elizabeth. A pattern is established for much of the narrative that follows: the announcement to Zachariah prepares us for Gabriel's announcement to Mary as John will prepare the way for Jesus; Zachariah's skeptical response to the angel contrasts with the humble acceptance of Mary, and so on. But there is also a major difference in the parallel accounts which may explain Luke's special interest in individual emotions and actions and in specific details. The events surrounding the birth of John, we notice, are heavily publicized; that is, many are involved—the multitude perplexed at the temple, the neighbors and kinfolk marveling at the circumcision, the countryside gossiping about "what then will this child be?" By contrast, the events surrounding the birth of Jesus are private and isolated: Gabriel appears to Mary when she is alone, her news is shared only with Elizabeth and presumably with Joseph, the narrative takes Joseph and his family away from their home town, and therefore away from their neighbors and kinfolk, to be enrolled in Bethlehem; and even in that town, there is no room at the inn and the child must be born in a manger, out of sight, unnoticed by those who fill the inn. The good news of the birth is told to shepherds in the fields, not to multitudes in the temple or to assemblies in the city or court. We know from 1:65, in fact, that the big news in Judea—where Jesus is born—the news "talked about through all the hill country," is the birth of John. Only when Jesus goes to Jerusalem does he begin to receive public attention. The differences between the multitudes who know about John and the few who know about Jesus is striking; perhaps more striking is the difference between Luke's emphasis on the privacy and isolation of the birth of Jesus and Matthew's emphasis on the birth's fulfillment of Old Testament prophecies and its impact on Herod and the entire city of Jerusalem.

The contrasts may suggest Luke's different understanding of this birth, of its significance for the individual in history. For Luke, perhaps events become major events, become "history," only after the fact; they are made up of seemingly minor events, involving people we do not know, the results of births we did not hear about. Those in Luke marvel at John's conception and birth, not realizing that unknown to them a more important conception and birth is taking place elsewhere. Luke seems to recognize the literary implications of this irony; he picks up and makes into literature a strand that runs through the Old Testament—in the still small voice, for example, at the sound of which Elijah covers his face with his mantle, or in the suffering servant who is despised and rejected by many.

The differences in the accounts of the birth of Jesus in the Gospels are not simply alternate versions of an oral tradition. The characters in Luke wonder, exclaim, rejoice, marvel, ponder; they are troubled, perplexed, filled with fear. By contrast, only the wise men rejoice in Matthew, and only Herod expresses emotion of any kind. For Luke, Jesus' birth has altered the meaning of individual actions and responses, any one of which might become significant for history, for literature. For Matthew, Jesus' birth is part of a predetermined plan that prophecies have predicted and that instructions given in dreams will help to fulfill. There is not one Jesus birth story in the Gospels, but two, told in profoundly different narrative styles, offering us two different interpretations of history and the individual's role in its creation, two different ways of representing the same reality, ways as different as these reflected in the contrast between:

> We three Kings of orient are
> Bearing gifts we travel afar . . .

and

> A cold coming we had of it,
> Just the worst time of the year
> For a journey, and such a long journey:
> The ways deep and the weather sharp,
> The very dead of winter.

18. ENCOUNTERS IN THE NEW TESTAMENT

Jonathan Bishop

There is obviously more than one way to have to do with some other thing or person. We may ignore it, or him, or her; we may attend, in various modes from "take for granted" up to "study intensively." Or we may embark on one version or another of actual relation. The simplest is probably identification: I become the other, more or less, in order to comprehend it, or him, or her. Often this elementary notion of sympathy works in reverse: I assume, unconsciously, that the other is already the same as myself, and proceed accordingly. The negative of this is rejection—which leaves Me standing alone in the world, unchanged. Or I may admit the other as different but equally real, in which case I will experience our engagement as a confrontation—of which again there are many species, from the mildest conversation up to warfare. But the most interesting, and surely the most advanced, mode of relation takes place on the farther side of confrontation. We may call it, following various authorities, the mode of encounter, which could then be defined as that kind of engagement with the world in which one comes into relation not merely with some opposite but with the absolutely other: that which has power to generate a change in the encountering self. One might understand one's own history, for instance, as the product of so many encounters as one may have had: with a life-changing teacher, say, or a lover, or some "crucial" situation that made a lasting difference to our identity.

And it is possible as well to reread the great novels as stories in which Somebody succeeds or fails to encounter Somebody Else.

The same is true, *a fortiori,* of scripture. There are many encounters in the Old Testament; indeed it is possible to read the whole as the story of a developing encounter between Israel and God, and therefore figuratively between any culture and the ground of its existence. The individual stories of the principal personages are all episodes of encounter in just the sense here proposed: Abraham, Jacob, Moses, to begin with, and then Joshua, Gideon, Samuel, and Saul. Each of the prophets experiences a moment of contact with God or his representative, in the course of which he receives an adult identity and work. Typically the book of any prophet begins with the story of his conversion. The more imaginative narratives, like Job or Judith, show the same structure: the prayer of Job, like that of the Psalmist, is *for* encounter, and Job gets what he asks for, though not quite in the form he thought he wanted.

The New Testament is, in this as in other ways, a concentration of the Old: encounter is so much the principle of what takes place that we may misunderstand, for no detail is allowed that does not prepare for the moment of contact, and this happens over and over, rapidly, so that an event which in a big novel or even a series of novels might with great effort occur once and at last may in a Gospel take place in a short paragraph or even a sentence, casually. In the Bible, too, most stories are of successful encounter, in contrast to secular literature. The differences might offer a generic definition: a Gospel is the announcement of an encounter that works, in content and form, for the character and therefore for the reader who can take the fiction seriously as a figure for himself. So the moment of transcendence is brought about quickly, through a minimum of explicit context. Less essential circumstances are simply left out. We have, in effect, to supply what will correspond to these out of our own ordinary life—and all of history before and since. The Gospels take that much for granted.

This does not mean we do not have what is needed. One could illustrate more or less from virtually any story, but the most illuminating structurally are those anecdotes in which the various stages of encounter remain distinct. For an instance, the story of the cure of the blind man in John will show very neatly what happens when an encounter is carried through all the way.

The story begins when Jesus meets "a man who had been blind from birth,"[1] apparently begging with others near the Temple gate, the customary place for that purpose. Jesus is asked a legal conundrum by those accompanying him: did this man sin in the womb, or were his parents guilty, to account for his deformity? Jesus' answer implies that explanations in such terms are irrelevant: the man was born blind in order that "the works of God might be displayed in him." Which Jesus then puts into effect: like God making Adam, he "spat upon the ground, made a paste with the spittle," anointed the blind man's eyes, and told him to go wash in the Pool of Siloam. There are overtones to this detail which the reader is expected to pick up. Elisha, when he cured Naaman the Leper, had told him to go wash in the river, and Elisha is often a figure for Jesus. More important, the water of the pool in question was employed in the liturgy of the Feast of Tabernacles, where it already symbolized the blessings of the kingdom of God. John situates this episode at the time of Jesus' visit to Jerusalem for that feast, and clearly wants his reader to realize these and other connections between the event and the occasion. These associations, as usual in the Gospels, constitute a background of allusion which deepens the imaginative import of the bare actions explicitly reported; allusion is often the concreteness of scripture. In any event the blind man goes off following instructions and finds that his sight has been restored.

So far the story is a miraculous cure of the sort frequent in the Gospels, though with the depth of meaning characteristic of John in particular which is supplied by the context of the action, by some of the details, and by the naturally metaphoric value any restoration of sight cannot but have. Light is restored to a man through water; it is this conjunction that presumably led the early church to employ the story in the liturgy of baptism. Any cure, though, is already an encounter worked out in terms of the natural body. To meet Jesus is in this way to be changed physically into somebody else.

But in this case the change is not only physical, for the focus now shifts to the ex-blind man's relation to the world. He no longer has to be the beggar he was before, but it is not clear immediately who he is instead. "His neighbors and people who earlier had seen him begging said, 'Isn't this the man who used to sit and beg?'" Some said yes, some no; whereupon the man himself speaks, acknowledging his *past* self: "I am the man." The words used are significant: in Greek his phrase is simply *ego eimi,* I am. That is, the man is now able to use for himself the expression which in all the anecdotes in John is employed by Jesus as the climax to a process of self-revelation. As Jesus uses it, the *ego eimi* is the divine name, the I AM communicated to Moses on Sinai. This is *how* Jesus exposes who he is; in the Word, literally enough, transcendence is revealed. We shall see the phrase used in just this way in a moment. But it is fascinating to observe that John apparently conceives it right for those who meet Jesus to find that as a result of encountering *his* being, they are entitled to use the same expression for their own. The encounter has transmitted, not the divine identity in some magical sense, but the man's *own* identity. To have met Jesus, to have had his sight restored, and to have become free to assert that he is indeed the man he has been, and so the man he now is, amounts to one action, an action that at the same time is a mode of expression. The miracle is continuing.[2]

The man explains what has occurred: "The man called Jesus . . . made a paste, daubed my eyes with it and said to me, 'Go and wash at Siloam'; so I went, and when I washed I could see." It sounds simple. *The man called Jesus* is all he can know so far of the identity of the person whose meeting with him has effected the cure. As a name it is incomplete but accurate as far as it goes. As the incident progresses the name of Jesus changes in proportion to the continuing alteration in the man himself: this too, I believe, is characteristic of encounter, and not only in the Gospels, though very typically there, again especially in John. The bystanders are not happy. They bring him before the Pharisees, where he tells his story over for the second time.

The Pharisees are concerned that the event has taken place on the Sabbath and so involved at least two illegalities—kneading dough as well as healing, for the man could have waited one more day. There is disagreement: disobedience of the Law would show that Jesus could not be from God; on the other hand, a sinful person could scarcely accomplish such a miracle. The Pharisees turn to the beneficiary of the ambiguous action. "What have you to say about him yourself, now he has opened your eyes?" One feels some condescension in their inquiry: this is a beggar still as far as they are concerned, and presumably a sinner as well, and the issue is in any case a matter to settle among their learned selves. The man speaks back as if indifferent to their attitude, but bound to accuracy. His name for Jesus enlarges a step. "'He is a prophet,' replied the man." Even to say this much involves a choice. He is affirming now that the person who cured him must be trustworthy and no sinner; and therefore the self that has become his own must be trustworthy too. This decision puts him into what we can fairly call a confrontation with the Pharisees.

They send for his parents, as if to prove the cure of no genuine deficiency. "Is this man really your son who you say was born blind? If so, how is it that he is now able to see?" The parents are afraid and stick to what they are sure of, no more: "We know he is our son and we know he was born blind, but we don't know how it is that he can see now, or who opened his eyes!" He is old enough, the parents continue; let him speak for himself.

So there is a third exchange: the structure of the story is a sequence of dialogues. "Give Glory to God!" they say, meaning, tell the truth, you rogue: "For our part, we know that this man is a sinner." And if you won't agree with us, the implication runs, and deny him, you will be guilty of the same blasphemy, and suffer accordingly. "I don't know," he replies, "if he is a sinner; I only know that I was blind and now I can see." So far he is simply rehearsing the stage he has already reached, though it takes courage to do so: he knows what he knows, and who he has become so far, never mind what else may be the case. And they ask him once again to tell over the story of the case.

And then something new happens: he becomes combative enough to break through any fear he may still have of the judicial threats lurking in the background, or the awe he may feel for the superior social position of his examiners. He proceeds to make concrete the selfhood he has acquired, and gives an aggressive reply to the badgering: "I have told you once and you wouldn't listen. Why do you want to hear it all again?" And then, most exhilaratingly, he is sarcastic: "Do you want to become his disciples too?" At this naturally they hurl abuse back: *he* can be Jesus' disciple if he wishes, *they* are satisfied to remain disciples of

Moses, whom they know was from God, "but as for this man, we don't know where he comes from." Whereupon the cured man progresses from rebuttal, which was bold enough, to instruction. "Now here is an astonishing thing! He has opened my eyes, and you don't know where he comes from!" The Pharisees are affronted by this challenge to their academic authority and repudiate his remarks as if he were still blind and therefore a sinner with no right to speak. "'Are you trying to teach us,' they replied, 'and you a sinner through and through, since you were born!'" Their definition of him, as of the situation, is obsolete, but it is practically effective, for he is driven away, presumably excommunicated—as many converted Jews of John's own generation may have been.

Then comes the completion of the episode. For only now does Jesus return to the man, after he has heard he was driven off. "'Do you believe in the Son of Man?' 'Sir,' the man replied, 'tell me who he is so that I may believe in him.'" A prophet, which he has already confessed Jesus to be, would have that kind of authority. And then Jesus completes the connection: *he is* the fulfillment of that traditional metaphor too. "Jesus said, 'You are looking at him; he is speaking to you.'" This speech is the divine I AM for this context, and thus a revelation in words of the being implied by the physical miracle, which the man has already proved he accepts as a change in his social self too. This entitles him to the moment of consciousness which follows the appropriation of a valid sign. His last response is final: "The man said, 'Lord, I believe,'" and threw himself at Jesus' feet. Whereupon Jesus' speech alters to poetry, to generalize what has happened, in the usual Johannine style:

> It is for judgment
> that I have come into this world,
> so that those without sight may see
> and those with sight turn blind.

To which the Pharisees attempt a last word in defense of themselves, and are answered again: if you were really blind, you would be innocent; as it is, by claiming to see when you do not, you are guilty. But this exchange takes place apart from the relation with the man who has been cured, who now has completed his education in Jesus' identity, and so in his own as well. Henceforth he is a disciple, which makes the story paradigmatic for the like change in anybody who has been brought to the same conclusion, in those days or since.

This is always the point to which the Gospels wish to bring matters. It is necessary imaginatively for Jesus to provoke representatives of every human and social type to acknowledge him as fully as they can in order to make the story universally applicable, that is, a Gospel, indeed. And so we see him doing through the other encounters which crowd all the versions of the story. Indeed, if John's version stands a little apart from the others in this respect, it is perhaps because John, writing later, had the advantage of seeing more clearly than the three previous writers how the function of a history of this kind could be precisely to demonstrate how Jesus met with representatives of the whole human race, converting some and provoking others to denial, in order that any reader might fulfill the intention thus variously enfigured, and so make the fictions true, the word a Word, and imagination a figure for identity.

To the extent that Jesus *is* whom he finds him to be, the blind man cured is a type of the elect; he has, in fact, what we are repeatedly told is required to enter the Kingdom: "faith." For faith within the Gospels seems precisely to mean the ability to recognize Jesus. Any such recognition constitutes the objective half of an encounter of which the subjective half is the corresponding response within a recipient. Not me but Christ in me, the cured man might have said (as Paul did say) inspired those brave words with which he repelled the effort of his enemies to persuade him that he was not himself. Yet that familiar mode of summing up what occurs in such cases could still leave an impression that the self of the believer is, as it were, occupied by Christ—which would make "Christ" mean a demon. The story makes clear that encounter does *not* result in possession; if that were so, the Pharisees would be right. To meet Jesus as the Christ is rather to recognize him as the man who is entitled to say, I AM. Whatever is done, miraculous or otherwise, is comprehensible as expressive of this identity. And to recognize him is not to become him, empathetically or mythically, but to become *ourselves*. The blind man is cured, and becomes who he was and is, and thus strong enough to identify with his own existence. In this way the Kingdom is not merely announced but created.

Further: since Jesus in the Gospels is himself a figure for the Christ of faith, and the persons who meet him figures of ourselves, the relation of encounter between him and them will act as a paradigm in multiple for the relation any one of us can have at any time, not with Jesus (him we do not meet, except as a character in these and other stories) nor, of course, with a theological idea, but with *any other person* who says I AM in some language or other. This would be the final import of the gospel as Gospel: unless it can be so understood, the text would not be a real Good Word at all, but only an interestingly compressed nonfiction novel.

Naturally this fulfillment of content in form and imagination in truth *need* not happen. If the Gospels include story after story of completed encounter which exhibit to the reader what any one of us might do in our circumstances as we meet our "neighbor," so too they show what occurs when encounter is refused. If faith is recognition, even very partial recognition, of Somebody Else, then lack of faith is within the story an unwillingness to see in Jesus whatever aspect of his identity is most significant to the character who meets him. We have a beautiful, virtually Jamesian, illustration of what can fail to happen in the story of Nicodemus. This man, we are told, was one of the Pharisees and a member of the Jewish Council. He comes to Jesus by night and says: "'Rabbi, we know that you are a teacher who comes from God; for no one could perform the signs that you do unless God were with him.'"

By speaking this way Nicodemus shows he is among those who ought to know; by position, learning, and devotion, he should be prepared in his ordinary capacity as rabbi to interpret such Messianic figures as Jesus has been giving. In fact—it is the largest irony of the Gospels as a whole—those best prepared cannot act when the chance comes, precisely *because* their expectations are too built into character and culture. Men like Nicodemus have identified themselves with definitions they know too exactly. They want someone new to confirm a notion already fixed inside the heads of those who know best. For them revelation has become, quite unconsciously, a kind of technology.

So we see here. Nicodemus comes, which is in his favor; indeed, he is an appealing character, caught in a predicament it should be easy for academic intellectuals to sympathize with. He makes what clearly seems to him the generous liberal gesture: he acknowledges that Jesus is a genuine teacher who has really come from God. This had been in doubt among his associates, as we know from other episodes. But from the side of faith, the point is that he already "knows" this fact he supposes himself to be conceding. He has worked it out by ordinary inference. The conclusion is still very much his possession, worked out from observation of or hearing about the miracles: it is *logical* for a careful and scrupulous man to believe this much. His consciousness can readily expand to that extent; information is increased, and with it himself. But it is still the same old Nicodemus. He is in control of what he knows. That is the point about knowledge of this sort; one remains in control of it.

Nicodemus would clearly like to go discussing the matter on the level he has started upon. Perhaps he would like some additional "sign," which he could communicate to wavering friends on the Council. But the Johannine Jesus does not continue the discussion within the terms in which his interlocutor has unconsciously established it. He leaps ahead, out of the game Nicodemus had begun to play:

> "I tell you most solemnly,
> unless a man is born from above,
> he cannot see the kingdom of God."

Nicodemus said, "How can a grown man be born? Can he go back into his mother's womb and be born again?" Jesus replied:

> "I tell you most solemnly,
> unless a man is born through water and the Spirit,
> he cannot enter the kingdom of God."

We have just seen, in the miracle of the blind man, how this rebirth *can* happen. To be "born again" is precisely to suffer encounter, and so take part in whatever action communicates the meaning of encounter. That action will be the "water" to the "spirit" revealed, in or out of any liturgy. Jesus brings up what Nicodemus is *not* doing, and the presence of this absence makes emphatic what happens instead. Nicodemus turns stupid, and understands a metaphor as if it were only a natural test, as others do on similar occasions. This is regressive; he swallows a word, as it were, the wrong way, rejecting not simply the possibility of a meaning for symbols but the imagination itself.

So nothing happens. "How can that be possible?" remains his best answer and last contribution to the scene; he goes out, shaking his head. Much later, at the other end of the whole story, he reappears again to help bury Jesus: "Nicodemus came as well—the same one who had first come to Jesus at night-time—and he brought a mixture of myrrh and aloes, weighing about a hundred pounds." This is *his* imaginative action, which allows us to suppose could have been completed later, offstage in a full conversion; which would be to imagine a happy ending, completing the story we have. There are legends to that effect. And other actual lives since have shown how a death can be a converting ordinance when a life has been only a life. As it is, though, Nicodemus remains a type of those who stop short of response to a new presence because they are overattached to some *a priori* scheme in terms of which the presence is only one more fact, though of course a very interesting one. He should be, if one might call him so, the patron of those who cannot quite encounter—not, as things are, a small party, which will always include most of ourselves.

19. JOHN 9: A LITERARY-CRITICAL ANALYSIS

James L. Resseguie

C. H. Dodd refers to John 9 as "one of the most brilliant passages in the gospel."[1] The imagery, the structure, the movement of the plot, and the characterization all work together to form a tightly knit narrative. The narrative has been carefully shaped so that everything it shows serves to tell.[2] The purpose of this paper is to show how the form and content of John 9 are closely woven together to form a unity.

The chapter may be divided into seven scenes with each scene containing a dialogue between two characters or sets of characters. In scene 1 the dialogue occurs between the disciples and Jesus; in scene 2, the blind man and his neighbors; in scenes 3 and 5, the blind man and the religious authorities; in scene 4, the religious authorities and the parents of the blind man; in scene 6, Jesus and the blind man; and in scene 7, the authorities and Jesus.

Scene 1: vv. 1-7. The opening scene introduces a blind man and two other characters, Jesus and the disciples. If we compare the structure of chapter 9 with other healing stories in the Gospel, we see that this chapter does not conform to the basic form of other similar stories. John 9 departs from the structural pattern of the other stories in one significant way: the characterization of the healed man is fully developed. In John 5, for example, a lame man at the pool of Bethzatha is healed by Jesus; yet within the miracle story itself there is no attempt by the narrator to develop the character of the lame man. Only once does the lame man speak, and that is in response to a question by Jesus. The blind man of chapter 9, however, not only speaks in 13 of 41 verses, but he uses irony and sarcasm, and he even takes the initiative to lecture the religious authorities on some basic theological insights. Unlike any other healing story of the Gospel of John, the blind man in chapter 9 does not fade into the background. He remains not only in the foreground but as the center of attention for the entire chapter.

As the scene opens, the disciples ask Jesus to make a judgment concerning the cause of the man's blindness. However, Jesus prefers not to answer that question; instead he points to the purpose of the man's blindness (v. 3: "that the works of God might be made manifest in him"). The literary import of this should not go unnoticed. By having the disciples raise a question that is not immediately answered, the entire narrative can then be structured so that the reader is shown the answer to that question instead of being told the answer. Also, postponing the answer to the disciples' question creates a dramatic tension for the readers. Ironically, it will be the religious authorities who will illustrate the cause of blindness, not the blind man.

The opening scene introduces some important images, which create a mood of urgency and set a tone of opposition. The images of night and day are set in opposition to each other in v. 4: "we must work the works of him who sent me while it is day; night comes, when no one can work." Verse 5 introduces the imagery of night with the saying by Jesus: "I am the light of the world," while the healing of the man's blindness sets before the readers another pair of images: blindness and sight. The dualistic imagery of day and night, of blindness and sight, of light and darkness, creates a pronounced tone of opposition and helps to establish a mood of urgency. The works of the day and of light can not be delayed even for a short period of time, for the night and the darkness may come at any time. For this reason the healing of the blind man cannot be postponed one day, even though the laws that govern the sabbath are violated in the process (cf. v. 14).

The imagery of the opening scene also has the effect of establishing a figurative context for the interpretation of the narrative. Similar imagery of light and of darkness is used figuratively in the prologue of the Gospel. There light is not only opposed to darkness, but light also represents the "enlighten-ment" that Jesus brings. "The true light that enlightens every man was coming into the world" (1:9). Therefore, the reader is already alert to the figurative significance of John 9. Light and the reception of sight represents enlightenment, while night and darkness represent blindness and continued opposition to the light.

The method of healing the blind man is striking; yet similar techniques are recorded in the Synoptics (cf. Mark 7:31-36; 8:22-26). Jesus spits on the ground, makes clay, and anoints the man's eyes. He then sends him to the pool of Siloam to wash. At this point the narrator intrudes into the narrative to inform the reader that the word Siloam means "sent." Although it is not unusual for the narrator to translate Hebrew words or to explain Jewish customs, the translation of Siloam as "sent" draws the reader's attention to the symbolic meaning of washing in the pool of Siloam. The narrator expects the reader to make a connection between Siloam, which means "Sent," and Jesus as the "one who is sent." Several times throughout the Gospel Jesus refers to himself or is referred to as the "one who is sent" from the Father (e.g., John 3:17; 3:34; 5:35, etc.). As recently as verse 4 of chapter 9 we are told that Jesus does the works of "him who sent me." The blind man received his sight after washing in the pool of Siloam. By association "enlightenment" comes from the "one who is sent." Scene 1 closes with the creation of the blind man's sight, and Jesus moves offstage.

Scene 2: vv. 8-12. The neighbors of the blind man enter and discuss among themselves whether this man who received sight was "the man who used to sit and beg." There is a division among them. Some say he is the man; others say he is someone else. The contrasting imagery of scene 1 is now replaced by contrasting opinions. Several times throughout the Gospel the narrator draws attention to divided opinion. In chapter 7, for example, some believe that Jesus is the Christ, but others are doubtful (vv. 40-41). The narrator, therefore, pointedly draws attention of the divided opinion: "there was a division among the people over him" (v. 43). In chapter 10 there is a division among some of the Jews over who Jesus is. Some say that he has a demon; yet others believe that he could not open the eyes of the blind if he had a demon (vv. 19-21).

Again the narrator specifically underscores the division with the narrative comment: "there was again a division" (v. 19). Later in this chapter the Pharisees will be divided over who Jesus is (9:16). Some conclude that Jesus is not from God; others remain uncertain. The narrator once again feels it is important to draw attention to the division: "There was a division among them." First the narrator shaped for us contrasting images (day/night; light/darkness; blindness/sight); now he molds contrasting opinions, pro/con. The dualistic imagery of light and darkness is reflected in the divided opinions, and the tone of opposition created by the imagery becomes concrete in the contrasting opinion.

The scene closes with the healed man's story of how Jesus healed him. When asked where Jesus is, he confesses his ignorance. "I do not know."

Scene 3: vv. 13-17. We have seen the development of contrasting imagery and of divided opinion, and now the narrative focuses on the development of the characters. The antagonists, the religious authorities, appear on the scene. Because Jesus healed the blind man on the sabbath and kneaded clay—a double violation of the laws governing the sabbath—the religious authorities are consulted by the neighbors of the healed man. The breach of the sabbath laws suggests that Jesus is a sinner and not from God, and yet the miracle itself seems to demonstrate that he is from God. The authorities are divided in their opinion concerning Jesus' action. This division serves not only to focus attention upon who Jesus is, but it sets an atmosphere for a trial. A verdict concerning Jesus' action of healing on the sabbath needs to be reached.

Therefore, the narrative takes the form of a trial. At first the religious authorities interrogate the healed man; then the parents of the healed man will testify, followed by a second interrogation of the man born blind. Finally, in a dramatic peripeteia, the verdict will be pronounced not on Jesus by the religious authorities, but on the authorities by Jesus.

Scene 3 closes with the testimony of the healed man concerning Jesus. "He is a prophet."

Scene 4: vv. 18-23. Unwilling to accept the testimony of the healed man, the religious authorities attempt another course of action. Perhaps the man was not born blind. Therefore, the authorities call the parents to testify. "Is this your son, who you say was born blind? How then does he now see?" The parents, however, seem reluctant to get involved in the trial. In fact their response is so evasive that the narrator intrudes to provide an explanation for their curt response to the authorities. "His parents said this because they feared the Jews, for the Jews had already agreed that if any one should confess him to be Christ, he was to be put out of the synagogue." It seems to make no difference to the narrator that the parents were not asked who Jesus is, only to provide an explanation for the fact that their son now sees. This puzzing comment by the narrator has been seen by many scholars as a later redaction added to the narrative. J. Louis Martyn,[3] for example, suggests that the community of the Fourth Evangelist is experiencing a situation similar to this comment. If the members of the community confess that Jesus is the Messiah, they are in danger of being expelled from the synagogue. Therefore, the narrative intrusion serves to identify the *Sitz-im-Leben* of the Fourth Evangelist, but it does not fit into the present narrative.

However, if the intrusion is seen as a rhetorical device on the part of the narrator, it does fit smoothly into its context. The parents are a foil for the action of the healed man in the subsequent scene. While the parents are fearful of the authorities and are afraid to confess Jesus as Messiah, the man born blind is fearless and bold in his confrontation with the authorities. The characterization of the healed man is markedly enhanced by contrasting his response to the authorities with that of his parents.

Scene 5: vv. 24-34. The scene shifts now to a dialogue between the religious authorities and the healed man; for the second time, they interrogate him. The division among the religious authorities concerning who Jesus is, is now replaced with a single authoritative voice. "We know that this man is a sinner." The confident assertion of the first person plural, "we know," clearly states the judgment of the religious authorities concerning who Jesus is.

The characterization of the healed man is most pronounced in this scene. With biting irony he asks the authorities if they too want to become disciples of Jesus. In the opening scene the blind man appeared more as an object to settle a theological discussion than as a person in his own right. In the third scene he still lacks color: to the questions of the authorities he responds with short, declarative sentences. He takes no initiative of his own, and his comments lack the biting sarcasm of the fifth scene. This scene, however, marks the development of the healed man as a person in his own right. His irony leads to sarcasm, and his sarcasm opens the way for him to lecture the religious authorities on some basic theological principles. When the authorities admit that they do not know from where Jesus comes the healed man sarcastically says, "Why, this is a marvel! You do not know where he comes from, and yet he opened my eyes." The lecture continues: "We know that God does not listen to sinners, but if any one is a worshiper of God and does his will, God listens to him. Never since the world began has it been heard that any one opened the eyes of a man born blind. If this man were not from God, he could do nothing." The confident assertion of the first person plural, "we know," underscores the authoritative posture of the healed man. His singular action of lecturing the authorities has penetrated the barriers of a stratified society. The narrative's development of the healed man's character is actually the development of his personhood. It is not accidental that the blind man appeared in scene 1 as a colorless object of theological speculation and that not until this scene does he appear as a character in his own right. The reception of sight in scene 1 and the "enlightenment" he receives concerning who Jesus is parallels the development of his own character. When he comes to the point of seeing who Jesus is, he also comes to the point of seeing who he himself is. No longer is he that nameless blind man of scene 1; now he is confident of his own identity, and he confronts the religious authorities.

The scene closes with the expulsion of the healed man by the religious authorities from their midst.

Scene 6: vv. 35-38. Jesus comes back onstage. When he hears that the healed man has been cast out by the authorities, he goes and finds him. The narrative places the final set of contrasts before us. First the narrative shaped for us the opposing contrasts of day and night, of light and darkness, of blindness and sight; they were followed by the divided opinions, pro and con, toward Jesus; then there were the contrasting responses of the parents and of their son to the religious authorities. Finally we have the contrast of the blind man's being cast out and then found by Jesus, the contrast of rejection and acceptance.

The scene closes with the healed man's confession of Jesus as the Son of man.[4]

Scene 7: vv. 39-41. The final scene of the narrative is an exchange between Jesus and some of the religious authorities. It opens with a solemn pronouncement by Jesus concerning his mission. "For judgment I came into this world, that those who do not see may see, and that those who see may become blind." Some of the religious authorities overhearing what Jesus said ask, "Are we also blind?" In the opening scene the disciples asked Jesus to make a judgment concerning the cause of blindness. That judgment, however, was deferred so that the narrative could show the reader the true cause of blindness. The closing scene now has Jesus make the judgment so that the reader is told as well as shown the cause of blindness, which is simply the reluctance of some of the religious authorities to see the light when given the opportunity. As a result the verdict is pronounced upon them. "If you were blind, you would have no guilt; but now that you say, 'We see,' your guilt remains." With the verdict given, the trial is now completed.

The literary unity of form and of content makes John 9 a brilliant passage in the Gospel. The imagery, the structure, the movement of the plot, and the characterization work together to form a unified whole. Each part contributes to the whole and advances the plot, no action or event is unrelated to the main theme of the narrative. The theme that shapes the form and content is the concept of judgment found in verse 39: "For judgment I came into this world, that those who do not see may see, and that those who see may become blind."

At the heart of the dualistic imagery of light, darkness, and blindness, on the one hand, and of day, light, and sight, on the other, is the concept of judgment. It is the individual's response or judgment concerning the light that determines whether he or she remains in darkness or enters into the light. The man born blind receives his sight because he is healed by the One who is the Light, and his positive judgment concerning Jesus parallels the reception of sight. But when the religious authorities are confronted with the

Light or knowledge of the Light, they remain obdurate and unwilling to see the Light.

The structure of John 9 also derives its meaning from the theme of judgment. The form of a trial is singularly appropriate to show the dramatic reversals brought about by the presence of light and the resulting judgment. Light and judgment are interrelated concepts in this Gospel, for light causes division or separation so that light and darkness cannot coexist. Actually the judgment that Jesus brings is nothing more than the specific manifestation of this process of division, which results because the light has come into the world. Although John 3:19 brings together the concepts of light and judgment ("And this is the judgment, that the light has come into the world, and men loved darkness rather than light, because their deeds were evil"), it is John 9 that shows the reader the relationship between light and judgment.

The movement of the plot is also directly related to the theme of judgment. The comic movement, or the movement from ill-being to well-being on the part of the healed man, parallels the judgment he makes concerning who Jesus is. The narrative shows the man born blind moving in an upward direction from spiritual blindness to spiritual enlightenment. As the trial progresses the healed man gives voice to statements that reveal an ever-deepening knowledge of who Jesus is. In the second scene he refers to Jesus merely as "the man called Jesus" (v. 11). In scene 3 he confesses that Jesus is a prophet (v. 17), and by scene 5 he has become an ardent defender of Jesus as one from God (v. 33). Finally, in scene 6 he sees that Jesus is the Son of man.

The comic movement of the plot contrasts with the tragic movement, or downward movement from well-being to ill-being on the part of the religious authorities. Initially the authorities' opinion concerning Jesus is divided; some say that he is not from God, but others are uncertain (v. 16). However, by scene 5 this divided opinion is replaced by the judgment that Jesus is not from God (v. 24). The last scene completes the tragedy when the authorities, not Jesus, are pronounced guilty.

Finally, the characterization contributes to the theme of judgment and to the unity of John 9. The contrasting characterizations of the religious authorities and of the blind man parallel the opposing judgments made by the characters concerning Jesus. The characterization of the religious authorities keenly illustrates their tragic fate because they believe that they do see, when in fact they are the ones who are blind to who Jesus is. It is with tragic irony that they ask at the end of the trial, "Are we also blind?"

The development of the blind man's character on the other hand, parallels his positive judgment concerning Jesus' identity. He moves from a colorless character in scene 1 to an engaging, attractive personality in scene 5 who badgers the authorities with irony and sarcasm. In the process of confrontation he discovers who he is. In other words, the development of the blind man's character is also the development of a person, of a newfound selfhood that penetrates a stratified society and that breaks down the walls that divide. John 9 shows us a new selfhood developing, one that is no longer captive to one's own sin or to the sin of one's parents. The creative act of giving the man sight enabled him for the first time to see both who Jesus is and who he himself really is.

Because the form and content are so carefully woven together, John 9 is a superb piece of literature. Dualistic images, contrasting opinions, opposing movement of plot, and diverse characterizations all work together to show the reader the interrelationship between light and judgment. At the same time everything John 9 shows also serves to tell.

NOTES

6. Joseph, Judah, and Jacob

1. I wish to acknowledge my indebtedness and express my gratitude to Robert Alter, Thayer Warshaw, and George Savran for their many helpful suggestions.
2. For a convenient listing and brief discussion of the doubled elements, see H. Donner, *Die literarische Gestalt der alttestamentlichen Josephsgeschichte* (Heidelberg: Carl Winter, 1976), pp. 36-43.
3. D. B. Redford, *A Study of the Biblical Story of Joseph (Genesis 37–50)*, vol. 20 of *Supplements to Vetus Testamentum* (Leiden: E. J. Brill), p. 75.
4. Ibid., pp. 75-76.
5. N. Leibowitz, *Studies in the Book of Genesis* (Jerusalem: World Zionist Organization Department for Torah Education and Culture, 1972), pp. 458-59.
6. Leibowitz, pp. 480-81. Both the Septuagint and the Samaritan Pentateuch read "your one *[hā 'ehad]* brother" rather than "your brother-another *['ahēr]*." While it must be admitted that the Hebrew syntactical construction is unusual, the Septuagint and Samaritan Pentateuch renderings seem to be emendations based on Gen. 42:19. The two contexts require different meanings.
7. It is interesting to note that Deut. 21:15-17, in discussing the duty of a man having two wives toward the firstborn when he is the son of the hated wife, states that he must "recognize" him as the firstborn. Are the brothers ironically alluding to this legal custom in asking Jacob to "recognize" the garment of his favored son?
8. E.g., Gen. 9:22-23; Exod. 20:26; Lev. 18:6-18; 20:11-21.
9. See Leibowitz, pp. 464-67.
10. L. Ruppert, *Die Josephserzählung der Genesis* (Munich: Kösel, 1965), p. 102.
11. G. von Rad, *Genesis* (Philadelphia: Westminster Press, 1966), p. 388.
12. Exod. 8:8, 26; 9:33; 10:6, 18; 11:8; I Sam. 20:5; cf. 9:19.

13. See F. Brown, S. R. Driver, and C. A. Briggs, *A Hebrew and English Lexicon of the Old Testament* (Oxford: Clarendon, 1955), p. 87: "'*ēt* expresses closer association than '*im*"—comparing I Sam. 14:17—Saul's "Who has gone from those about us *[mē 'immānû]*"—with Gen. 44:28—Jacob's "and the one has gone from with me *[mē 'ittî]*.

14. Cf. Exod. 2:14; Judg. 9:7-15; I Sam. 8, etc.

15. H. Gunkel, *Genesis* (Göttingen: Vandenhoeck & Ruprecht, 1917), p. 401; G. Von Rad, *Genesis*, pp. 348-49; E. A. Speiser, *Genesis* (Garden City, N.Y.: Doubleday, 1964), pp. 293-94; B. Vawter, *On Genesis: A New Reading* (Doubleday, 1977), pp. 386-87.

16. Redford, pp. 132-35.

17. Cf. Exod. 21:16; Deut. 24:7. M. Greenberg, "Some Postulates of Biblical Criminal Law," in J. Goldin, ed., *The Jewish Expression* (New Haven: Yale University Press, 1976), pp. 24-29, demonstrates that biblical law, in distinction from Babylonian or Hittite, prescribes the death penalty for murder and prohibits the death penalty for theft. Since kidnapping involved selling a person into slavery, Israelite law treated it as a form of murder.

18. Leibowitz, pp. 396-97.

19. "The Youngest Son or Where Does Genesis 38 Belong?" *Journal of Biblical Literature* 96 (1977): 27-44.

20. Cf. II Sam. 3:7-11; 16:20-23; I Kings 2:22.

21. "The Youngest Son," pp. 38-40.

22. Ibid., p. 40.

23. Ibid., esp. pp. 38-42.

24. "A Literary Approach to the Bible," *Commentary* 60 (1975): 70-77.

25. "Paradox and Symmetry in the Joseph Narrative," in *Literary Interpretations of Biblical Narratives,* ed. K. R. R. Gros Louis, with J. S. Ackerman and T. S. Warshaw (Nashville: Abingdon, 1974), pp. 67-69.

26. Ibid., 62-64.

27. Jer. 37:16.

28. My interpretation of Gen. 49:8-12 is following the general lines of E. M. Good, "The 'Blessing' on Judah, Gen. 49:8-12," *Journal of Biblical Literature* 82 (1963): 427-32, although I do not agree with Good's conclusion that the poem in its present setting is a polemic against Judah. Cf. also C. Carmichael, "Some Sayings in Gen. 49," *Journal of Biblical Literature* 88 (1969): 435-44.

29. Job 31:10; perhaps Judg. 5:27 is playing on this connotation in describing Sisera's encounter with Jael.

30. The Hebrew term for "staff" in Gen. 49:10 is not the same as in Gen. 38:18, 25; but both terms occur in poetic parallelism in Isa. 14:5 and Ezek. 19:11, 14.

31. Carmichael, "Some Sayings in Gen. 49," 441-42.

32. Ibid.

33. The Hebrew text (*ʿad kî yābōʾ šîlô*) is very problematic.

34. "Joseph and His Brothers," *Commentary* 65 (1980): 59-69.

35. Ibid., esp. pp. 59-61, 69.

36. Ibid., p. 60.

7. An Equivocal Reading of the Sale of Joseph

1. Versions of this study were presented at the Columbia University Hebrew Bible Seminar (December, 1979) and at the annual meeting of the American

Academy of Religion in Dallas, Texas (November, 1980). I wish to thank in particular William Herbrechtsmeier, David Marcus, Alan Mintz, and Thayer Warshaw for their helpful suggestions, and the Abbell Research Fund of the Jewish Theological Seminary for helping to support the preparation of this study. Throughout this essay, I use my own translation from the Hebrew.

2. That the text employs both the names "Jacob" (37:1, 2, 34) and "Israel" (37:3, 13) is attributed by source-criticism to two hypothetical documents from which our text appears to have been composed. One document used the name "Jacob," the other "Israel." Whatever the validity of this explanation based on the analysis of sources, from a literary perspective this explanation is irrelevant. Since the text is a literary whole—however it was composed— shifting between the two names of the patriarch may now carry literary significance. Literary analysis of the entire chapter demonstrates that there is more at work here than an author's "desire for literary variety" (Donald B. Redford, *A Study of the Biblical Story of Joseph, Vetus Testamentum* Supplement 20 [Leiden, 1970], 106; so, too, M. H. Segal, "The Composition of the Pentateuch," in Chaim Rabin, ed., *Studies in the Bible,* Scripta Hierosolymitana 8 [Jerusalem, 1961], 90). Briefly stated, a theme running through the entire story, most intensely perhaps in chap. 37, is the dialectic between what is and what will be, reality and destiny (as, for example, in the dreams). Now, once we recall from preceding narratives that the name "Jacob" connotes the scheming man of this world while "Israel" connotes the man of vision and destiny, who had "striven with God and with men and prevailed" (Gen. 32:28), we may perceive the dialectic of reality/destiny in the alternation "Jacob"/"Israel."

3. Cf. Burke O. Long, "Recent Field Studies in Oral Literature and Their Bearing on OT Criticism," *Vetus Testamentum* 26 (1976): 187-98, esp. 194-95.

4. Redford, *A Study of the Biblical Story of Joseph,* p. 106.

5. Cf. ibid., pp. 140ff.; Samuel Sandmel, *The Enjoyment of Scripture* (New York: Oxford University Press, 1972), p. 113.

6. Cf., e.g., Zvi Adar, *Teaching the Joseph Story* (Jerusalem, 1966), p. 9, n. 1 (in Hebrew); Nahum M. Sarna, *Understanding Genesis* (New York: McGraw-Hill, 1966), p. 214.

7. See, e.g., O. S. Wintermute, "Joseph Son of Jacob," *Interpreter's Dictionary of the Bible* (Nashville: Abingdon Press, 1962), p. 983*b*: "Gen. 37 is one of the most convincing illustrations of the 'documentary hypothesis'"; cf. recently Bruce Vawter, *On Genesis* (Garden City, N.Y.: Doubleday, 1977), pp. 386-87.

8. E. A. Speiser, *Genesis,* Anchor Bible #1 (Garden City, N.Y.: Doubleday, 1964), p. 293; cf. W. F. Albright, *Yahweh and the Gods of Canaan* (Doubleday, 1968), p. 39: "It is most improbable that the original editors of the Pentateuch can have left such an obvious discrepancy standing." For a recent description of the source-critical analysis of Genesis 37, see Alan W. Jenks, *The Elohist and North Israelite Traditions,* Society of Biblical Literature Monograph Series 22 (Missoula, Montana, 1977), esp. pp. 27-29.

9. Cf. Roland Barthes, *Writing Degree Zero,* trans. A. Lavers and C. Smith (New York: Hill & Wang, 1968), p. 58: "In actual fact, clarity is a purely rhetorical attribute, not a quality of language in general, which is possible at all times and in all places, but only the ideal appendage to a certain type of discourse, that which is given over to a permanent intention to persuade."

10. E.G., Sarna, *Understanding Genesis,* 214, who ignores the statement in verse 28 relating that the Midianites pulled Joseph out of the pit. Troubled by the

apparent discrepancies, George W. Coats removes the Midianites from the story altogether by hypothesizing that the mention of the Midianites was interpolated into the narrative by a later hand (*From Canaan to Egypt: Structural and Theological Context for the Joseph Story* [Washington, D.C.: Catholic Biblical Association of America, 1976], pp. 17, 61). This is also the reading of Andrew Lloyd Webber and Tim Rice for their rock operetta *Joseph and the Amazing Technicolor Dreamcoat.*

11. E.g., Donald A. Seybold, "Paradox and Symmetry in the Joseph Narrative," in Kenneth R. R. Gros Louis, et al., eds., *Literary Interpretations of Biblical Narratives* (Nashville: Abingdon Press, 1974), pp. 60-61: Mary Savage, "Literary Criticism and Biblical Studies: A Rhetorical Analysis of the Joseph Narrative," in C. C. Evans, et al., eds., *Scripture in Context,* Pittsburgh Theological Monograph Series #34 (Pittsburgh, 1980), pp. 79-100.

12. Cf. Sarna, *Understanding Genesis,* p. 214; Sandmel, *The Enjoyment of Scripture,* p. 111. See already the commentary of the medieval exegete Rabbi Abraham Ibn Ezra; but contrast the commentary of his older contemporary Rashi, who perceived that these Midianites are not Ishmaelites and that the text refers to more than one sale.

13. Shemaryahu Talmon sees the alternation "Ishmaelite"/"Midianite" as "but an instance of (stylistic) variation" ("The Presentation of Synchroneity and Simultaneity in Biblical Narratives," in J. Heimann and S. Werses, eds., *Studies in Hebrew Narrative Art,* Scripta Hierosolymitana 27 [Jerusalem, 1978], pp. 9-26, here p. 19). However, such a reading ignores the divergent references to these groups, as I explain below.

14. The narrative sequence in chap. 37 is interrupted by the episode involving Judah and Tamar in chap. 38, after which chap. 39 opens with a resumption of the action at the end of chap. 37. Such a "resumptive repetition" has been characterized as a typical feature of biblical narrative, for which see Talmon, "The Presentation of Synchroneity," with reference to our case on p. 18 (see preceding note), and cf. G. W. Coats, "Redactional Unity in Genesis 37-50," *Journal of Biblical Literature* 93 (1974): 15-21, esp. 16, n. 2.

15. Benno Jacob has tried to get around this contradiction by interpreting "to Egypt" in 37:36 to mean the Ishmaelites (*The First Book of the Bible: Genesis,* abridged, ed., and trans. E. I. Jacob and W. Jacob [New York: Ktav, 1974], p. 255). But his attempt is hardly convincing. In order to avoid finding any contradiction in this episode, one would have to interpret the passage in a manner like that of Isaac Caro, a fifteenth-century Spanish rabbi, in his commentary *Sefer Toledot Yitzhaq.* According to Caro, the brothers instructed the Midianites to remove Joseph from the pit and sell him on their behalf to the Ishmaelites. After this sale, the Midianites accompanied the Ishmaelites to Egypt, where the Ishmaelites asked the Midianites to sell Joseph to Potiphar for them. Thus, for Caro, 39:1 means that Potiphar purchased Joseph from the ownership of the Ishmaelites, not from them directly. Needless to say, such a reading goes far beyond the limits of the text itself.

16. Edwin M. Good, *Irony in the Old Testament* (Philadelphia: Westminster Press, 1965), p. 107; cf. Eric I. Lowenthal, *The Joseph Narrative in Genesis* (New York: Ktav, 1973), pp. 27-28.

17. See the title essay of Susan Sontag, *Against Interpretation* (New York: Farrar, Straus, 1966), pp. 3-14.

18. Cf. Louis Z. Hammer, "The Relevance of Buber's Thought to Aesthetics," in Paul A. Schilpp and M. Friedman, eds., *The Philosophy of Martin Buber*

(LaSalle, Ill.: Open Court, 1967), esp. p. 627. This phenomenological approach to literature has received extended articulation recently in the works of Stanley Fish and Wolfgang Iser. For bibliography and discussion of Fish, see William Ray, "Supersession and the Subject: A Reconsideration of Stanley Fish's 'Affective Stylistics,'" *Diacritics* 8/3 (Fall, 1978): 60-71. And see Iser's *Implied Reader* (Baltimore: Johns Hopkins Press, 1974) and *The Act of Reading* (Johns Hopkins Press, 1978).

19. See in particular his "Introduction to the Structural Analysis of Narratives," *Image/Music/Text*, trans. S. Heath (New York: Farrar, Straus, 1977), pp. 79-124; *Elements of Semiology*, trans. A. Lavers and C. Smith (New York: Jonathan Cape, 1968); and *S/Z*, trans. R. Miller (New York: Hill & Wang, 1974).

20. R. Barthes, "The Struggle with the Angel," in Barthes, et al., eds., *Structural Analysis and Biblical Exegesis*, Pittsburgh Theological Monograph Series #3 (Pittsburgh, 1974), pp. 21-33 = *Image/Music/Text*, pp. 125-41. For a discussion of this study by Barthes, see Hugh C. White, "French Structuralism and OT Narrative Analysis: Roland Barthes," *Semeia* 3 (1975):99-127.

21. Barthes, *Image/Music/Text*, pp. 140-41.

22. Ibid., p. 131.

23. Cf. e.g., Joel Rosenberg, "Meanings, Morals, and Mysteries: Literary Approaches to Torah," *Response* 26 (1975): 67-94, esp. 83 ff. Additional supporting evidence is presented in the Epilogue to this essay.

24. We would only want to eliminate scribal errors in the transmission of the text since the time at which the text was integrated.

25. In the article by B. O. Long referred to above in n. 2, it is made clear that "repetitions, doublets, false starts, digressions, rough transitions and the like, so dear to the heart of biblical critics" (p. 195) are in fact characteristic of orally recited prose narrative in various illiterate cultures. They are also common in mythology in general and in ancient Near Eastern literature, too. Thus, even if the present form of our biblical text comes to us through a process of literary redaction, its form may be regarded as conforming to the conventions of its culture.

26. Cf., e.g., the studies cited above in notes 5, 6, and 11. So also Jacob Licht, *Storytelling in the Bible* (Jerusalem, 1978), pp. 70-71, in discussing the story of Balaam (Numbers 22–24). In that narrative the text presents what appear as contradictory behaviors on God's part. On the one hand, God encourages Balaam to go on his mission (Num. 22:20), but on the other, God attempts to block his way (22:22 ff.). Because he can make no sense of the story, Licht resorts to source criticism, attributing the contradictory statements to different genetic origins. But, of course, this does nothing to assist the reader to experience this text rather than the hypothetical sources of this text. Here, too, we would recognize the Bible's logic as "metonymic," or thematic, rather than linear, or sequential. In this way we may infer that through relating God's conflicting actions, the text conveys the sense that God is ambivalent about how to thwart Balaam—by preventing him from going in the first place, or by allowing him to go but transforming his words of execration into blessings. For a complementary approach to the story of Balaam, see now Alexander Rofé, *The Book of Balaam* (Jerusalem, 1979; in Hebrew).

27. Cf. Barthes, *S/Z*, p. 213.

28. The preceding passage describing Joseph's naïve zeal in seeking out his brothers is one of the most ironic in the Bible. Surprisingly, the irony seems to

have eluded such sensitive readers as Good *(Irony in the Old Testament)* and Redford *(A Study of the Biblical Story of Joseph,* esp. pp. 144-45); cf. now Licht, *Storytelling in the Bible,* p. 48.

29. The combination of verbs here does not necessarily reflect a chronological sequence. They may have intended to kill him and then cast him into the pit, but the pronominal suffix on the verb "to throw" seems to refer to a live Joseph. The verbs may well mean "Let us kill him by throwing him into the pit." One finds a similar combination of verbs without implying chronological order in Gen. 34:2, where "he took her, he lay with her, he forced/humbled her" may mean either he lay with her and thereby humbled her (the Revised Standard Version) or he forced her to lie with him (the New Jewish Version).

30. Reynolds Price, *A Palpable God* (New York: Atheneum, 1978), p. 127; cf. Benno Jacob, *The First Book of the Bible.*

31. Speiser, *Genesis,* p. 289; cf. his commentary on p. 291. Cf. also Gerhard von Rad, *Genesis,* trans. J. Marks, Old Testament Library (Philadelphia: Westminster Press, 1961), p. 348; Jenks, *The Elohist and North Israelite Traditions,* p. 28.

32. For re-analysis in biblical poetry, with reference to music, visual art, and other literature, see my "Two Variations of Grammatical Parallelism in Canaanite Poetry and Their Psycholinguistic Background," *Journal of the Ancient Near Eastern Society of Columbia University* 6 (1974), esp. 97-101; and "One More Step on the Staircase," *Ugarit-Forschungen* 9 (1977): 77-86. For the phenomenon in general, see Barbara Herrnstein Smith, *Poetic Closure* (Chicago: University of Chicago Press, 1968).

33. Interestingly enough, Freud refers to the technique of projecting "two images on to a single plate, so that certain features common to both are emphasized, while those which fail to fit in with one another cancel each other out and are indistinct in the picture" *(The Interpretation of Dreams,* trans. and ed. James Strachey [New York: Discus Books, 1965], p. 328 [VI.A.iii]).

34. I thank Dr. Blossom Feinstein for calling this parallel to mind. For a discussion of the film, see Parker Tyler, "Rashomon as Modern Art," in Julius Bellone, ed., *Renaissance of the Film* (New York and Toronto: Collier, 1970), pp. 198-210.

35. See, e.g., Seybold, "Paradox and Symmetry in the Joseph Narrative," pp. 71-73; Licht, *Storytelling in the Bible,* pp. 139-40.

36. As an illustration of a notable advance in this direction, see Bernhard W. Anderson, "From Analysis to Synthesis: The Interpretation of Genesis 1–11," *Journal of Biblical Literature* 97 (1978): 23-39. In an article on the Joseph story published too recently to be incorporated into the body of my discussion, Robert Alter also deals with the literary interpretation of the conflicting sequences surrounding Joseph's removal to Egypt; "Joseph and His Brothers," *Commentary* 75/5 (November, 1980): 59-69. Alter proposes that the juxtaposition of the Ishmaelite and Midianite versions "suggests that selling (Joseph) into Egypt is a virtual murder and thus undermines Judah's claim that by selling the boy the brothers will avoid the horror of blood guilt" (p. 64b). This is fairly close to part of my own analysis, but I think Alter's interpretation wrongly confines itself to the episode at hand since the ambiguity concerning the circumstances of Joseph's descent to Egypt persists in the continuation of the story. My reading has the additional virtue of relating the sale-of-Joseph episode to an overarching theme of the entire narrative.

8. The Unity of Genesis

1. Another version of this essay was previously published in *Theology Digest,* vol. 24, no. 4 (winter, 1976), pp. 360-67.
2. Such "literary heterogeneity" consists of *duplications* of narrative accounts, with substantial *variations* and even *contradictions* in details between the duplicates, as well as *differences in the names of the Deity,* marked *differences in language and writing styles,* and much else. Examples can be found in a comparison of the two creation stories (1:1–2:4*a* with 2:4*b*–3:24); the two genealogies, in 4:17-26 and 5:1-31; the two promises of Isaac's birth, in 17:1-27 and 18:1-15; and many other instances in Genesis. What is *most* significant is that any one of these points of comparison correlates with all the others. That is, where we encounter a duplicate narrative, there also has the language style changes, the name favored for Deity changes, and so on. Each feature changes *in phase* with the others. This is not the same phenomenon as the litany-like repetitions we find in ancient oral composition as such. The evidence cited and much else like it suggests diverse narrative traditions in Genesis *whether* oral or written.
3. The distinction between narrative strands in Genesis is a simplification, for this particular discussion, of what is known to several generations of biblical scholarship as the "Documentary Hypothesis" concerning the composition of Genesis and the rest of the first six books of the Bible. Some form of this hypothesis seems to me inescapable for an understanding of the history of that composition; that such a view does not fragment the book is part of the argument of this essay.
4. Gerhard von Rad, *Genesis: A Commentary,* rev. ed. (Philadelphia: Westminster Press, 1973), p. 13.
5. George W. Coats, *From Canaan to Egypt: Structural and Theological Context for the Joseph Story,* Catholic Biblical Quarterly Monograph Series, No. 4 (Washington, D.C.: Catholic Biblical Association of America, 1976), p. 73. See also p. 79.
6. Ibid., p. 89.

10. Samson's Dry Bones

1. *Religio Medici,* Sec. 21, ed. L. C. Martin (London: Oxford University Press, 1964), p. 21.
2. A reader who wishes other references to these standard theories may consult with profit F. Michael Krouse, *Milton's Samson and the Christian Tradition* (Princeton: Princeton University Press, 1949). I supply the following samples of traditional exegesis, which he does not mention, to orient readers whose primary interest is modern studies. They are necessarily brief.
   Literal: Samson is said to be a sociopolitical figure who lived in a relatively restricted geographical area (about twenty square miles), was a Danite, and gained a reputation for strength. Eusebius' *Chronicle* claims he lived eight hundred years after Abraham (summarized in Jack Finegan, *Handbook of Biblical Chronology* [Princeton University Press, 1964], p. 161). His career is fully given by Judges, but restated by many subsequent literalists (e.g., Josephus, *Antiquities of the Jews* 5.8; Sulpitius Severus, *The Sacred History*

27-28). For secular modern students, there is some difficulty in reading Samson's private prayers to God or pillow talk to Delilah as anything more than literary convention similar to orations in Thucydides or soliloquies in Shakespeare.

Typological: Samson's "every action announces Christ the Lord symbolically" (*Quodvultdeus: Liber Promissionum* 2.21.39, ed. Rene Braun [Paris, 1964], p. 388. My translation of this fifth-century phrase). With symmetry and flashes of insight, typologists point to actions of the judge that prefigured those of the Messiah (e.g., Samson "signified Christ" when he extended his arms to the pillars since he presents the initiated viewer with "an image of the cross." So St. Caesarius of Arles, *Sermons* 118, trans. Mary Magdeleine Mueller [Washington, 1964], II, 184, 189). Despite the historical and esthetic virtues of typology, it deals with the Samson story not as a unified narrative but rather as a collection of isolated gestures whose greater significance is not realized until they are fulfilled by deeds of Jesus. A lovely painting of Rogier van der Weyden, *Christ Appearing to His Mother* (Metropolitan Museum, New York), illustrates the strengths and weaknesses of a typological viewing: in the foreground, the resurrected Savior bends solicitously to the kneeling Mary. Behind them, two minutely carved capitals support gothic arches and, figuratively, the triumph over death. There, Samson kills a lion and carries off Gaza's gates, the σκία (shadow) foretelling how his ἀντίτυπος (antitype) will accomplish the miraculous victory over mortality. Not only does typology imply that Samson's real vigor springs from the life of Jesus, but it also makes assertions whose authority may seem arbitrary (e.g., St. Caesarius expands his Samson/Jesus parallel by saying the dead lion also symbolizes the Lord [*Sermons*, p. 185]. Similarly, "the razor . . . is Christ our Lord, who cuts wicked, hurtful thoughts out of our heart" [p. 194]. But Caesarius likewise asserts that "the lion can further be understood as the Gentiles who believed," a popular identification repeated by Ambrose ["The Holy Spirit," 9], Augustine ["Against Faustus," 12.32], and Paulinus of Nola [*Letters*, 23.16], but confusing to moderns who do not share Caesarius' premise: "In Sacred Scripture, . . . one and the same person can have a different signification, depending upon the time and situation" [p. 198]).

Tropological: The Samson material contains lessons to guide our moral behavior on earth. In general, the warning is against women. Examples of this anti-feminism are, sadly, too easy to find (e.g., Clement of Rome, "Second Epistle on Virginity": "This man, a Nazirite, one consecrated to God, gifted with powerful strength, was ruined by a woman's vile body and shameful lust. Are you such a man? Know yourself." [My translation.] Ephraim of Syria, *Hymns About Paradise* 7.7: Samson overcame a lion but a snake conquered him. Brunetto Latini, *Li Livres dou Tresor* 2.2.89: women can despoil ordinary men since they have already ravaged Adam and Samson). Despite their focus on a reader's ethical life, tropologists often seem to neglect more than they discover. I think most of us sense a complexity in the Samson tale more general than the rubric drawn from it by Chaucer's Monk: "Beth war by this ensample oold and playn/That no men tele hir conseil til his wyves" (*Canterbury Tales*, "The Monk's Tale," lines 2091-92, in *The Works*, ed. F. N. Robinson [Cambridge: Harvard University Press, 1957], p. 190).

Anagogical: Samson's career offers the reader a comment upon his own spiritual condition. Julian of Vezelay, *Sermons* 27, lines 267 ff., explains that our souls are strong as long as they remain vigilant. But once they sleep, they can, like Samson, be captured, blinded, and gloated over by Satan the

Philistine. However true such admonitions may be, they leave unexamined the internal relation of episodes in the original texts. Also, anagogical interpretations may be hard to share with readers who lack the exegete's insight into pneumatology, the study of the soul.

Rationalist: Samson's deeds conform to verifiable facts about topography, animal lore, wedding customs, city gates, looms, temple architecture, and so forth. While we all recognize a solid foundation of archaeologically demonstrated data in both Testaments, a rationalist interpretation sometimes jettisons miracle to stress physicality, certainly the last editor who produced our present Samson material accepted as central fact the intrusion into human life of God's noumenal power. Also, rationalists sometimes destroy the story's texture by rationalizing: Richard Rogers' pragmatic *Commentary Vpon the Whole Booke of Iudges* (London, 1615) claims that Samson was a holy man who self-consciously did the Lord's work among "idolaters." The wedding bet with the Philistines, venial though it may seem, was merely "a pleasant whetting of their wits, and . . . occasion of mirth . . . so . . . they might bee kept from manifolde offendings" (p. 676).

Mythological: Samson may be a lone hero, but he exists in twice- and thrice-told tales from many countries. Mythological critics point to parallels between, say, Samson and Hercules. (Augustine does so in *The City of God* 18.19. E. Meier has an elaborate list of supposed correspondences in *Geschichte der Poetischen Nationalliteratur der Hebraer* [Leipzig, 1856]. John M'Clintock and James Strong summarize these nineteenth-century claims in their *Cyclopaedia of Biblical, Theological and Ecclesiastical Literature* [New York, 1880], *s.v.* Samson.)

Samson as a mere avatar of the sun who is defeated by ללה—laylah or "night,"—yet who regains his strength, occupies other mythologists (C. F. Burney conveniently sums up the solar hypothesis in *The Book of Judges* [London, 1930], p. 407). A third group of mythologists sees Samson's betrayal of Delilah to please the Philistines as the Hebrew version of Nisus/Scylla/ Minos, Pterelaus/Comaetho/Amphitryon, Curoi/Blathnat/Cuchulain, or Llewllaw/ Blodenwedd/Gronw. (Building on the work of James Frazer, Robert Graves points to these sequences in *The Greek Myths* [Baltimore: Penguin Books, 1961], I, 310.)

Clearly the number of motifs common to Judges and other literatures is limited only by the ardor of individual mythologists. While valuable in illustrating Cyrus Gordon's provocative thesis that the Mediterranean littoral shares much (*The Common Background of Greek and Hebrew Civilizations* [New York: W. W. Norton, 1965]; *Homer and Bible* [Ventnor, N.J.: Ventnor Publishers, 1967]), a mythological approach still neglects the question of plot. How beginning, middle, and end are linked does not concern mythologists except tangentially. Cleomedes and Samson both pull down pillars, but for radically different reasons. At least one modern commentator denies the presence of mythological clichés in Samson: "There is little or no correspondence with the mythical Babylonian and Greek heroes" (Arthur E. Cundall, *Judges: An Introduction and Commentary* [Chicago: Inter-varsity Fellowship, 1968], p. 155). Even if other cultures talk of men who kill lions—Enkidu, for instance, Polydamas, Iwain, David, and Benaiah—their acts do not sufficiently explain the particular dynamics of Samson. (A reasonable survey of this entire school is A. Smythe Palmer, *The Samson-Saga and Its Place in Comparative Religion* [London, 1913].)

3. Kenneth R. R. Gros Louis, "The Book of Judges," in *Literary Interpretations of Biblical Narratives,* ed. Gros Louis, et al. (Nashville: Abingdon Press, 1974), pp. 159-60.

4. J. Blenkinsopp, "Structure and Style in Judges 13–16," in *Journal of Biblical Literature,* 82 (1963): 72-73. A second useful article by the same author is "Some Notes on the Saga of Samson and the Historical Milieu," in *Scripture,* 11 (1959): 81-89. Both contain assertions that there are structural patterns. Another informative essay is James Muilenburg's "A Study in Hebrew Rhetoric: Repetition and Style," in *Vetus Testamentum: Supplement, I,* Congress Volume, Copenhagen (Leiden, 1953), pp. 97-111. Also, there are some good comments on word play in A. D. Crown's "Judges IX in the Light of Its Humor," *Abr-Nahrain,* 3 (1961–62): 90-98. The Anchor *Judges,* ed. Robert G. Boling (Garden City, N.Y.: Doubleday, 1975), which I use for quotations, is likewise valuable throughout.

5. Readers who wish to see how various structural systems operate in these works may consult: Michael Fishbane, "Composition and Structure in the Jacob Cycle (Genesis 16:19–35:22)," *Journal of Jewish Studies,* 36 (1975): 19-32; Edmund Leach, *Genesis as Myth and Other Essays* (London: Jonathan Cape, 1969); Cedric Whitman, *Homer and the Heroic Tradition* (Cambridge: Harvard University Press, 1958); *Odi et Amo: The Complete Poetry of Catullus,* trans. Roy Arthur Swanson (Indianapolis: Liberal Arts Press, 1959), ix-x; Kenneth Quinn, *Virgil's Aeneid: A Critical Description* (Ann Arbor: University of Michigan Press, 1968); John D. Niles, "Ring Composition and the Structure of *Beowulf,*" *PMLA,* 94 (1979):924-35; Maren-Sofie Ristvig, *The Hidden Sense and Other Essays* (New York: Humanities Press, 1963).

11. A Human Comedy

1. On the genre of Ruth, see Edward F. Cambell, Jr., "The Hebrew Short Story: A Study of Ruth," in *A Light Unto My Path: Old Testament Studies in Honor of Jacob M. Myers,* ed. Howard N. Bream, et al. (Philadelphia: Temple University Press, 1974), pp. 83-101; for a detailed exegesis, see also Edward F. Campbell, Jr., *Ruth, AB* (New York: Doubleday, 1975). My debt to this commentary is evident throughout, even where my views differ. Translations of Ruth that follow Campbell are indicated by the abbreviation *AB;* translations that alter the Revised Standard Version are designated by an asterisk after the abbreviation RSV (RSV*); my own translations are unmarked.

2. Cf. Stephen Bertman, "Symmetrical Design in the Book of Ruth," *Journal of Biblical Literature* 84 (1965): 165-68; Yehuda T. Radday, "Chiasm in Joshua, Judges and Others," *Linguistica Biblica* 3 (1973): 7-9.

3. Though this language indicates my debt to structuralism, I do not develop a structuralist analysis of Ruth; instead, I explore surface structure. On Ruth and structuralism, see Hagia Hildegard Witzenrath, *Das Buch Rut: Eine literatur wissenschaftliche Untersuchung,* Studien zum Alten und Neutestament 40 (Munich: Kösel, 1975).

4. Note also that Elimelech is called Naomi's husband in v. 3, in contrast to her being "his wife" in v. 1; thus, the focus of the narrative shifts to the woman.

5. Cf. Edmund Leach, "The Legitimacy of Solomon: Some Structural Aspects of

Old Testament History," in *Introduction to Structuralism,* ed. Michael Lane (New York: Basic Books, 1970), pp. 268-77.

6. For attempts to posit poetic antecedents to Ruth, see Jacob M. Myers, *The Linguistic and Literary Form of the Book of Ruth* (Leiden: E. J. Brill, 1955); George S. Glanzman, "The Origin and Date of the Book of Ruth," *Catholic Biblical Quarterly* 21 (1959): 201-7.

7. See SS 3:4; 8:2; also Gen. 24:28.

8. For other interpretations of the phrase "mother's house," see Campbell, *Ruth,* pp. 64-65.

9. *Kindness* is hardly an adequate translation of *ḥesed;* see Nelson Glueck, *Hesed in the Bible* (Cincinnati: Hebrew Union College Press, 1967); Katharine D. Sakenfeld, "Studies in the Usage of the Hebrew Word *Hesed*" (Ph.D. dissertation, Harvard University, 1970).

10. On the motif *return,* see Werner Dommershausen, "Leitwortstil in der Ruthrolle," in *Theologie im Wandel* (Munich and Freiburg: Wewel, 1967), pp. 394-407.

11. See Phyllis Trible, "The Radical Faith of Ruth," in *To Be a Person of Integrity,* ed. R. James Ogden (Valley Forge: Judson Press, 1975), p. 47; Campbell, *Ruth,* p. 82.

12. The description of Ruth as clinging *(dbq)* to Naomi (1:14), as well as Ruth's words to Naomi, "Entreat me not to abandon *['zb]* you," recall the primeval man in Gen. 2:24 abandoning *('zb)* his father and his mother to cleave *(dbq)* to his woman.

13. On the name *Naomi,* see Campbell, *Ruth,* pp. 52-53.

14. The pattern of emptiness/fullness is explored by D. F. Rauber, "Literary Values in the Bible: The Book of Ruth," *Journal of Biblical Literature* 89 (1970): 27-37.

15. For the translation "a man of substance," see Campbell, *Ruth,* p. 90.

16. I take this phrase to have an indefinite meaning rather than to be a specific reference to Boaz. In 2:1 the narrator prepares the reader for the eventual link between Boaz and the one in whose sight Ruth will find favor, but the two women themselves do not make this connection until 2:19-20; cf. Campbell, *Ruth,* pp. 92, 109. For the alternative reading, see Jack M. Sasson, "Divine Providence or Human Plan?" (a review of Campbell's *Ruth*), *Interpretation* 30 (1976): 418.

17. See Ronald M. Hals, *The Theology of the Book of Ruth* (Philadelphia: Fortress Press, 1969), pp. 11ff.

18. Boaz's words to Ruth, "Keep close *[dbq]* to my young women" (2:8c), employ the same verb that described Ruth's clinging to Naomi in 1:14c; also cf. its use in 2:21, 23.

19. Cf. Sasson's resistance to theological interpretation ("Divine Providence or Human Plan?" pp. 417-18).

20. For a different reading, see Campbell, who interprets at least most of the masculine-plural endings on the nouns *harvesters* and *young people* as including both sexes (*Ruth,* p. 97).

21. The question "Where did you glean today?" (2:19b) is perhaps another indication that the reference in 2:2 is indefinite rather than a specific mention of Boaz.

22. Note the juxtaposition of the two terms *kinsman* (*mydᶜ,* 2:1) and *redeemer* (*go'el,* 2:20) at the beginning and end of this scene. Though *kinsman* occurs also in 3:2, thereafter only *redeemer* is used. For a discussion of these terms, cf.

Notes for Pages 174-187

Campbell, *Ruth,* pp. 88-90, 132-37. For the term *myd',* I follow the traditional translation *kinsman* rather than *covenant-brother* as proposed by Campbell.

23. The moun *marg⁴lōtāw* in 3:4, 7, 8, 14, which is usually translated "feet," probably functions as a euphemism for the genitals; cf. Campbell, *Ruth,* pp. 121, 131-32. I should prefer that Campbell had left intact the ambiguity of this episode in the dark of night rather than conclude "that there was no sexual intercourse at the threshing floor" (p. 134). For the opposite conclusion, see D. R. G. Beattie, "Kethibh and Qere in Ruth IV 5," *Vetus Testamentum* 21 (1971): 493.

24. Cf. the woman in the Song of Songs who goes out into the streets at night to find her mate and then brings him home for lovemaking (SS 3:2-4).

25. Discussions about the meaning of *redeemer* in relation to levirate marriage are legion; see, e.g., H. H. Rowley, "The Marriage of Ruth," in *The Servant of the Lord and Other Essays* (London: Lutterworth Press, 1952), pp. 161-86; Thomas and Dorothy Thompson, "Some Legal Problems in the Book of Ruth," *Vetus Testamentum* 18 (1968): 79-99 and the bibliography cited there; also Campbell, *Ruth,* pp. 132-37.

26. For a perceptive interpretation of this occasion, see Leszek Kolakowski, "Ruth, or the Dialogue Between Love and Bread," in *The Key to Heaven and Conversations with the Devil* (New York: Grove Press, 1972), pp. 53-56.

27. Cf. in 3:8 the narrator's use of the words "the man" and "a woman" rather than the names Boaz and Ruth. Darkness hides identity. Moreover, after 3:9, this screening of personal identity is maintained throughout the rest of scene three. But, although darkness, privacy, and secrecy hide the names of Boaz, Ruth, and Noami, these phenomena do not conceal the divine name; see below on 3:10, 13.

28. See Hals, *The Theology of the Book of Ruth,* pp. 13 ff.

29. For the translation "so-and-so," see Campbell, *Ruth,* pp. 141-43.

30. On the topic of land and related issues in Ruth 4, see Robert Gordis, "Love, Marriage, and Business in the Book of Ruth: A Chapter in Hebrew Customary Law," in *A Light Unto My Path,* pp. 146-64.

31. I follow the *qere* here rather than the *kethib;* for the opposite reading, see Beattie, "Kethibh and Qere," pp. 490-94; also "The Book of Ruth as Evidence for Israelite Legal Practice," *Vetus Testamentum* 24 (1974): 251-67.

32. Note that this interruption is set apart by an inclusion: "this was the [custom] formerly in Israel . . . this was the manner of attesting in Israel" (4:7 RSV*). On the symbolism of the sandal, see Calum M. Carmichael, "A Ceremonial Crux: Removing a Man's Sandal as a Female Gesture of Contempt," *Journal of Biblical Literature* 96 (1977): 321-36, esp. 332-36.

33. Note the symmetrical arrangement of the proper names in this statement: two women and one man at the beginning; two men and one woman at the end. Cf. "house of Israel" and "house of Perez" with "mother's house" in 1:8; the last occurs in an episode void of males; the other two in an episode void of females.

34. An alternative interpretation suggests that Boaz is protecting Ruth in public.

35. Cf. the reversal on the theme of exogamy in 1:4: marriage in Moab vs. marriage in Bethlehem.

36. Cf. Gen. 2:24, where third-person narration also distanced the privacy of intercourse.

37. This statement, "Yahweh gave *[ntn]* her conception" (RSV*), corresponds in structure and function to 1:6: "Yahweh had visited his people and given *[ntn]* them food" (RSV*). As the first and last narrative references to the deity, these statements accent two blessings of life: food and posterity.

38. *Contra* Oswald Loretz, "The Theme of the Ruth Story," *Catholic Biblical Quarterly* 22 (1960): 391-99.
39. On comedy, cf. Northrop Frye, *Anatomy of Criticism* (Princeton: Princeton University Press, 1957), pp. 163-86.

12. I Samuel 3: Historical and Narrative Poetics

1. See A. Leo Oppenheim, "The Interpretation of Dreams in the Ancient Near East," *Transactions of the American Philosophical Society*, 46.3 (1956): 188-90, 199-201.
2. Cf. Licht, *Storytelling in the Bible* (Jerusalem: Magnes, 1978), chap. 3.
3. The Massoretic text reads *meqallelîm lāhem*, "cursed them," but this is clearly a pious scribal correction of the original *'elōhîm* ("cursed God"), preserved in the Septuaguint.
4. Cf. the two possible references of the expression noted earlier.
5. The word *tahat* ("instead of"; "in place of"; "after") is regularly used.
6. The fourth call uses a different, "intensifying form": YHWH came . . . and called *kefa'am befa'am*, "as aforetimes"; it also repeats the name of Samuel twice, not once as earlier.
7. See, e.g., I. Burke, "On Musicality in Verse," *The Philosophy of Literary Form* (Baton Rouge: Louisiana State University Press, 1941), pp. 369-78; and M. Bloomfield, "The Syncategorematic in Poetry: From Semantics to Syntactics," *To Honor Roman Jacobson* (Paris: Moulon, 1967), pp. 309-17.
8. See my *Text and Texture; Close Readings of Selected Biblical Texts* (New York: Schocken, 1979), chap. 7, esp. pp. 99-101.
9. E.g., Genesis 11:9 *(lebēnāh/nābelāh)*, and my discussion in *Text and Texture*, p. 38.

14. I Samuel 25 as Literature and History

1. An earlier and somewhat different version of this essay was published under the title "I Samuel 25 as Literature and as History" in the *Catholic Biblical Quarterly*, 40 (1978): 11-28. I thank the publishers of that journal for permission to reproduce parts of that article herein and Prof. James S. Ackerman for his very constructive suggestions for revising it.
   I Samuel 25:1-42 is one unit of literature. In v. 1, read *Mā 'ôn* with LXX Instead of Paran. If David ever fled to Paran, we have no other reference to it. The notice about David's wives at the very end of the chapter (vv. 43-44) does not belong to the action of the narrative, but seems to have been attracted quite naturally by the reference in the conclusion of the narrative to his marriage with Abigail, to which the notice alludes (v. 43). There is no reason to assume that the last two verses were ever separate from the rest of the chapter.
2. Prov. 17:21; 30:22; Jer. 17:11; Ps. 14:1; 53:1.
3. The wording is significant for the theme of heartlessness: *wēlēb Nābāl tôb 'ālāyw*, literally, "Nabal's heart was good on him," v. 36.
4. II Sam. 13:23-28; perhaps Gen. 38:12.
5. I Sam. 16:2; see also 18:1, 16, 20.
6. But compare the opinion of P. Kyle McCarter, Jr. (*I Samuel*, Anchor Bible 8

[Garden City, N.Y.: Doubleday, 1980], p. 398), who argues that the meaning is simply, "Let any burden of blame that might arise from our conversation rest upon me and not you," and that the sentence is only "the polite way of initiating conversation with a superior" and "has nothing to do with Nabal's misbehavior." On the most superficial level of analysis, McCarter is right. The narrator's use of language throughout, however, is multidimensional and connotative. It is unlikely (*contra* McCarter) that only modern commentators would attribute significance to Abigail's choice of opening words. Note (as does McCarter) that she does not employ the more ordinary, but in this instance less suggestive locution *bî ădōnî*, "upon me, my lord."

7. As long recognized, the phrase might mean either "males" or (as with Rashi and other Rabbinic commentators) "dogs." If "dogs" is the meaning of the euphemism, then we may have another jab at Nabal, whose ancestor Caleb *(Kālēb)* bore a name that sounded like and was indentical in writing to the word for dog *(keleb)*.

8. Jacob does refer to his gift once as *běrākâ* (Gen. 33:11), but here there is an obvious play ("Please take my blessing which has been brought for you") on Jacob's deceitful acquisition of Esau's blessing (Genesis 27).

9. It is important not to miss the fact that the term *nāgîd* in the Hebrew Bible tends to refer to a future king.

10. It becomes a refrain of the pre-Exilic Deuteronomistic historian. On this, see Frank Moore Cross, *Canaanite Myth and Hebrew Epic* (Combridge: Harvard University Press, 1973), pp. 274-89; and Jon D. Levenson, "Who Inserted the Book of the Torah," *Harvard Theological Review* 68 (1975): 203-33.

11. Erich Auerbach, *Mimesis: The Representation of Reality in Western Literature* (Princeton: Princeton University Press, 1953), pp. 11-12.

12. Robert Alter, "A Literary Approach to the Bible," *Commentary*, vol. 60, no. 6 (December, 1975): pp. 71-72.

13. Note the contrasting parallelism of this construction to David's greeting to Nabal: "Prosperity to you, prosperity to your household, and prosperity to all that you own" (v. 6).

14. Alter, "A Literary Approach," p. 73.

15. I speak, of course, of an Israelite king killing another Israelite. The taboo does not apply to warfare.

16. William McKane, *I and II Samuel* (London: SCM, 1963), p. 152.

17. I Sam. 27:3; 30:5; II Sam. 2:2; 3:3; I Chron. 3:1.

18. On this passage, see B. Mazar, "David's Reign in Hebron and the Conquest of Jerusalem," in *In the Time of Harvest: Essays in Honor of Abba Hillel Silver,* ed. D. J. Silver (New York: Macmillan, 1963), pp. 235-44. On the historical background, see H. J. Zobel, "Beiträge zur Geschichte Gross-Judas in Früh—und Vor-davidischer Zeit," *Vetus Testamentum Supplements* 28 (1974): 253-77.

19. Num. 14:20-25; Deut. 1:22-36; Josh. 14:6-15; 15:13-19; Judg. 1:20.

20. Matitiahu Tsevat, "Marriage and Monarchical Legitimacy in Ugarit and Israel," *Journal of Semitic Studies* 3 (1958): 241.

21. Tsevat, "Marriage," pp. 237-43; Roland de Vaux, *Ancient Israel* I (New York: McGraw-Hill, 1965), 116.

22. James A. Montgomery, *A Critical and Exegetical Commentary on the Books of Kings,* International Critical Commentary (Edinburgh: Clark, 1951), pp. 127-28.

23. I Chron. 2:9-17; 50-51. The full implications are drawn in Jon D. Levenson and

Baruch Helpern, "The Political Import of David's Marriages," *Journal of Biblical Literature* 99 (1980): 507-18.

24. On the sociopolitical dimension of genealogies, see Robert R. Wilson, *Genealogy and History in the Biblical World,* Yale Near Eastern Researches 7 (New Haven: Yale University Press, 1977).

25. The word used in the construct plural of *'iššâ,* "woman," "wife." It might be argued that the reference is to David's marriage to another woman of Saul's, his daughter Michal (I Sam. 18:20-29), except that (1) *iššâ* does not mean "daughter" and (2) David married only one daughter of Saul's. Qimchi (Radaq to II Sam. 3:5), aware of the problem, suggests that the reference is to Eglah, who one rabbinic tradition maintained was first Saul's spouse, then David's. It is interesting that the rabbis were willing to see this process in the case of Eglah, but not in the case of Ahinoam, where the evidence is stronger. Probably, they preferred not to believe that David took Saul's wife while the old king still lived. We should assume that after Saul's death David acquired his other wives and concubines as well.

26. I Sam. 27:3; 30:5; 2:2; 3:2; I Chron. 3:1.

27. The tendency of the commentaries to say that the Jezreel in question is the one in Judah rather than that in the north is based on nothing more than the fact of Ahinoam's first mention here in connection with Abigail of (the southern) Carmel. But if David had already married her (so that *lāqaḥ* in v. 43 is pluperfect), there is no way to tell which Jezreel is inteded. There is, incidentally, no reason why Saul could not have taken a southern wife. For an argument that Judah was indeed part of Saul's kingdom, see A. D. H. Mayes, *Israel in the Period of the Judges,* Studies in Biblical Theology, 2nd Series, no. 29 (Naperville: Allenson, 1974), pp. 3-4.

28. See D. N. Freedman, "Early Israelite History in the Light of Early Israelite Poetry," in *Unity and Diversity,* H. Goedicke and J. J. M. Roberts, eds. (Baltimore: Johns Hopkins Press, 1975), p. 16.

16. Narrative Art in the Book of Judith

1. Charles Torrey, *The Apocryphal Literature* (Hamden, Conn.: Archon Books, 1963), p. 90.
2. Robert Dentan, *The Apocrypha, Bridge of the Testaments* (Greenwhich, Conn.: Seabury Press, 1954), p. 55.

18. Encounters in the New Testament

1. Scripture quotations in this chapter are from the Jerusalem Bible, copyright © 1966 by Darton, Longman & Todd, Ltd. and Doubleday and Company, Inc. Used by permission of the publisher.
2. My discussion of John owes much in general to the notes in the Jerusalem Bible, from which all my biblical quotations are taken, and the commentaries of C. H. Dodd and Raymond Brown. The link between Jesus' *ego eimi* and that of the man cured is briefly made by John Marsh in his excellent *Gospel of St. John,* Pelican Gospel Commentaries (Harmondsworth, 1968), p. 380. J. L. Martyn's *History and Theology in the Fourth Gospel* (Nashville: Abingdon,

1979) has an excellent analysis of this episode which may be taken as paralleling the one offered here.

19. *John 9: A Literary-Critical Analysis*

1. *The Interpretation of the Fourth Gospel* (Cambridge: University Press, 1953).
2. Cf. Wayne C. Booth, *The Rhetoric of Fiction* (Chicago: University of Chicago Press, 1961) for the distinction between telling and showing, chap. 1. The Gospel of John itself provides ample illustrations of the distinction between telling and showing. Whereas the author *tells* the reader in the prologue that "the true light that enlightens every man was coming into the world," we are *shown* what that means in the narrative of John 9. Or whereas John 1:11 *tells* us that Jesus "came to his own home, and his own people received him not," John 9 *shows* us what that statement means. The "showing" aspect of John is so effective that everything it "shows" also serves to "tell."
3. *History and Theology in the Fourth Gospel,* 2nd ed. (Nashville: Abingdon, 1979).
4. Some early manuscripts lack the words "and he said . . . Jesus said" in vv. 38-39. Yet the external attestation clearly favors the longer text, and therefore vv. 38-39 should not be omitted from the narrative.